The Crisis in South Africa

The Crisis in South Africa

by John S. Saul and Stephen Gelb

REVISED EDITION

Monthly Review Press
New York

10.3534

Chapter 2, "The Crisis in South Africa: Class Defense, Class
Revolution," originally appeared as the July-August 1981 issue of
Monthly Review, copyright © 1981 by Monthly Review Press.

Library of Congress Cataloging-in-Publication Data

Saul, John S.
    The crisis in South Africa.

    Includes bibliographical references.
    1. South Africa—Politics and government—
1978–   . 2. South Africa—Economic conditions—1961–
3. South Africa—Social conditions—1961–   . I. Gelb,
Stephen. II. Title.
DT779.952.S28 1986   305.8'00968   86-12882
ISBN 0-85345-707-7
ISBN 0-85345-706-9 (pbk.)

Monthly Review Press
155 West 23rd Street
New York, N.Y. 10011

Manufactured in the United States of America

10 9 8 7 6 5 4 3 2 1

Contents

ACKNOWLEDGMENTS

The first edition of this book included the following note of acknowledgment, which is still applicable: "Both authors wish to thank TCLSAC (the Toronto Committee for the Liberation of Southern Africa) as a group for freely giving various kinds of support, logistical and financial, to the present project; and to thank, as well, a large number of comrades in and around the committee (not to mention all those who have participated in P.S. 657.6, 'The Politics of Liberation in Southern Africa,' at York University in the past two years) for providing a stimulating context of political commitment and intellectual concern within which to pursue many of the themes elaborated upon here. Stephen Gelb would like to thank, in particular, Carole Houlihan and Pat Baker of the committee for the support given him most directly. In addition, we owe a considerable debt of gratitude to a number of South African comrades who have been of great assistance but must remain nameless. And a debt of gratitude, too, to our editor, Susan Lowes of Monthly Review Press, both for her initial confidence in the project and her essential role in bringing it to fruition."

For assistance in preparing this revised edition I must thank, especially, my original co-author Stephen Gelb and, once again, my friend and editor Susan Lowes. In addition, fellow members of the editorial collective of *Southern Africa Report* (published by the aforementioned TCLSAC), comrades at the Centre

7

d'Information et de Documentation sur le Mozambique et l'Afrique Australe (CIDMAA) in Montreal, Alicia Fernandez at *Monthly Review* and Dean Ron Bordessa of Atkinson College, York University, Toronto, have all facilitated my work in invaluable ways.

Finally, I would like to dedicate this revised edition of *The Crisis in South Africa* to all those who are seeking to build a new and egalitarian future for that country.

—John S. Saul

Introduction:
The Revolutionary Prospect
by JOHN S. SAUL

The Crisis in South Africa first appeared as the expanded summer issue of *Monthly Review* in 1981 and shortly thereafter in a paperback edition. We took Bill Freund's subsequent recommendation of the book as "a compressed and perceptive accounting with an emphasis on the latest developments" (in the bibliography of his *The Making of Contemporary Africa)* as some indication that we had succeeded in our effort to provide a useful overview that could help orient readers to the complexities of South Africa in the 1980s.[1] The book also received favorable mention from reviewers in such diverse forums as the *New York Review of Books* and the (New York) *Guardian.* Most importantly to us—and in spite of the fact that the book was quickly banned by the South African government—we learned, largely by word of mouth, that our analysis had been found useful by many South Africans themselves; gratifyingly, it was deemed "fascinating and readable" in the admirable Johannesburg-based *Work in Progress*[2] and "a stimulating monograph" in the African National Congress's own *Sechaba.*[3] Of course, the reviewers in both these latter publications had criticism to make, criticisms that will be alluded to further in this introduction. Still, the book's initial reception has encouraged us to think that now, some five years later, a second, updated edition will prove welcome.

We have chosen to leave intact the body of that original

9

book. Compressed as it is, it would in any event not lend itself easily to minor alterations. Besides, it seems to us to have stood up quite well to the test of time, having identified patterns both of ruling-class response to crisis and of popular-class resistance that have, if anything, become all the more clear in the years since 1981. Of course, at that time we were seeking to address ourselves to a stereotype that was still surprisingly widespread, at least in North America. This was the stereotype of a relatively motionless apartheid system, immoral enough to many, but not yet so contested a terrain as to demand much political commitment, beyond mere moralizing, from liberals or the left. We sought to demonstrate that, in fact, the system of racial capitalism was in real crisis, enough so to force the regime at least to contemplate the unthinkable—"reform" or, better put, new kinds of "formative action" (as we termed this option, following Gramsci and Stuart Hall)—albeit without abandoning, as we also emphasized, the simultaneous use of the stick of repression. Invoking Rosa Luxemburg's model of the "mass strike," we sought to document, as well, the inexorable reawakening and rise of a formidable and commited resistance, one that had already, in 1981, placed revolution on the agenda in South Africa more firmly than ever before.

Such has been the pace of events in South Africa since then that few would now doubt either the depth of that country's crisis or the strength of the resistance. We think that the original chapters of *The Crisis in South Africa* can, as they stand, still help to structure for the reader a useful explanation of these now even more salient realities. But to have left matters there would not have been sufficient either. For this reason, a new concluding chapter has been added to the book, one that seeks briefly to trace the deepening of the crisis of racial capitalism and the heightening of resistance. And there is also this new introduction, designed to deal with certain questions raised regarding our first edition and to further clarify certain premises of our argument. Here, too, some crucial features of South Africa's crisis not dealt with adequately in our original book will be sketched out, notably the regional implications of that crisis. For, as we shall see, the death agonies of South Africa's cancerous regime have also found that regime spilling over its borders and subjecting its neighbors to vicious wars of destabilization—in effect transforming the "crisis in South Africa" into a southern Africa crisis. Finally, it should be noted that both this new introduction and the concluding chapter have been written by only one of the original authors, John S. Saul—Stephen Gelb having been unable to participate at first hand in the updating of the book that this second edition represents. Although the present author has benefitted greatly from a number of discussions with his original co-author in preparing these new materials, the latter is in no way responsible for them or for the interpretations they contain.

The Crisis of Racial Capitalism

Our 1981 text was premised on the understanding that by that date South Africa already faced an "organic crisis," that is, a crisis that was not merely economic—although certainly the conditions for the expanded reproduction of South African capitalism had been placed in sharp question even in narrowly economic terms—but also one cast in even more broadly political terms. In other words, economic contradictions meshed with the fact of intensified political mobilization against the established racial capitalist system in such a way as to create a pre-revolutionary situation. This seemed obvious enough even in commonsensical terms, and all the more so in the period since our first writing. As will be discussed in the new concluding chapter to this volume, 1986 found capital, worldwide and local, acting in such a way as to suggest its possibly terminal lack of confidence in the ability of a structure of domination premised on apartheid to continue to guarantee its long-term interests. This was true in part because of the pressure capital was beginning to feel from anti-apartheid, pro-sanctions lobbies in Western countries. Even more important was the growing suspicion that capitalism cannot easily defend itself if it continues to be linked, as it has been for so long, to a parallel structure of racial oppression.

Viewed from a Marxist perspective capitalism is, by definition, a tension-ridden system. Economic crises, whether "general" or partial, are seen to spring from the fact that "in capitalist production the individual desire for profit periodically collides with the objective necessity of a social division of labor." Obviously this is an unavoidable tension or contradiction within the capitalist mode of production, yet only under certain circumstances does it give rise to crisis. So, too, when the crisis of capitalism becomes more "organic" (when, that is, the very continuation of the capitalist system itself is cast in doubt), this reflects the mere intensification—the effective politicization—of an ever present contradiction, that between labor and capital. Such contradictions characterize the South African capitalist system as well, as do certain more specific tensions peculiar to the rather idiosyncratic form of capitalism that has emerged there.

Thus in South Africa, for extended periods of time, the structure of racial domination has interpenetrated with and reinforced a structure of capitalist exploitation, producing what we have called a system of *racial capitalism*. Yet it need come as no surprise that this linkage between racial domination and capitalist exploitation is as potentially contradictory as, for long stretches of time in South Africa, it has been mutually reinforcing. Indeed, we argue below that one important dimension of the various crises of South Africa's racial capitalism has been, precisely, the surfacing of a real strain between these two aspects of the South African system.* Moreover, severe crises must generally be resolved in one of two ways: either by revolution from below or by "formative action" taken by the dominant classes, the better to renovate and reconsolidate their rule. In the 1940s

---

* At least one author, Deborah Posel, does query the approach to crisis adopted in our book, suggesting that the "crises" we identify (the 1940s, the later 1970s-early 1980s) reflect merely the intensification of tensions which have all along been present in the system.[4] It is difficult to know why Posel considers this to be so telling a point since, as noted, this is a commonplace of crisis theory. Posel may appear to be on stronger ground when she charges us with failing "to distinguish the onset of the 'crisis' according to a particular—specified—*degree* or mode of development of these structural tensions." Yet it is not easy to do this with the precision of a chemical experiment. Although mere commonsensical identification of the threshold of crisis is not adequate, the analyst must nonetheless deal with the specificity of a complex, overdetermined conjuncture and this is inevitably a somewhat imprecise and qualitative exercise in judgment. Readers can decide for themselves our success in this respect.

the response from ruling circles was a marked intensification of racial oppression—the apartheid option—an outcome that capital came to live with quite comfortably despite a certain initial temptation (at least on the part of some of its "fractions") to attempt something different. In the 1980s, in contrast, the stripping away of certain racist dimensions of the system has begun to seem more necessary to many in such circles, albeit formidably difficult to achieve.

Race and class? Several generations of liberal analysts of South Africa have chosen to counterpose these two variables quite starkly, overstating in the process the degree of contradiction said to exist between an "irrational" racism and the "rational" workings of a capitalism whose color-blind and liberating tendencies the institutionalization of white supremacy is said to block. Marxists do better here; nonetheless, they have in turn been accused by their critics of economic reductionism, of underestimating the autonomous determinacy of the racial factor, of mounting a "functionalist" argument and seeing manifestations of racism in South Africa as little more than quite straightforward expressions of the requirements of capital.[5] However overstated much of this latter criticism may be, it behooves us to take it seriously; for there can be little doubt that, even for Marxists, the "race-class" question remains the most difficult aspect of the South African situation to come to terms with, both analytically and politically. And this is as true for the attempt to characterize the manner in which the dominant system operates (racial oppression? class exploitation?) as it is for the attempt to characterize the composition of the movement (national liberation? class struggle?) that much form up to oppose that system.

Marxists do indeed tend to give explanatory primacy to the production process and the class variable. However, Marx's own pronouncements on such matters are not by any means definitive. Recall his well-known statement that

the specific economic form in which unpaid surplus-labour is pumped out of the direct producers determines the relationship of rulers and ruled, as it grows directly out of production itself. . . . It is always the direct relationship of the owners of the conditions of production to the direct producers . . . which reveals the inner-most secret, the hidden basis of the entire social structure, and with it the political form of the relation of sovereignty and de-pendence, in short, the corresponding specific form of the state.[6]

Yet immediately Marx adds a proviso:

This does not prevent the same economic basis—the same from the standpoint of its main conditions—due to innumerable different empirical circumstances, natural environment, *racial relations,* ex-ternal historical influences, etc., from showing infinite variations and gradations in appearances, which can be ascertained only by analysis of empirically given circumstances. (Emphasis added)

How then to conceptualize, how to weigh up, the importance of such "racial relations"?

Erik Olin Wright has attempted, in a useful manner, to clarify things here, suggesting that "while it may be the case that different forms of domination reciprocally condition each other, Marxists are generally agreed that only class relations have an internal logic of development," a tendency toward transformation of the class structure being inherent in the process of economic development (in the development of the productive forces). "The apparent symmetry in the relationship between class and gender or class and race, therefore, is dis-rupted by the developmental tendencies of class relations. No such developmental trajectory has been persuasively argued for other forms of domination."[7] Yet even this may be a trifle too "economistic" a formulation. The South African experience cer-tainly does confirm that historically resonant ideologies and congealed political practices retain an autonomy and weight that can have pertinent effects upon the presumed "development tendencies of class relations." Even more important, perhaps, is the need to reemphasize the very "materiality" of racism itself in a setting like the South African one. For racism and much of the concrete structure of racial oppression has been a product of the expansion of Western capitalism and of the fact of colonial conquest. In addition, quite specific class forces and class alli-ances (including, more often than not, large numbers of the white working class) have grouped around the resultant structure of racial oppression—the better to defend their "material" advantage.

Of course, there can be little doubt that capitalist development has often breathed fresh life into the pattern of racial hierarchization in South Africa, shaping it to its needs around the turn of the century, for example, the better to guarantee supplies of cheap labor. Nor have any potential contradictions that might, in theory, be thought to exist between racial oppression on the one hand and capitalist exploitation on the other tended to turn fundamentally antagonistic.* Small wonder that "South Africa's major extra-parliamentary opposition movements bristle with anti-capitalist sentiments. There is no doubt that there is a growing hostility towards capitalism among black youth. The reason is simple: capitalism is seen as the driving force behind apartheid."[8] Yet even if this is true, it does not lay to rest the race-class debate. For it must be emphasized that it is not merely liberal writers in the academy who are worried about reductionist readings of racism in South Africa. It is just such a concern that also informs the review of our book by "ZPJ" (Pallo Jordan, now a member of the ANC's National Executive Commitee) in the ANC's own journal *Sechaba*. Noting our "terminological inadequacies," Jordan pinpoints "racial capitalism," in particular, as being "a term fraught with severe limitations." There is also the much more intemperate article— one that scatters unhelpful venom and personalistic attacks in all directions—in *The African Communist* (journal of the South African Communist Party, which is closely linked to the ANC). There "Nyawuza" criticizes Gelb's deploying (albeit in another context but with a usage closely paralleling our own in the present book) of the "racial capitalism" concept.[9] In both cases,

---

* At least, it could perhaps be argued, until recently. This is a theme for our final chapter, where we will find even so compromised an erstwhile apologist for apartheid as Afrikaner businessperson Louis Luyt not only admitting that "whether business likes it or not, it has benefitted from apartheid" ("a system," he adds, that "has been wrong for forty years"!), but continuing on to say that "it is only now that apartheid has turned against it that they [businesspeople] are seeking its removal." As we shall see in this book, however, it is far easier for capital to make such "reformist" pronouncements than it is for it to implement any seriously "formative" program.

the charge is that this concept, like our analysis more generally, tends to downplay—even when acknowledging—the weight of national-cum-racial oppression and to overestimate the centrality of capitalism per se and of class exploitation.

National Liberation and Class Struggle

Readers can judge for themselves the accuracy of these kinds of criticism when reading what follows. At its most extreme, a related concern leads one academic observer to ascribe to Gelb and myself—because of our alleged "functionalism," in which any "dysfunction" must necessarily be deemed "abnormal"! —an almost apocalyptic vision of the crisis in South Africa: "The idea of a 'structural crises' developed from a functionalist perspective on the last decade in South Africa gives the misleading impression that irresistible structural pressures will do the work of exacting fundamental change in this country."[10] When, with an apparent air of fresh discovery, the author (Deborah Posel) contrasts this bizarre fatalism that she has attributed to Marxists with the (obvious) point that the "eradication of economic and political inequities in South Africa is still, as it always was, a matter of on-going and fluctuating struggle," one wonders just which book it is that she has been reading. Faced with such incomprehension we can merely reiterate our understanding that there is an "organic crisis" in South Africa—and that its outcome is *not* predetermined. As we argue in the text which follows, such a crisis gives unique opportunities for the forces of opposition to organize, even as it impels the forces of domination to seek to refashion the terms of their rule.

Pallo Jordan is much more subtle, concretizing his criticisms, for example, by underlining our "annoying habit of mistaking the ruling class's wishful-thinking and fine-sounding rhetoric for reality."[11] I doubt that even this is a charge that will stand up, however. Certainly we do argue that the novel attempts by various fractions of the dominant classes to mount effective "formative action" in their own interests has been, and will continue to be, of significance. But that emphasis in our book is no more prominent than a parallel emphasis upon the extreme difficulties these elements are having in conceptualizing, let alone implementing, such action. In part these difficulties reflect the "drag" of racist ideas, in part the strength of sub-classes that have an even more vested interest than does big capital in the day-to-day privileges afforded them by apartheid. But, as we point out on numerous occasions, capital is also aware that realizing the hypothetical option of a deracialized capital-ism implies risks—not least the risk of merely further fueling, rather than coopting, the revolutionary momentum—that even the most enlightened businesspeople are extremely nervous about running. This does indeed render their concrete actions as much "reactive" (in Jordan's term) as formative; in consequence, there seems little reason to quarrel with Jordan's summation that "much that the ruling class and the racist state propose and have already implemented are an attempt to keep pace with an extremely fluid situation, in which they can no longer take their opponents for granted." In fact, for all the talk of reform, it is probably the case that, to the present, the further militariza-tion of South African society in defense of the status quo is the most prominent aspect of the ruling classes' response.

The criticisms in *Sechaba* and *The African Communist* are, in any case, less about the nature and flexibility of the structures of domination than about the kind of movement of the forces of opposition which is most appropriate under South African conditions. For Jordan, what is ultimately at stake is Gelb's and my "very shallow conception of the relationship between the national and class aspects of the liberation struggle"—our failure "to grasp the centrality of the national question to the revo-lutionary struggle." For Nyawuza the situation is even more cut and dried. Thus the concert of "racial capitalism" as a cap-sule theorization of the South African situation is counterposed to the characterization of South Africa as exemplifying "colonial-ism of a special type": "The programme of the South African Communist Party, adopted in 1962, advances the thesis of 'Colonialism of a Special Type' and the two-stage revolution. In 1969 the Morogoro Conference of the ANC adopted the *Strategy and Tactics* document, which took some of the Communist Party programme a stage further."[12] Consequently, the very use of the concept "racial capitalism" is deemed to signal an insidious assault on the fundamental principles of both the ANC and the SACP:

> The real . . . aim of these new "Marxists" is to reject the *two-stage* theory of our revolution. To do this successfully, they have to question the validity of the thesis of "colonialism of a special type" and then proceed to demolish the national-democratic stage thesis and question the role and genuineness of the non-proletarian forces in the struggle. They want to change the orientation and the language and all that we stand for.

To give him his due, Jordan recognizes that things are not quite so straightforward. In his words, "Much of the confusion among our friends in the international community is probably attributable to the imprecise terms our movement's discourse is usually couched in. Though we all employ the formulation, 'colonialism of a special type,' how many of us have bothered to define it?"* Moreover, as he goes on to ask, "what implications does this formulation have for the question of class leadership over the liberation movement as a whole?" Such queries suggest the kind of tightrope the ANC is forced to walk, not just theoretically but also practically, in building an effective resistance movement. Thus it seeks to speak to the real and legitimate grievances all blacks have against a racially oppressive, quasi-colonial system, and to draw on the political energies that a multi-class, nationalist-minded alliance can, in consequence, be expected to contribute to the struggle against such a system.

---

* Might one suggest, in this context, that Jordan was a little too precipitous in his dismissal (as quoted earlier) of the notion of "racial capitalism"? He did not, in any case, explain clearly why he considers that concept to be so "fraught with serious limitations." It at least has the virtue of attempting to capture the *simultaneity* of racially defined and class-based oppression in South Africa, something the "colonialism of a special type" formulation fails to do. Indeed the latter, by so exclusively concentrating on the fact of racially defined oppression, seems better designed to mask the multi-dimensional complexities of South African reality —and the consequent challengers facing the liberation movement—than to illuminate them. Fortunately there are other activists—like Jordan, but some even writing in *The African Communist* (as we shall see)—who are not entirely comfortable with the kind of verbal shell-game which can so readily postpone the question of class struggle to a later "stage."

But there is also a strong tendency afoot in the liberation movement to go much further, toward a confrontation with the class exploitation dimensions of the system. The resultant tension is fully manifest in the wavering focus of Jordan's own review: even as he criticizes Gelb and myself for misguided "speculation about the various class forces that constitute the ANC," he simultaneously twits Nolutshungu (whose book he is also reviewing) for tending "to treat the multi-class nature of the liberation movement as unproblematic"!

The tightrope which the ANC must walk regarding the national question is nothing new, of course. Historically the ANC has experienced attack from both right and left over the issue, although most vociferously from various groupings of black nationalists. Thus in the early 1950s there was the dissident "National-Minded bloc" and in the late 1950s the "Africanists" (who were to break away to establish the Pan Africanist Congress). In the 1970s it was the turn of a group of cultural nationalist critics within the ANC who surfaced, albeit momentarily, as the "ANC African Nationalists" group. And all through the recent period there have been the various spokespersons of the loosely defined Black Consciousness movement who have criticized the ANC and its Freedom Charter, this current being presently represented on the ground inside South Africa by the Azanian People's Organization (AZAPO) and the National Forum. True, this school of thought has more often than not represented a critique of the ANC for being too "multi-" or "non-racial" in its emphasis, rather than a critique of the movement for being too preoccupied with class struggle. But the latter has certainly not been absent as a consideration.*

And then, paradoxically, there is the critique from the left

---

* The picture is a complex one, however, and too complicated, certainly, to be fully elaborated here. Thus, one telling public critique of the ANC's presumed weakness vis-à-vis the national question came from a loyal and dedicated voice within the movement itself (see Ben Turok, *Strategic Problem in South Africa's Liberation Struggle: A Critical Analysis* [Richmond, B.C., 1974]). It is also the case that some recent critics of the ANC from within the Black Consciousness tradition have sought to argue that the ANC is, simultaneously, neither "nationalist" enough nor sufficiently oriented toward a working-class project!

of the movement's "petty-bourgeois nationalism," most publically exemplified in recent years by the (admittedly shrill and
jejune) intervention of the self-styled "ANC—Marxist Tendency," which is discussed in the body of our text. Indeed,
it was in response to a particularly sloganized quasi-academic
defense (by Robert Fatton, Jr.) of the latter group's viewpoint
that one senior ANC cadre, Thabo Mbeki, was moved to
exclaim:

> . . . the ANC is not a socialist party. It has never pretended to be
> one, it has never said it was, and is not trying to be. It will not
> become one by decree or for the purpose of pleasing its "left"
> critics. To accuse the ANC of having "failed to develop a truly
> socialist revolutionary strategy" is akin to criticizing Fatton for
> failing to give birth to babies.[13]

Yet Mbeki is reluctant—the tightrope again—to let the
matter rest there, invoking the "notion of *both* an all-class common front *and* the determined mobilization of the black proletariat and peasantry." Indeed, the "ANC is convinced that
within the alliance of democratic forces that will bring about
the outcome (i.e., 'the defeat and overthrow of the present ruling class and the birth of a new democratic state'), the black
working class must play the leading role, not as an appendage of
the petty bourgeoisie but as a conscious vanguard class, capable
of advancing and defending its own democratic interests" (socialism?). In a related presentation, Joe Slovo, a leading cadre
of both the ANC and the SACP, uses even stronger language
to critique (*pace* Nyawuza) any rigid, two-stage model of the
South African revolution: he argues that the "dominant ingre-
dients of later stages must already have begun to mature within
the womb of the earlier stage" and that in South Africa there is
indeed a certain simultaneity to the struggles "for social as well
as national emancipation."[14] Moreover, the "most important"
determination of whether the revolution will move toward
the "true liberation" which socialism represents is precisely
the "role played by the working class in the alliance of class
forces during the first stage of the continuing revolution."

It was the search for a conceptualization that would help
make sense of the lived simultaneity of the national and class

struggles that led Gelb and myself to emphasize the interplay of "popular democratic" and proletarian assertions. In the text that follows we argue that the possibility that these will come to reinforce each other is at least as great as the possibility that they will stand in contradiction. Nor are "popular democratic" assertions—of "nationalism, racial consciousness, and democratic self-assertion" (as we identify them)—presented as being any less real or less legitimate under South African conditions than currents that might be expected to place socialism more firmly on the agenda. We were surprised, therefore, at Jordan's charge, cited earlier, that we had failed "to grasp the centrality of the national question to the revolutionary struggle," and that we tended "to regard the sense of national grievance in a purely instrumentalist light." We would urge Jordan to reconsider the possibility that the notion of a dialectical relationship between "popular-democratic" and "proletarian" emphases can help clarify the coexistence of diverse moments within the South African struggle.

We would agree, therefore, with Thabo Mbeki when he attacks "the strange view that national consciousness and national liberation are the deadly enemies of class consciousness and class emancipation." In our text, in fact, we suggest that the popular-democratic cast of the struggle in South Africa can actually help give a more broadly revolutionary thrust to working-class self-assertion than might otherwise be the case; moreover, as the new concluding chapter makes clear, this has undoubtedly proven to be the case with respect to the increased politicization of the workers' movement in recent years. However, we have also underscored some of the ambiguities of popular democratic assertions (including "national consciousness and national liberation"), not least the danger, so familiar elsewhere in Africa, of the petty bourgeoisie hijacking the struggle.*

---

* Critics like Pallo Jordan might also note that by examining the prospects for a socialist denouement to the South African freedom struggle, one is *not* suggesting that even the "mere" emergence of a color-blind, bourgeois-democratic system, or some other form of genuinely "nationalist" government, would be anything other than a heroic advance over the tyrannical pigmentocracy that currently exists.

Perhaps this danger seems less pressing for Jordan and Mbeki because of their awareness of the relative weakness of any African petty bourgeoisie that does exist and of the extent to which it too suffers under white domination.[15] This is correct up to a point, but whether it is adequate as a guide to the much more complex interclass politics that is likely to play itself out (even within the liberation movement) during the later stages of the transition to black majority rule must be open to doubt. Here Slovo may be closer to the mark: "The high level of capitalist development in South Africa has given birth to a distinctive form of class stratification, not only in the enemy camp but also among the black oppressed." In consequence, "as the national liberation struggle approaches its climax, we must expect a stronger urge from the non-working-class black forces to stop the revolution in its tracks and to opt for a bourgeois solution."

There is another point. Mbeki's formulation, quoted above, was not entirely clear regarding the manner in which, in practice, the working class comes to play its "leading role . . . within the alliance of democratic forces." However, there is a particular reason why some within the Congress movement—possibly including Mbeki himself—have little problem in conceptualizing the kind of interplay between the "national-democratic" and "proletarian" dimensions of the South African struggle that might be expected to strengthen the prospect of a socialist denouement. For them, the guarantor that the revolution will, in Slovo's term, be made "on-going," and that the proletarian-cum-socialist card will ultimately be played, is the South African Communist Party. Although both are writing in *The African Communist*, Slovo is, in fact, much more forthright than Nyawuza in making this point. Thus the "ANC remains a mass nationalist movement. . . . It correctly welcomes within its ranks all liberation fighters, whatever their class affiliation, who support its revolutionary nationalism. While its policy for the future, as set out in the Freedom Charter, is not inconsistent with an advance towards socialism, the ANC does not and should not demand a commitment to a socialist South Africa as a precondition of membership." The SACP, on the other hand, "is not a mass movement; it represents the aspirations of a single class—the proletariat." In consequence,

the party's mobilizing propaganda will have a special content which the ANC's intervention should not and cannot have. There is not a daily problem facing the working people, whether in town or countryside, which cannot be linked to the ravages of capitalism: and *it is only our party* which can present this connection in an undiluted way. (Emphasis added)

As we suggest in the text that follows, many socialists will be uneasy with this, uneasy with the idea of yet another "official" Communist Party defining itself as the (more or less exclusive) vanguard of the working class. Not that the SACP is without an honorable and often heroic history of commitment and struggle; indeed, more than many such parties elsewhere, it has shown a capacity to adjust its perspectives to keep pace with the evolution of popular aspirations in its own country, and it may well continue to do so.[16] Yet it is also true (as we argue later in the book) that as regards many of the most questionable canons of Soviet-influenced orthodoxy, the SACP has not been one of the more open and independent of Communist parties. It is fortunate, therefore, that the misgivings that the latter fact might give rise to can be placed in a much broader and more promising context.

After all, one of the most striking things about the South African working class is that it has not spent much time, in recent years, waiting upon some promised vanguard to "mobilize" it. Indeed, it has exemplified a dramatic dynamism both within and without the Congress movement, creating vibrant new institutions for itself, including the freshly minted Congress of South African Trade Unions (COSATU). And it has become increasingly articulate about its long-term goals. Later in this book we quote a recent statement by Jay Naidoo, COSATU's general secretary, made in the wake of a meeting he had with the ANC in Zimbabwe. It seems worthwhile anticipating the citation here in order to underscore the general point:

I told the ANC and SACTU delegations we did not want superficial changes or black bosses to replace white bosses, while the repressive machinery of state and capital remained intact. I expressed very clearly to them our commitment to see a society which was not only free of apartheid, but also free of the exploitative, degrading, and brutalizing system under which black workers suffered. This meant a restructuring of society so that the wealth of the country would be shared among the people. . . . COSATU was looking at alternatives which would ensure that any society that emerged would accurately reflect the interests of the working class.[17]

Of course, the radicalization which this statement reflects cuts right across South African society, as "popular democratic" and "proletarian" demands reinforce and push each other forward. This is why such a statement as that by Naidoo need not automatically be interpreted as embodying some fundamental contradiction between the organized workers and the Congress movement. Nor need it be seen as casting any very profound shadow over the ANC's claim to centrality within the struggle for liberation broadly defined. Indeed, at a subsequent meeting between the ANC and COSATU (a meeting in which the South African Congress of Trade Unions—SACTU—also participated), all parties "recognized that the emergence of COSATU as the giant democratic and progressive trade union federation in our country is an historic event in the process of uniting our working class and will immeasurably strengthen the democratic movement as a whole."[18] Yet it was also "recognized that the fundamental problem facing our country, the question of political power, cannot be resolved without the full participation of the ANC, which is regarded by the majority of the people of South Africa as the overall leader and genuine representative." And what of the future which these kinds of "recognitions" are likely to define?

They [the three delegations] agreed that the solution to the problems facing our country lie in the establishment of a system of majority rule in a united, democratic, and non-racial South Africa. Further, that in the specific conditions of our country it is inconceivable that such a system can be separated from economic emancipation. Our people have been robbed of their land, deprived of their due share in the country's wealth, their skills have been suppressed and poverty and starvation have been their life experience.

The correction of these centuries-old economic injustices lies at the core of our national aspirations. Accordingly they are united not only in their opposition to the entire apartheid system, but also in their common understanding that victory must embrace more than formal political democracy.

In short, even if the distinction which we have sought to establish between popular democratic and proletarian assertions has a certain analytical utility, in practice the two overlap in important ways. Certainly, as already hinted, much is lost if these two dimensions of the struggle are conceived to be readily compartmentalized, whether as distinct "stages" of the revolution or in entirely separate organizations. To repeat, the radicalization referred to above thrusts its way into all of South African political life and into all of the organizations of the oppressed. And this is all to the good.

Of course, there can be little doubt that the extent and precise terms of this radicalization will be sharply contested both within and without such organizations. Nor, in any case, are the precise modalities of a further deepening of the South African revolution entirely self-evident. Thus Eddie Webster, in his perceptive review of the first edition of this book (published in *Work in Progress*), turned upon Gelb and myself exactly the same criticism I have just made of certain of the extant formulations from within the camp of liberation itself: "It is not enough simply to assert the centrality of the working class within the national liberation movement. The question surely is *how* this centrality is to be asserted."[19] Webster then suggests that in order "adequately to capture the depth of the crisis facing South Africa" in this respect, "a materialist analysis would have to locate itself more firmly in the contradictions generated *within* the accumulation process. In particular such an analysis would have to recognize the implication of the growing concentration of economic power and the transformation of the labour process in South Africa for the possibilities of creating a workers' movement."

Needless to say, this is an on-going challenge for both analysts and practitioners. Fortunately, the past five years have seen some answers, in practice, to Webster's central question, as workers have further organized and politicized themselves. It is true that their most dramatic political actions have tended to be carried out—alongside students, members of the petty bourgeoisie, and the like—in the townships and at the level of the polity. In an economy so dependent upon black labor one might, perhaps, have hoped that the collective power of the workers could have been wielded at the point of production itself in an even more dramatic and crippling manner than it has been to date. In fact, a further deepening of the South African crisis along these lines—complementing the intensification of the armed struggle which is also certain to occur—can be expected, with profound implications both for the liberation struggle and for post-liberation South African society.

Destabilization: A Regional Crisis

A preoccupation with such possible strategic innovations on the part of the ruling classes in South Africa as the various attempts at formative action that we analyze in our text is appropriate. But it is even more important that any discussion of South Africa not downplay the centrality of the formidable repressive apparatus at the disposal of South African power-wielders—or the latter's willingness to use it. Although certainly not overlooked in our book, it may be that our postponing the discussion of that aspect of the situation to the very end of the second chapter gave it too much the appearance of being some kind of residual category, almost too obvious a one to give it its proper due. Yet there is at least as much reason to keep front and center the reality of repression—and the ever growing prominence of the military and police in South African decision-making circles—in 1986 as there was in 1981. I shall have reason to underscore this point again in the concluding chapter, but here it is a closely related point that bears emphasizing. For, as stated earlier, the regional costs of South Africa's deepening crises are even clearer than they were five years ago, as the brutal destabilization of its neighbors has become an ever more prominent tactical dimension of South Africa's aggressive strategy of defending the status quo at home and abroad.

Domination of its regional environment: South Africa's specific goals in this regard are multiple, the most overt being its desire to undermine support for the ANC in the neighboring states, in particular concrete support in the form of bases, supply lines, and freedom of passage. Clearly, some of South Africa's professed concern here has a primarily propagandistic intent—the better to project its own internal conflicts onto the rest of the subcontinent and present them as coming from outside, from "Communist-backed," hit-and-run "terrorists." Needless to say, this approach seeks to blur the fact that the ANC is, first and foremost, rooted not outside South Africa but in the ongoing struggle within; it manages, too, to overstate the degree of support (in logistical as distinct from rhetorical terms) that has come to the ANC from states in the region. Still, as the Nkomati Accord (signed with Mozambique in 1984) demonstrated, South African pressure can do the ANC some damage.[20]

There are other, perhaps more important, reasons for South Africa's assertiveness vis-à-vis its neighbors, however. One is economic. The southern African economy developed, historically, as a hinterland for South Africa, and the latter is prepared to try various means to retain its economic hegemony—to retain it as market, labor pool, transport outlet. In consequence, one key target of South African-sponsored incursions into neighboring countries has been the infrastructure of transport and communications among these states which, under the auspices of such initiatives as the Southern African Development Coordination Conference (SADCC), might be seen to be contributing to the emergence of a regional economic grid outside the orbit of South African control. Moreover, vis-à-vis individual states and economies, South Africa can hope to so weaken them as to make them more vulnerable to economic penetration, both by its own and other international capitalist actors.

South Africa also relishes the possibility that failed economies and shattered societies beyond its immediate borders will redound to its benefit in propaganda terms, both externally and domestically. If, on the one hand, South Africa's own responsibility for these outcomes can be blurred somewhat, then it might be made to appear that it is "socialism" and "black majority rule" that are not working in Africa. If, on the other hand, significant economic and political concessions can be extorted from its neighbors, some might be convinced to hail South Africa's "positive" role as peacemaker and help-mate in the region. So, at least momentarily, was South Africa able to present the Nkomati Accord, parlaying it into Botha's 1984 tour of Western European capitals, during which he found a few more doors than usual open to him.

Not that South Africa's tactic of destabilization, *qua* tactic, is entirely free of internal tensions and contradictions. Thus, at one extreme, destabilization might be geared to actually overthrowing the target government, or at least keeping it so bogged down in internal turmoil as to virtually neutralize it militarily. At the other extreme it might be aimed merely at weakening its target just enough to make it more vulnerable to economic penetration (by state-sponsored aid and trade agreements, by the activities of multilateral agencies—the IMF, the World Bank—and/or by private corporations), which could serve, in turn, to reinforce the target's subordination to the circuits of regional and international capital and ensure its consequent political docility. Clearly, there are difficulties in employing both instruments—the carrot and the stick—simultaneously, if only because a number of key potential protagonists of economic penetration, particularly in the private sector, are unlikely to want to enter as long as the socioeconomic disruption caused by destabilization continues. When, then, is it safe to drop the stick of destabilization in order to proffer the carrot of economic cooptation?

Certainly the South African state has seemed reluctant to desist from the use of force (its continued strong support for the MNR in Mozambique, long after the signing of the Nkomati Accord, for example),[21] even when some other relevant actors have begun to feel that the moment for the "peaceful" consolidation of neocolonialism has arrived. Perhaps, it has been suggested, the ambiguity of South African policy in this regard reflects the existence of different factions or "lines"

jockeying for position within South African policymaking circles
(e.g., the "militarists" vs. the "liberal capitalists"). Or, more
likely, it evidences hesitancy and uncertainty in such circles over
how best to deal with the situation. Can even more profitable
concessions be wrung out of a target state by applying just a
little more force for just a little while longer? Can a movement
like FRELIMO really be trusted not to try eventually to re-
activate its socialist project, even if it has made a significant
range of concessions in the short run in order to lift the weight
of our aggression? So their minds may run.

There are also real ambiguities as regards the nature of
the involvement of other Western actors beyond South Africa
in the regional destabilization of southern Africa. There is no
doubt, for example, that the South Africans took the election
of Ronald Reagan in 1980 to be a green light for their more
widespread use of the tactic (particularly against Mozambique);
moreover, at the time U.S. officials hailed uncritically both the
adoption of the Nkomati Accord (with its undermining of the
ANC's position in Mozambique) and the FRELIMO government's further opening to Western capital, without showing the
least uneasiness about the aggressive manner in which this
"peace" was won and these "compromises" extorted.[22] It is true,
as we shall see, that a heated debate continues about the further
logic of this situation, with an eminent liberal Republican opin-
ing, in the *Washington Post* of June 1985, that the ideal
moment for the cooptation has now arrived[23]—even as, in sharp
contrast, right-wing Republicans like Jesse Helms act to stem,
in the name of global anti-communism, any such opening toward a FRELIMO-led Mozambique. For its part, the Reagan
administration may be, literally, caught between these two positions, both attempting to proffer the economic carrot while
also—or so Mozambicans suspect—helping to prime the pump
of destabilization. And, of course, in Angola the destructive role
played by the Americans, alongside the South Africans, is far
more overt.

We have suggested that destabilization is merely one tactic
used by South Africa within its overall regional strategy, a tactic
to be applied primarily against those of its neighbors that are

the most recalcitrant. Not that the use of force beyond its borders is new to South Africa: it had already played some such aggressive role—militarily assisting the Portuguese and the Rhodesians in their defense of white minority rule, for example—well before the collapse of Portuguese colonialism. But when, in 1974, the latter event seemed to deprive South Africa of its familiar buffers against the continental advance of black majority rule, the denizens of the South African state felt the need for an even more active and formative policy in the region. At first the Vorster government sought to carry the day by means of diplomacy—its "détente" initiative emerging as an extension of an earlier Vorster emphasis on "dialogue" with black Africa—and by reliance on the apparently ineluctable logic of its economic hegemony (this latter already successful, it was felt, in ensnaring such countries as Swaziland, Botswana, and Lesotho in the South African net after their independence). But the temptation to adopt more aggressive means to control a changing environment was clearly very strong.

Thus, in 1975 South Africa launched its (unsuccessful) invasion of Angola and, in a move pregnant with implications for the region, also began to develop its sponsorship of the UNITA movement there. To be sure, when Botha replaced Vorster in 1978 the most overt policy emphasis remained the economic one, this centered on the notion of a regional "Constellation of States" within which the South African government and South African business could deepen their already considerable economic advantage and thus domesticate any potential enemies. But with the victory—so disappointing to South Africa—of Mugabe, not Muzorewa, in the Zimbabwe elections of 1980, and with the launching of the SADCC initiative that same year, the balance of South African regional policy reverted more firmly toward aggression. This was, in any case, something that fitted easily within the "Total Strategy" (including, as it did, the development of an ever more powerful and diversified military machine) which Botha and his strategists had already begun to define in order to defend the status quo.

Thus, if neighboring states could not be counted on to

accept "realistically" and relatively passively the logic of South Africa's regional economic and military hegemony, they would have to be forced to do so. Not only would they have to be reminded of their own weakness vis-à-vis South Africa; they might even have to be *further weakened*—to the point where there was no real alternative but to fall more supinely into line with South Africa's demands in the region. From this starting point a formula for destabilization was slowly but surely put together.

From the start, direct incursions by the South African state into neighboring countries were part of the package. Cross-border raids into Angola recommenced not long after the abortive invasion of 1975 and have continued, even intensified, ever since. Using the excuse that such raids are directed at "SWAPO bases" (true in part but no excuse, given the legitimacy of SWAPO's struggle), as well as the excuse provided by the Cuban presence in Angola,* South Africa has managed, quite unjustifiably, to avoid paying any very heavy price internationally for its efforts to destroy Angola—while also managing to drag its feet over any withdrawal from its own illegal occupation of Namibia. Moreover, cross-border raids were soon to take their place elsewhere in the region as an important part of South Africa's new hard-line approach to disciplining its neighbors. On January 12, 1981, a raid on Maputo killed 12; on December 9, 1982, 44 were killed in Maseru, Lesotho; May 1983, Maputo again, leaving 19 dead. More recently it was Botswana's turn as, on June 14, 1985, 12 people died in Gabarone. Although such raids were ostensibly directed against ANC targets, as often as not it was local citizens who died; clearly, first and foremost these attacks were intended as a reminder to

---

* In fact, there is good reason to suspect that it has become South African policy to act in such a way as to keep the Cubans tied down in Angola—the better to encourage the Reagan team to view the whole southern African situation in simplistic global Cold War terms. It was, after all, Chester Crocker who so outrageously handed the issue of a necessary linkage between a Namibia setlement and the withdrawal of Cubans from Angola (these latter in any case present from the outset only to stem a more aggressive South African advance) to the South Africans as a bargaining counter. The South Africans have, in turn, exploited this opening expertly.

African states of South Africa's might. To such raids must also be added the ruthless elimination of individuals—Ruth First, Joe Gqabi, and others—and the presence of South African commandoes both in sabotage raids (the death of South African Defense Force lieutenant Alan Gingles in 1981 by his own bomb while attempting to destroy a railway line deep inside Mozambique is a case in point) and alongside counter-revolutionary guerrillas in neighboring countries.

Nonetheless, South Africa's real military innovation lay in this latter phenomenon, the *counter-revolutionary guerrilla*. A word of explanation is in order here. There is, of course, nothing new about counter-revolutionaries. Nor is it unusual for them to coordinate their actions with external forces that wish a particular revolution ill. But the prominence of the counter-revolutionary guerrilla in recent years has, nonetheless, a new and grisly feel to it. The operations in which the counter-revolutionary guerrilla plays a leading role are being mounted with a new sophistication and a new ruthlessness. One cautionary note: it would be wrong to think of this guerrilla as having taken a leaf out of the book on classical guerrilla warfare. To a surprising degree—as exemplified by the contras in Nicaragua and, as we shall see, the MNR in Mozambique—he disdains actively to seek the support of the peasantry. More often intimidation and naked terror against the local population are the tactic. No, the textbook the guerrilla—and his backers—use is the textbook on social, economic, and political development. And they turn it inside out!

In other words, the experience of countries like Nicaragua and Mozambique suggests that the planners of this kind of warfare have developed a sophisticated sense of just what kind of linkages are necessary to begin to move an underdeveloped country forward. And they have crafted their intelligence and operational capacities quite self-consciously to identify such linkages-in-the-making and to destroy them in the countries that have been targeted. One graphic and quite overt example of this surfaced recently from another kind of textbook, the leaked ninety-page manual in Spanish entitled *Psychological Operations in Guerrilla War*, prepared by the CIA for its contra henchmen in Nicaragua. Among other things, the manual suggested the hiring of professional criminals "to carry out specific selective jobs," including the "neutralization" of Nicaraguan judges and other key Sandinista cadres. I wrote of the pattern underlying such grotesqueries in a personal account of a recent trip to Nicaragua and I will repeat one passage here since it also bears directly on the southern African situation:

Déjà vu. Nicaragua had too much the feel for me of Mozambique two or three years ago, on the way to the Nkomati Accord with South Africa: an inspiring struggle, a humane and vital revolution, being slowly bled to death. A Jesuit priest, now working in Nicaragua's agrarian reform sector but also active in Chile before the coup, put the point to me with scalding simplicity. "In Chile," he said, "the Americans made a mistake. They cut off the revolution too abruptly. They killed the revolution but, as we can see from recent developments there, they didn't kill the dream. In Nicaragua they're trying to kill the dream."

Of course, the possibility of Reagan attempting a quick kill remains. Nicaraguans are bracing themselves for a possible invasion, as well they should. But in the meantime the U.S.-backed contras are not merely, perhaps not even primarily, a military threat per se—though people are dying. They're also part of an overall strategy of slow strangulation—attacking economic targets and disrupting normal economic life on the one hand, draining off scarce Sandinista resources—internal funds, foreign exchange, personnel—into the defense effort on the other. Such wrecking complements an all-too-familiar gamut of international economic pressures which have been brought into play as well: leaning on debts, boycotting exports, and the like. Its hard to know who wrote the book on this kind of warfare, South Africa or the United States; it does at least seem certain that they have compared notes. And the result in Nicaragua does begin to approximate that achieved by the South Africans in Mozambique, even if the process has not gone nearly so far: an economy in tatters, with lack of foreign exchange a severe constraint, a goods shortage, rising prices.

Needless to say, these developments hit the proverbial man (and woman) in the street pretty hard. Such economic difficulties are the first thing many people wanted to talk about as I walked about Managua. Even when they could see the U.S.-cum-contra role in all of this, some people grumbled—not going over to the other side, it seemed, but a little less wholeheartedly enthusiastic about the revolution than before. Some of the blame for economic crisis must stick to socialism, so the Americans apparently calculate.

Who'll dare to raise their heads for another fifty years after we get through, who'll dare to dream: this too seems part of the calculation. When I gave a public talk in Managua about South Africa's war of aggression in Mozambique, Nicaraguans shook their heads; the parallels jumped off the page.[24]

In Angola, as noted earlier, the use of this particular tactic has meant cultivating and beefing up UNITA, an existing movement already notorious for its opportunism and tribalist politics. Massive South African support quickly became the most important key to UNITA's success in extending its presence in southern Angola and in its becoming such a costly running-sore for the beleaguered MPLA government. South Africa has nourished in similar fashion dissident groups in Lesotho (the self-styled Lesotho Liberation Army) and has also attempted to exacerbate the ZANU government's difficulties (otherwise self-inflicted) in the Ndebele area of Zimbabwe, beaming its "Radio Truth" into this area while helping to underwrite the so-called super-ZAPU band of marauders as a disruptive force.

But it is Mozambique that provides the purest case of this counter-revolutionary tactic. It was Rhodesian intelligence that first stitched together the MNR (or "Renamo," the Mozambique National Resistance) from the detritus of Portugal's defeated colonialism—from former policemen and special forces members, among others.[25] But with the collapse of Rhodesia, South Africa was prepared to pick up the slack, moving the whole operation south, providing training and military bases in the Transvaal, as well as supplies and essential logistical support. As noted above, the MNR has done relatively little to ground its activities in a popular base. There have been occasional rhetorical outbursts of "anti-communism" and some attempt to mobilize ethnic resentments; moreover, the combination of destabilization, natural disaster, and policy failures that have ground Mozambique's rural economy to a virtual standstill may well have tended to neutralize the peasant population—rendering their link to the Frelimo government a much more passive one than previously—in some parts of the country. But the basic reality has remained the MNR's intimidation of the local population, often carried out with unimaginable bestiality, and the press-ganging of fresh recruits into the ranks. Even though no real alternative to FRELIMO has been established, this particularly gross and cynical form of destabilization has been the primary cause of a downward spiral of economic decay and social distemper in Mozambique that has profoundly shaken the FRELIMO government's fragile structures and unleashed anarchic forces of truly disturbing proportions.

Particularly striking, then, is just how willfully destructive this tactic of counter-revolutionary guerrilla warfare has been designed to be in economic terms. Of course, South Africa has been prepared to use, in a variety of ways, the considerable economic leverage it has inherited from the historically warped, South Africa-centered pattern of economic growth in the region. It can threaten such countries as Lesotho, Zimbabwe, and Mozambique with cutting off their labor flows into South Africa and has, from time to time, acted upon such threats (as in the case of Mozambique, for example). It juggles trade and customs agreements vis-à-vis its dependent neighbors; it rations out locomotives and rolling stock essential to the regional rail network as a bargaining counter; it harasses the movement of Zimbabwe's and Lesotho's imports and exports through its ports, while turning off and on the tap of its own traffic to the sea via the port of Maputo as its manipulative purposes warrant. This latter ploy is merely one additional way in which economic warfare has been directed against the FRELIMO government, but perhaps, in the end, it is President Samora Machel's own words, presented as part of an explanation for Mozambique's signing of the Nkomati Accord, that capture best something of the impact of South Africa's war of destabilization on Mozambique's domestic development efforts:

Only future generations will show the precise extent of the social trauma caused by the horrors and barbarity of the armed gangs. The children who witnessed atrocities and repugnant acts of violence and destruction will grow up with the nightmare of their tragic memories. Men and women have been permanently mutilated and maimed, both physically and psychologically. They will be the living evidence of the cruelty of the war waged against us.

Our people had their property looted, their houses destroyed, their granaries raided, their crops pillaged and flattened, their cattle stolen and killed, their tools burnt and destroyed. The communal villages and cooperatives, the schools and clinics, the wells and dams built by the people with so much effort and sacrifice became targets for the enemy's criminal fury. The systematic destruction of economic infrastructure, bridges and roads, shops and warehouses, sawmills, plantations, agricultural and industrial machinery, electricity supply lines, fuel tanks, lorries and buses, locomotives and carriages has prevented the implementation of economic development projects of the utmost importance for the well being of the Mozambican people.

Eight hundred and forty schools have been destroyed or closed, affecting more than 150,000 schoolchildren. Twelve health centers, 24 maternity clinics, 174 health posts, and 2 centers for the physically handicapped have been sacked and destroyed. Nine hundred shops have been destroyed, hampering marketing and supplies for about 4.5 million citizens.

The bandits have murdered and kidnapped peasants and members of cooperatives, parliamentary deputies and party militants, teachers and students, nurses, lorry drivers, engine drivers, agricultural, construction, and commercial workers, technicians in various sectors, nuns, priests, private shopkeepers, journalists, and civil servants. . . .

This is the enemy's cruel nature—kill everything, steal everything, burn everything.[26]

The Mozambican case also demonstrates that South Africa's destabilization tactic has had its successes. Thus, at Nkomati the Mozambican government—literally bludgeoned into submission—sought to offer sufficient concessions to South Africa and its Western allies to lift the cruel weight of aggression from its back (albeit with no great success). Small wonder that when Lesotho was forced to evacuate certain ANC personnel from its territory in 1983, its foreign minister explained quite candidly that the country "could no longer withstand South African military and economic pressure."[27] And the truth of this remark was to become all the clearer when, in early 1986, South African economic blackmail was a key factor in facilitating the military coup that brought down the Jonathan government in that country.[28] Under such circumstances, the summary of the situation offered by Zambia's President Kenneth Kaunda remains much too close to the truth of the matter for us to take any easy comfort:

> Yes, humble Swaziland agrees, humble Mozambique accepts, humble Zambia hosts meetings of unequal neighbors like South Africa and Angola. What else can we do? But we are not doing it with happy hearts. We do it out of fear, but that fear will end one day. It is bound to.[29]

The final note struck by Kaunda is important, however. South Africa's brutal approach to the region may have bought it some further room for maneuver; it momentarily inflicted a blow—though very far from a mortal one—on the ANC and, as noted, it facilitated a semi-successful tour by Botha of Western Europe shortly after the signing of the Nkomati Accord. Nonetheless, any such advantage was bound to be short-lived. For destabilization can do nothing whatsoever to resolve South Africa's own internal contradictions. Indeed, as these latter contradictions have sharpened—since Nkomati—in 1984's dramatic resistance to the new South African constitution and amidst 1985's deepening crisis, the ANC's star has continued to rise and the apartheid regime's isolation continued to grow. Of course, these developments—and what they indicate as to the long-term vulnerability of the apartheid regime—cannot make any more palatable the fact that, thanks to Pretoria's ongoing wars of destabilization, it is South Africa's neighbors who still must pay much of the price for the defensive death agonies of racial capitalism in the region. As a result, none can hope even to begin to realize their full potential for development as long as an untransformed South Africa hovers over them, stick and carrot in hand. Moreover, ominously enough for such neighbors, the apartheid regime presently seems prepared to give renewed currency to its characteristic rationale for aggression: a shrill rhetoric, downplayed somewhat at the time of Nkomati, which stresses the threat of a "total onslaught," mounted, globally and regionally, against South Africa by that old bogeyman, the "communist menace"! For southern Africa, in short, worse may be yet to come. This is one more reason why we must not allow the drama of South Africa's internal crisis—crucial though that crisis undoubtedly is—to displace a simultaneous focus upon Pretoria's wars of destabilization from the agenda of the worldwide anti-apartheid movement.

The Imperatives of Anti-Apartheid Work

Fortunately anti-apartheid work has been on the upswing in recent years, and not least in the United States. There the Reagan administration has provided a particularly ripe and worthy target for the mobilization that has occurred. Gelb and I originally wrote in the very first days of the Reagan administration, but even then the political and moral bankruptcy of the policy that came to be known as "constructive engagement" was (as we note in the brief concluding section to the original text) perfectly apparent. True, some academic observers have since argued—however fatuously—that "Americans must understand that something like constructive engagement had to be tried and found wanting so that preconditions for truly effective United States pressure on South Africa could emerge." Yet even such time-serving "experts" must now admit the emptiness of Chester Crocker's "modernizing autocracy option": "The past fifteen months have shown that white-led change cannot succeed."[30] Moreover, the most forthright critics of constructive engagement worry—with good reason—that the powers-that-be in Washington have not yet fully grasped the folly of such a policy. Writing in *Foreign Affairs,* Sanford Unger and Peter Vale discuss Reagan's mid-1985 imposition of economic sanctions upon South Africa—this being a narrow and highly qualified gesture primarily designed to sidetrack more assertive initiatives by the Congress—and note that these merely

continue the recent American practice of attempting to reform the South African system by working entirely within it and honoring its rules. "Active constructive engagement" (the new, impromptu name the President seems to have given his policy during a press conference) is still a policy that engages the attention and the interests of only a small, privileged stratum of South Africans. It relies almost entirely on white-led change, as designed and defined by a regime that is becoming more embattled by the day. And it ignores the needs, the politics and the passions of the black majority in South Africa.[31]

But the Reagan record is actually much worse than even these formulations imply. For far more is at stake than merely adding credibility to the wrong side in the struggle for South Africa. Thus there is little doubt that the U.S. administration's perceived racism and the simpleminded primacy it has granted to "anti-terrorist" and "anti-communist" preoccupations in its policymaking have actually served to strengthen South African intransigence. More important, "during its first four years in office, the United States gave more economic, military, and diplomatic support to South Africa than any previous administration."[32] This is a record—memorably described by Bishop Desmond Tutu as being "immoral, evil, and un-Christian"—that has been well documented elsewhere. It is also a continuing reality, although it is the case that the escalating struggle in South Africa—and the burgeoning anti-apartheid movement in the United States and elsewhere—has given imperial policymakers some pause. Even within the Republican camp there are apparent divisions, views ranging from the died-in-the-wool racist support for South Africa of "Die-hards" like Jesse Helms and Jerry Falwell to the much more sophisticated approach of a new breed of right-wing Republicans; these latter "Young Turks"—in the interests both of cleaning up the image of America's anti-communist crusade abroad and of building a "Republican majority" (including some black support) at home—seek to distance, to some extent at least, the United States (and the Republican Party) from embarrassing entanglements with the apartheid regime.[33]

Meanwhile, the policies of the "Bureaucrats" within the Reagan administration appear merely to gyrate unsteadily and inconsistently from pole to pole, one week scorning the very idea of sanctions, the next week (as seen) opportunistically embracing certain of them, one day accepting the goal of "majority rule" for South Africa and legitimating the ANC as "freedom fighters" (thus spake Assistant Secretary of State for African Affairs Chester Crocker), the next day (literally) withdrawing both such assertions (thus spake "administration officials").[34]

True, there is a greater felt need than ever before, even in the White House, to contemplate the unthinkable regarding South Africa. Who would have anticipated, even a year or two ago, any reversal whatsoever regarding sanctions, let alone the strong condemnations of police brutality and calls for negotiations with the likes of Nelson Mandela which we have heard. Nonetheless, the answer to the question of how best to deal with South Africa's crisis remains elusive, especially for all those who are not prepared to accept the imperatives of a revolutionary resolution there.

Not surprisingly, the same observation applies equally to liberals. The incoherence and inadequacy of the response *inside* South Africa, even by those who represent the most "enlightened" and "reform-minded" capitalist circles, is documented in our concluding chapter. But the same is true of liberals outside South Africa. There has been, for example, the grotesque case of those congressional Democrats who find themselves so cowed by the Cold War atmospherics prevalent in Reagan's America as to side with pro-UNITA, and hence pro-South African, legislative initiatives—even as, simultaneously, they push for sanctions against South Africa.[35] But what is the likely response of such liberals to possible developments in South Africa itself as the struggle there advances through various novel stages. It may be true that "there is no longer any question that change will occur in South Africa," but (as Ungar and Vale proceed to say) there *are* crucial questions to be asked regarding this change: "How, according to whose timetable, and with what sort of outside involvement?" And even if, for the United States, the only hope can lie in "establishing much more direct communication with the South African majority and . . . granting it far greater and more practical assistance," just what can this be expected to mean in concrete terms?[36]

There are some suggestions on offer, of course, most recently those of the influential Irish writer Conor Cruse O'Brien.[37] No friend of socialist revolution, O'Brien seems equally concerned about the possibility that sheer anarchy will eventuate during the transition period in South Africa. Indeed, his controlling metaphor for structuring an analysis of current developments is the "necklace," a flaming, petrol-filled tire which has been used, in the townships, to assassinate police informers and other collaborators. His fear: ". . . the rule of the children, or rather of whichever ominous child emerged as victor out of the internecine competition for power within a political movement whose sanction, symbol, and signature is the burning alive of people in the street." Evocative stuff which, by both overstating the prevalence of such practices and by systematically under-stating the importance of the impressive organizational infra-structure that has given much shape to township political life (civic associations, trade unions, student associations more or less disappear in his sensationalist account), helps rationalize his preference for a "multi-racial bourgeois coalition."

Such a coalition, he notes, might not be "wholly attractive," although "it might, with luck, work quite well." For it could help stave off the demands, in particular, "of all the 'outs' of black society, including the politicized unemployed." Fortunate, then, that the "new black South Africa, unlike other African countries, will have a large black middle class," a "black bour-geoisie" ready to form a "middle class government," ready to "find allies among the whites," ready to facilitate the emergence of "a multi-racial coalition," a "coalition of all those with some-thing to lose, whatever the color of their skin." Moreover, O'Brien seems confident of the ability to enlist both "organizer labor" and the ANC to the service of this projected domestication of the liberation struggle, citing as an example—but seeming to imply much more—that Oliver Tambo, the ANC's president, "is essentially a liberal; he will get on well with Dr. Slabbert"[38]— the reference being to Frederik van Zyl Slabbert, leading South African liberal and, until recently, head of the opposition Pro-gressive Federal Party, who is among those most concerned about the future perils of "majority domination."

Opinions will differ (for reasons discussed in this book) as to the likely cooptability of the ANC and other actors into the "multi-racial bourgeois coalition" of the future. There are im-portant voices of South African capital who still feel much more comfortable with the likes of Gatsha Buthelezi, selected by the influential business journal *The Financial Mail* as its "Man of the Year" for 1985—this despite the fact he had spent the best part of the year further discrediting himself by acting as principal hammer of the UDF and other anti-apartheid organizations in Natal. What bears noting here, however, is that numerous external actors, faced with the deepening crisis of apartheid, have begun working to turn O'Brien's projected scenario into a reality. Taking off from the early-1986 announcement by Coca-Cola of the formation of a "series of 'Equal Opportunity Funds' to support black economic development in South Africa" (and the possible inclusion of such notables as Alan Boesak and Desmond Tutu on the board of this project), a recent article by James Cason and Mike Fleshman documents

a broader—and growing—effort by corporations, universities, foundations, and private groups to promote the development of a black, pro-capitalist middle class in South Africa. It did not go unnoticed among U.S. business and government leaders that workers at the formation of COSATU late last year denounced not only apartheid but also capitalism. The angry denunciations of apartheid, the U.S., and capitalism in general that have become regular features at mass demonstrations and funerals in recent years have conjured up fears that a future, black majority-ruled South Africa might adopt a harshly anti-capitalist, pro-socialist perspective. In reacting to the trend, the U.S. has developed a number of programs that are designed ultimately to direct any future transition in South Africa in a more capitalist direction.[39]*

---

* Of particular interest is a U.S.-based but Anglo American-funded study project, "South Africa Beyond Apartheid," which seeks to "outline and evaluate a range of strategic options" and which includes on its "research team" such worthies as the above mentioned Professor Adam (see n. 38), conservative U.S. churchman Richard Niehaus, and Chief Buthelezi's sinister house pollster, Lawrence Schlemmer of South Africa's Natal University. The activities of the Johnson Foundation, Mobil Oil, Harvard and Tufts universities, and Bayard Rustin's "Project South Africa" are also mentioned in the article. Attention should also be paid to the most Cold War-oriented of international trade union organizations, which have been even quicker off the mark than most business interests with respect to containing the long-term radicalization of South Africa. See, for example, Mark Gandell, "Foreign Affairs: The CLC [Canadian Labour Congress] Abroad," *This Magazine* (Toronto) 19, no. 6 (February 1986). Among other things, the CLC is revealed as being particularly responsive to business's concern (in the words of CLC International Affairs director John Harker) not "to leave a political vacuum which could be filled by political agitators."

Not that we should permit a preoccupation with various possible scenarios for a future, post-liberation South Africa to get out of hand; the struggle to reach that phase is still very far from having been concluded. O'Brien, to give him his due, emphasizes this fact as well, suggesting "a hardening of mood, especially in the Afrikaner community" and invoking "the model [of] General Jacques Massu's successful repression of the FLN in Algeria in the late·1970s." In his view, "a military—or more deeply militarized—government in South Africa might be expected to get a lot tougher than the government of P. W. Botha has yet felt able to be."[40] True or not, one can agree (as is argued in our concluding chapter) that a great deal more pressure, political and military, by the popular classes will have to be brought to bear on the South African state before any stage of genuine "end-game" bargaining can be said to have begun. All the more reason to reiterate the call with which Gelb and I concluded the first edition of this book, the call to complement the more familiar range of anti-apartheid activities in Western countries with ever more "overt support for the full range of militant activities [by South Africans] on the ground and for the African National Congress as it increasingly focuses that militancy." This is a call recently reiterated by the Afro-American anti-apartheid activist Prexy Nesbitt:

At this stage our movement has been organized on simply an anti-apartheid basis, which is insufficient for our tasks in the coming period. We must go from being merely anti-apartheid to being supportive of the specific national liberation movements in their quests for the total destruction of apartheid and in their creation of new societies in southern Africa. . . . The moment has never been more crucial to see the mobilization of the Afro-American community and progressive peoples of all races across this country [the United States] to not only do more divestment work, but to also affirmatively and clearly move to assist the ANC and SWAPO [of Namibia] in the tasks they have. . . . This will involve lending political support to the program and tactics of these organizations, including the defense of armed struggle as a legitimate tactic in the struggle for freedom.[41]

This, in itself, is no small task, especially at a historical moment when the term "terrorist" has taken on such highly charged (and eminently manipulable) connotations. In itself, this would be problem enough but, as I have written elsewhere in discussing the challenges of anti-apartheid work in Canada, many North Americans' incomprehension of the need South Africans feel to fight for their freedom

is underwritten by a low-key yet pervasive ethos of racism. . . . Put quite bluntly, we have even more difficulty in taking black aspirations for freedom and social change seriously than we do roughly comparable aspirations on the part of whites. . . . Few of us are pacifists, and indeed when European liberation movements, like the Dutch and French undergrounds in the 1940s, fought against fascism (Germany and its local colaborators), Canadians not only applauded, but even sent troops to help. Yet the enemy in South Africa is clearly the same: it is no accident that John Vorster was interned during the Second World War as a pro-Nazi sympathizer. Surely there are many more Canadians than have thus far made themselves heard who can have a colour-blind response to two such similar struggles for freedom.[42]

Nesbitt invokes another historical parallel to make much the same point: "After all, the independence of our own nation [the United States] only came about as a result of a revolutionary war against Great Britain."[43]

One hopes that such parallels—as well as the clear justice of the black struggle in South Africa which they seek to illuminate—will in fact elicit the kinds of supportive response that are so necessary. But the challenge becomes all the greater when we find ourselves forced to take the argument a step further— and return, in doing so, to that very scenario-mongering about the nature of a post-apartheid South Africa that we were tempted to abandon only a paragraph or two ago. For even as we take steps to further and more effectively support those who must, literally, fight for their freedom in South Africa, we must also mark clearly the implications for our work of two additional facts that have been underscored in this introduction. There is, first of all, the fact that South Africans committed to fundamental change are themselves already discussing the nature of the society they hope to build; such discussions effect the nature of the alliances they form and the strategies they adopt, even as they have implications for the future. Secondly, there are powerful actors, within and without South Africa but united in their opposition to a full-blown revolutionary transformation of South African economy and society, who are already launching schemes themselves designed to shape that future. We ignore such facts at our peril.

There are, to be sure, those in the anti-apartheid movement who will argue, with conviction, that tieing any of our anti-apartheid work to a concern about the likely long-term content of South African liberation is a mistake. After all (Canadian Chris Leo writes), "the immediate priority vis-à-vis South Africa is to get rid of the regime":

> The main reasons for the regime's present difficulties, as I see it, are a combination of international pressure against apartheid and the extraordinary tenacity and courage of black resistance within South Africa. The international side of the equation grows out of an attack on apartheid based on liberal ideology. That works because it appeals to the vast majority of people in capitalist countries and because the South African system is transparently vulnerable to it. The attack has been very effective and has, in a couple of years, substantially changed the climate of opinion—in Canada at least—about South Africa.
>
> What is needed, in my view, is to intensify that kind of attack and to put pressure for more and more effective boycotting and economic sanctions. That's what's going to bring the regime down if anything does. There is, of course, a radical critique to be made of South African society, and of all other capitalist and so-called socialist societies. . . . but I don't think this is the time to be putting energy into it where Southern Africa is concerned. There the priority has to be an end to the obscenity of apartheid, which is an offense to anyone with a bit of humanity left, whether they be believers in capitalism or socialists. If a radical critique of South Africa has any effect at all in Canada today, it will be to undermine the liberal assault on apartheid by lending credence to propaganda about alleged Soviet domination of the ANC and other black political groups.[44]

Cogent, but not convincing. Take the notion of "lending credence." Surely the lesson for our work is precisely the opposite of what Leo implies. As argued, a distinctive radicalization of the South African resistance movement is taking place. Inevitably, as the current balance of forces shifts and as end-game approaches, the bearers of that radicalization will be red baited—the better, for those who do the red baiting, to guide in their own interests the process of change. The ANC, for example, has experienced something of a honeymoon period from such attacks, but it is unlikely to last.* Even if a right-wing ideologue in the United States like Richard Viguerie—who is on record as having said that South Africa will continue to "have white rule for the foreseeable future. The question is whether that white ruler will be South African or Soviet"—does not call all the shots, in the present American political climate his kind of emphasis will have some impact. Liberals are, in any case, eminently susceptible to less crude variants of the same general "anti-communist" line.† Better, then, that we take full cognizance of the set of facts I have adduced above and seek to build an anti-apartheid constituency that can (for example) make more intelligent distinctions between the bogey of "Soviet domination" on the one hand and, on the other, the reality of indigenous radicalization, of the consolidation of that genuinely revolutionary project that South Africa's deep-seated social, economic, and political inequalities demands. Otherwise we may be caught flat-footed— and be out-flanked by some quite sinister forces—as the process of change accelerates.

---

* Unless, of course, the ANC were to fulfill Conor Cruse O'Brien's fondest dreams and prove to be as servile to established economic interests as he suspects to be possible.

† This is all the more likely since the South African Communist Party is so real and legitimate a presence within the camp of liberation (see Patrick Lawrence, "Behind the Red Funeral Flags" and Howard Barrell, "The View from Abroad: Conditions Have Probably Never Favoured the Party More," both in *The Weekly Mail*, 11-17 April 1986). Viguerie's statement, from *Newsweek*, 2 September 1985, is quoted in E. Imafedia Okhamafe, "South Africa: A Story in Black and White," *The Black Scholar* 16, no. 6 (November-December 1985), where Viguerie is also quoted as saying, "If I were black, I would prefer communism to apartheid." Okhamafe's own comment: "Nevertheless, the issue is not what ideology is acceptable to me or the Fallwell's; such decision best rests with the people of South Africa. It is for this reason that I ask: what is wrong with South Africa going communist if such a decision is democratically determined? Does Viguerie's U.S. no longer stand for self-determination, or people choosing or deciding for themselves how they should govern themselves?" These are doubly cogent questions given the ease with which all forms of radical development strategy are collapsed, in so much Western discourse, into an identity with (large "C") Communism. Unfortunately, we know the answer to Okhamafe's questions all too well.

Finally, though it is legitimate—even necessary—to keep the debate about a future socialist South Africa on the current agenda of the anti-apartheid movement, this should not imply that consolidating a socialist development project in the next round will be a simple matter. In the sphere of economic policy alone there will be dilemmas such as those that have confronted other countries in the region, like Mozambique and Zimbabwe: push the pace of transformation too quickly and risk both disastrous economic collapse and foreign intervention, move too slowly and risk complete absorption into the established circuits of capital and at least a partial compromising of the drive to meet the needs of the broad mass of the population (the needs, that is, of precisely those "outs" whom O'Brien considers eminently abandonable). Indeed, the considerably greater complexity and sophistication of the South African economy, the density of its external linkages, and other features specific to it will make this and other dilemmas especially challenging.

Nor can the discovery of progressive solutions to such dilemmas be left merely to the more or less judicious decisions of the fresh cadre of leaders that emerges, important though the quality of leadership is likely to be in the difficult aftermath of a transfer of power in South Africa. Turning O'Brien upside down, we must stress the extent to which hopes for the future are also dependent upon the ability of the popular classes (the "outs," broadly defined, and *including* "organized labor") to sustain the drive to empower themselves that they have launched so dramatically in recent years. If history teaches us anything, it is that only an effective infrastructure of democratic control from the base up—within the liberation movement, on the shop floor, in the township and erstwhile bantustans, in representative institutions at the national level—can keep alive a creative and positive dialectic between leadership and mass action. Perhaps, too, it is only then that such key issues as the land question are likely to be kept firmly on the agenda, only then that such programs as the further nationalization of key industries will be pursued while being given real socialist content.

These are big questions (once again touching on the issue of the long-term relationship between the ANC and the trade union movement, for example), but ones that can merely be noted in passing in an introduction such as the present one. And there are many other crucial questions. Thus, socialism or no, "racism will not necessarily end with the end of apartheid, just as the official end of Jim Crow did not end racism in the U.S." (even though, as E. Imafedia Okhamafe then adds, "the end of apartheid will at least remove the government from the business of racism").[45] Add all the other inequalities and distortions inherent in South Africa's system, the inequalities and distortions which the architects of racial oppression and capitalist exploitation have, literally, willed into place in South Africa over the past several hundred years. Add potenial ethnic tensions (this variable having been given added saliency—and, in the form of the bantustan governments, an institutional infrastructure—by the apartheid government's divide-and-rule strategy), add gender oppression,[46] add so many other challenges that will have to be confronted and dealt with, and one can readily grasp that even with the fall of the current system, the struggle for a truly free South Africa will only have just begun. One need scarcely add that the next phase—when it comes—will be full of risk. Yet, self-evidently, it will also be full of promise, promise inherent in the fact that then, at last, all South Africans will have the opportunity to run their own risks, to conceive their own futures, to participate in the shaping of their own destinies. Risk—and promise—and a struggle that will continue. It is not too early for anti-apartheid activists to enlist for this phase of the South African revolution as well.

(April 1986)

Notes

1. Bill Freund, *The Making of Contemporary Africa* (Bloomington: Indiana University Press, 1984), p. 335.
2. Eddie Webster, "Book Review" in *Work in Progress* (Johannesburg), no. 23 (June 1982): 24.
3. Z.P.J. (Pallo Jordan), "Book Review: Black Middle Class—Eleventh-Hour Counter-Insurgency or Acquiescence in Continued Domination," *Sechaba* (Lusaka), May 1983, p. 24.
4. Deborah Posel, "Rethinking the 'Race-Class Debate' in South African Historiography," *Social Dynamics* (Capetown) 9, no. 1 (June 1983).

5. Deborah Posel (in ibid), for example, insists that Gelb and I reduce racial hierarchization to a mere reflex of the class structure and the imperatives of capital in precisely this "functionalist" manner. As a result, she argues, we cannot really theorize, even if we are sometimes forced to acknowledge, the contingent nature of the links between class exploitation and racial oppression. (Posel, for her part, and in her own chosen theoretical terms, sees the relationship between these two realities as being instead both "functional" and "dysfunctional.") Here one is tempted to respond, with Engels: "What these gentlemen [and ladies—JSS] all lack is dialectics. They see only here cause, there effect. That this is a hollow abstraction, that such metaphysical polar opposites exist in the real world only during crises, while the whole vast process goes on in the form of interaction—though of very unequal forces, the economic movement being by far the strongest, most primeval, most decisive—that here everything is relative and nothing absolute—this they never begin to see. Hegel has never existed for them." (See "Letter to Conrad Schmidt" in Robert Tucker, ed., *The Marx-Engels Reader* [New York: Norton: 1972], p. 645.)

6. Karl Marx, *Capital* (New York: International Publishers, 1967), vol. 3, pp. 791-92.

7. Erik Olin Wright, "Giddens' Critique of Marxism," *New Left Review* 138 (March/April 1983): 24.

8. Patrick Lawrence, "White Capitalism and Black Rage," *Weekly Mail* (Johannesburg), 13-19 September 1985.

9. Nyawuza, "New 'Marxist' Tendencies and the Battle of Ideas in South Africa," *The African Communist* (London) 103 (Fourth Quarter 1985).

10. Posel, "Rethinking the 'Race-Class Debate'"; see also n. 5 above.

11. Jordan, "Book Review."

12. Nyawuza, "New 'Marxist' Tendencies."

13. Thabo Mbeki, "The Fatton Thesis: A Rejoinder," *Canadian Journal of African Studies* 18, no. 3 (1984).

14. "Sol Dubula" [Joe Slovo], "The Two Pillars of Our Struggle: Reflections on the Relationship Between the ANC and SACP," *The African Communist* 87 (Fourth Quarter 1981).

15. Not that Jordan is ever tempted to fall back quite so comfortably as Nyawuza on an outright dismissal of any class analysis of the black population, Nyawuza preferring to use such concepts (sic) as "sell-outs" and "lost souls" to characterize those who abandon the cause of the "African people." This latter approach may also be contrasted with that of Slovo, below. Unfortunately Mbeki, too, appears to downgrade class analysis unduly, dismissing rather too easily and contemptuously Fatton's suggestion that there might be "ruling classes" in the bantustans, for example.

16. This is a process that is said to be more evident in various resolutions of the Central Committee than it is, certainly, in the pages of *The African Communist*. Indeed, so shrill is the attack on "workerism"

and related heresies in a number of recent articles in the latter journal (the abovementioned article by Nyawuza is a particularly depressing example) that some have even interpreted this tendency as evidencing a defensive reaction on the part of the more Stalinist right wing of the SACP uneasy about fresh winds of change that are gathering force within the party itself.

17. See the article entitled "COSATU Spells Out Its Aims to the ANC," *The Star* (Weekly), 23 December 1985.

18. These quotations are drawn from "Communique of the Meeting Between the Congress of South African Trade Unions, the South African Congress of Trade Unions, and the African National Congress," 7 March 1986.

19. Webster, "Book Review."

20. On this and related matters see my chapter "Nkomati and After" in John S. Saul, ed., *A Difficult Road: The Transition to Socialism in Mozambique* (New York: Monthly Review Press, 1985).

21. On this subject see my "Mozambique Socialism and South African Aggression: A Case Study in Destabilization," paper presented at the (American) African Studies Association, New Orleans, November 1985, and also Robert Davies, *South African Strategy Towards Mozambique in the Post-Nkomati Period: A Critical Analysis of Effects and Implications* (Montreal: CIDMAA, 1985); for a useful overview of the regional picture which is complementary to the present one see Robert Davies and Dan O'Meara, "Total Strategy in Southern Africa: An Analysis of South African Regional Policy since 1978," *Journal of Southern African Studies* 11, no. 2 (April 1985).

22. What is *not* heard in Washington—and seldom enough in Western Europe—is any significant defense of the integrity of the development efforts originally conceived by the Mozambicans or the Angolans. This in itself may indicate how difficult it is for Western countries to detach themselves—whatever the rhetorical flourishes they may indulge in vis-à-vis apartheid—from the role South Africa plays as the gendarme for capital in the southern African region. Indeed, this may explain why, in certain countries, South Africa's wars of destabilization have not been a more salient focus than they have been in circles ostensibly opposed to apartheid.

23. Melvin Laird, "Opening to Mozambique," *Washington Post,* 17 June 1985.

24. John S. Saul, "Nicaragua Under Fire," *Monthly Review* 36, no. 10 (March 1985).

25. For a further elaboration of material discussed in this paragraph see my paper, as cited in note 21 above.

26. Samora Machel, "Accord of Nkomati: A Victory for Peace," in the supplement to AIM (Mozambique Information Agency) *Bulletin No. 94* (Maputo), April 1985. In addition to destroying infrastructure relevant to Mozambique development per se, communications and transportation links of potential importance to an emerging SADCC-

based regional economy have also been an important target for the South African-sponsored "bandidos" in Mozambique.

27. Quoted in Robert M. Price, "Pretoria's Southern African Strategy," *African Affairs* (London) 83, no. 330 (January 1984).

28. See Dan O'Meara, "The Coup d'Etat in Lesotho," *Southern Africa Report* (Toronto) 1, no. 5 (April 1986).

29. Quoted in Kenneth W. Grundy, "Pax Pretoriana: South Africa's Regional Policy," *Current History* 84 (April 1985).

30. Michael Clough, "Beyond Constructive Engagement," *Foreign Policy* 61 (Winter 1985-86): 3, 23.

31. Sanford J. Unger and Peter Vale, "South Africa: Why Constructive Engagement Failed," *Foreign Affairs* 64, no. 2 (Winter 1985-86): 235.

32. Kevin Danaher, *The Political Economy of U.S. Policy Toward South Africa* (Boulder: Westview Press, 1985), p. 196. The point is well documented in this book, and also in Prexy Nesbitt, "South Africa, Reagan, and the 'Right' in the Time of the 'Toad,'" unpub. ms., n.d.

33. For an instructive article on this theme (one that introduces the terms "Die-hards," "Young Turks," and "Bureaucrats" to describe the different factions within the Republican Party), see William Finnegan, "Coming Apart over Apartheid: The Story Behind the Republicans Split on South Africa," *Mother Jones,* April/May 1986.

34. On this latter episode see the articles by David Ottaway entitled "U.S. Favors Black Rule in South Africa," *Washington Post,* 13 March 1986, and "African Policy Experts Asking How Long Crocker Can Last," *Washington Post,* 14 March 1986; also Leslie Gelb, "U.S. Vows to Resist Despots of Right as Well as of Left," *New York Times,* 14 March 1986. I am grateful to Mike Fleshman for making these articles available to me.

35. This is, of course, also the voting pattern of the "Young Turks," though they perhaps can do so with rather greater claim to logical consistency.

36. The latter formulations are quoted from Ungar and Vale, "South Africa: Why Constructive Engagement Failed," p. 237.

37. Conor Cruse O'Brien, "What Can Become of South Africa?" *The Atlantic,* March 1986, p. 68.

38. An academic variant of O'Brien's approach can be found in a recent paper by the notorious Heribert Adam, a Canadian-based professor who has built a career from affecting a coolly "objective" posture and a quasi-leftist vocabulary—the better to pour cold water over any and all revolutionary enthusiasms in South Africa. By now having to shift ground pretty frantically in order to keep pace with events, Adam suggests that the blandest form of "social democracy" is the most that one should look forward to. Arguing, characteristically, that South African "business" is "rational" enough to adjust to current pressures, Adam sees the cooptation of the trade unions as the best means for such business interests to control the possible socioeconomic fall-out of political transformation. Not that he is any more worried than

O'Brien about the revolutionary vocation of the ANC (this latter "to all intents and purposes [representing] an aspiring but hitherto excluded middle-class"). He takes Mbeki's statement (". . . the ANC is not a socialist party") pretty much at face value, ignoring the possible ambiguities (the centrality of the working class, the possible role of the SACP) which, as we have seen, Mbeki was careful to build into his formulation. See Heribert Adam, "Capitalism and the Future of Apartheid," lecture at Carleton University, Ottawa, 7 March 1986, mimeo.

39. James Cason and Michael Fleshman, "Coke Adds Artificial Sweetener: Buying into the Black Opposition," *Southern Africa Report* 1, no. 5 (April 1986).

40. O'Brien, "What Can Become of South Africa," p. 65.

41. Prexy Nesbitt, "Expanding the Horizons of the U.S. Anti-Apartheid Movement," *Black Scholar* 16, no. 6 (November-December 1986): 45.

42. John S. Saul, "In the Belly of the Beast," *This Magazine* (Toronto) 13, nos. 5-6 (November-December 1979): 52.

43. Nesbitt, "Expanding the Horizons."

44. Chris Leo of the University of Winnipeg in a letter published in *Southern Africa Report* (Toronto) 1, no. 4 (February 1986).

45. E. Imafedia Okhamafe, "South Africa: A Story in Black and White," *Black Scholar* 16, no. 6 (November-December 1985): 23.

46. See, on this issue, the review-article by Linzi Manicom, "The Lives of South African Women," *Southern Africa Report* 1, no. 2 (October 1985) and *Focus on Women*, a special issue of *Southern Africa Report* 1, no. 4 (February 1986), available from TCLSAC, 427 Bloor St. W, Toronto M5S 1X7, Canada.

The Crisis in South Africa: Class Defense, Class Revolution
by JOHN S. SAUL AND STEPHEN GELB

INTRODUCTION

The strikes by African workers first erupting in Durban in 1972 and spreading throughout the country ever since, the outbursts sparked by students in Soweto and elsewhere from 1976 to the present, the actions undertaken by the African National Congress's guerrillas on the ground (most dramatically evidenced) by the Sasolburg bombings of 1980): these and other developments have been clear signs that the tide has at last begun to turn against South Africa's apartheid system. In the 1960s, after the regime's fierce and effective crackdown on the burgeoning opposition movement of the preceding two decades, the forces of liberation were in a state of disarray, the South African people momentarily stunned. In North America, too, there was a danger that opposition to apartheid would be forced into the *cul-de-sac* of sterile moralizing about an indefensible but apparently unyielding situation. This need no longer be a temptation, and for that reason political work around South African issues takes on a new kind of urgency. Ronald Reagan, Alexander Haig, and their various minions will seek, no doubt, to persuade us that most of the actions mentioned above reflect the working of some sinister Soviet plot. It is, therefore, all the more essential that the real truth of the matter be presented: the efforts of the oppressed mass of South Africans to challenge their oppression must certainly find more effective focus and direction in the years ahead but, in a nutshell, it is these efforts which have already been the most crucial factor in placing *crisis*—deep and unavoidable—on the South African agenda for the 1980s.

Are there other indices of crisis? Consider the phrase "adapt or die." It was with this blunt statement to the white population of South Africa that P. W. Botha entered into the premiership in 1979. Such sentiments, accompanied by a flurry of rhetorical pronouncements to similar effect, and even by occasional "reforming" initiatives (the precise content and implications of which we shall explore below), earned Botha the accolade of 1979 "Man of the Year" from the prestigious Johannesburg-based business journal *Financial Mail*. The *FM* (November 30, 1979) found in Botha "a driving resolve . . . to move away from the narrow sectarian approach which had characterized the regime of other Nationalist Party Prime Ministers" and to move toward more straightforwardly liberal-capitalist solutions to South Africa's pressing problems, economic and political. Why was this necessary? Because, as the *Financial Mail* (February 1 and June 6, 1980) editorialized on other occasions, "In the coming decade of crisis, what South Africa needs is skilled crisis management. . . . If South Africa is to enter an era of (relative) stability and prosperity, government must ensure that as many people as possible share in that prosperity and find their interests best-served by an alliance with capitalism. . . . Defusing the social time-bomb . . . can only be achieved through negotiation—not with men with Kalashnikovs but with the authentic leaders of the black people." And this theme was reiterated recently by Harry Oppenheimer, chairman of South Africa's largest single business enterprise, the Anglo American Corporation, when, worried by the snail's pace of the Botha reform program he had originally praised, he "warned of possible revolution in white-minority-ruled South Africa in five years unless blacks get major concessions" (*Globe and Mail* [Toronto], February 4, 1981).

We shall see in due course that the "snail's pace" of reform is as revealing of South African realities as is the tendency toward reform itself. It is clear, too, that the very notion of reform, so much at play in South African ruling circles these days and almost certainly to be heard much more of in Western discussions regarding South Africa, must be viewed with considerable skepticism. It is therefore fortunate that much more enlightening theoretical ground exists upon which to locate the discussion of South Africa's crisis than that provided by sterile, liberal-minded agonizing over the extent, nature, and significance of such "reform." Thus Stuart Hall, in examining a rather different ruling-class project to manage the conditions of severe crisis—that advanced by Margaret Thatcher in the United Kingdom—returns to Gramsci to find a clue. Arguing that Great Britain's swing to the right is part of what Gramsci called an " 'organic' phenomenon," he quotes the *Prison Notebooks* (p. 178) as follows:

> A crisis occurs, sometimes lasting for decades. This exceptional duration means that uncurable structural contradictions have revealed themselves . . . and that, despite this, the political forces which are struggling to conserve and defend the existing structure itself are making efforts to cure them within certain limits, and to overcome them. These incessant and persistent efforts . . . form the terrain of the conjunctural and it is upon this terrain that the forces of opposition organize.

Hall then continues:

> Gramsci insisted that we get the "organic" and the "conjunctural" aspects of the crisis into a proper relationship. What defines the "conjunctural"—the immediate terrain of struggle—is not simply the given economic conditions, but precisely the "incessant and persistent" efforts which are being made to defend and conserve the position. If the crisis is deep —"organic"—these efforts cannot be merely defensive. They will be *formative:* a new balance of forces, the emergence of new elements, the attempt to put together a new "historical bloc," new political configurations and philosophies, a profound restructuring of the state and the ideological discourse which construct the crisis and represent it as it is "lived" as a practical reality; new programmes and policies, pointing to a new result, a new sort of "settlement"—"within certain limits." These do not "emerge": they have to be constructed. Political and ideological work is required to disarticulate old formations and to rework their elements into new configura-

tions. The "swing to the right" [in Great Britain] is not a re-flection of the crisis: it is itself a *response to* the crisis.[1]*

It is entirely appropriate to see much of this as directly applicable to the current moment in South Africa—even if, paradoxically, it is reform rather than a swing to the right that forms the potential centerpiece of the dominant classes' "response to the crisis." Needless to say, one must proceed with caution here. Hall has recently been criticized for overestimating the extent to which Thatcher can really hope to shift the terrain of class struggle in the U.K. formatively to the right and in her favor; certainly her attempt to do so is beginning to fray markedly at the seams.[2] The same is true in part for Botha: as we shall see, the deep-seated contradictions and balance of class forces (both within and between classes) that define the South African crisis narrow the scope for creative maneuver on the part of the ruling group. Moreover, so complex is the politico-economic minefield which South Africa presents that there is room for considerable difference of opinion, even among those who occupy precisely the same class position, as to the best strategy and tactics to pursue. Indeed, it is in this regard that Oppenheimer's frustration, mentioned above and elaborated upon in the same speech, becomes of considerable interest:

> Mr. Oppenheimer told the journalists that Mr. Botha and previous National Party governments, following the official policy of apartheid or racial separation, have squandered too much time in trying to reach an accommodation between South

---

* Perhaps it is worth specifying further the way in which these formulations cut through the ambiguities surrounding the use of the word "reform." Using it in one way, the Western media (and South Africa propagandists) seek to present reform as opposite to preservation of the status quo and to imply thereby that it involves changes much more fundamental than in fact it does. In extrapolating from Hall's analysis and contrasting "reform" to "revolution," we are emphasizing that reform is to be understood primarily as a more sophisticated and active ("formative") defense of that status quo. This is a distinction with implications which stretch beyond the South African case, but it is nonetheless a particularly important one to bear in mind there if we are to avoid being entrapped on a liberal terrain of debate. (Or, for that matter, on an "ultra-left" terrain of debate: "reform" is not genuine transformation, but it is not meaningless or irrelevant either, for it can affect the shape of the field of battle in ways which must be taken into account!)

Africa's 4½ million whites and 20 million blacks. During two years as Prime Minister, he said, Mr. Botha had raised the hopes of blacks with promises of a new deal, at the same time telling whites they must "adapt or die." But, he said, time is running out and unless "substantive changes" are made by the mid-1980s, South Africa could face violent revolution.

Of interest, too, is the response of the *Financial Mail* which, only eight months after naming him "Man of the Year," was editorializing that Botha had led businessmen "up the garden path," and by year's end could only resignedly call his track record one of "continuing to talk change while consolidating his power base—hopefully in order to be able to introduce some"!

Small wonder that others, approaching the Botha record even more skeptically but from the left, have called it merely a "facelift" for apartheid[3] or, locating "reform" within the framework of the government's self-proclaimed "total strategy" for meeting the crisis, have taken the increased ascendancy of the military and the increased repression of any real political challenge to white power to be the more fundamental dimension of the current moment in South Africa.[4] There is good reason for such an emphasis. The old Adam of apartheid is still with us: only a very dishonest observer would argue that the basic structures of the racial-capitalist system have even begun to be tampered with or that any shift, *à la* the apparent fondest wishes of Oppenheimer and the *Financial Mail,* to a more color-blind capitalism will be easily made.

This said, we would still argue that the "facelift" formula is somewhat too comfortable a starting point for analysis, one which, correct as far as it goes, may prejudge too many issues and foreclose, by metaphorical fiat, too many possibilities. To begin with, it may encourage an underestimation of the depth of the organic crisis (economic and political) to which South Africa's ruling class must respond. Though skyrocketing gold prices have bought that class some further room for maneuver (a point to which we will return), there is simply less scope than previously for business—or politics—as usual under apartheid. In short, the sparring between Oppenheimer and Botha—like that between Botha and, further to the right within the Nationalist Party camp, Andries Treurnicht—is real. And it is about something real: the crisis. Thus it behooves us, now more than ever, to take seriously, and to understand, such jockeying for position among the power wielders.

Moreover, it bears reasserting that the "incessant and persistent efforts" of some of the actors within this latter group *can* be "formative," *can* give rise to "elements"; which, in important ways, are indeed "new." Even the establishment of the "independent" bantustans—an early initiative in the attempted reconstruction of the situation—has had some impact on the balance of forces in South Africa, despite the obvious fraudulence of the ploy and its failure to win much legitimacy abroad. What of present attempts to free up some space for black trade union activity (the Wiehann report), for pursuit of (limited) privileges by select black urban strata, for (strictly circumscribed) black political activity (the President's Council, the "constellation of states")? What of any future adjustments that the crisis may squeeze out of the established structures of racial capitalism? Of course, to ask these questions is not to mistake the scope or the intent of any such initiatives, or to enthuse with *Business Week* (March 4, 1981) that Botha is really "trying to make radical changes in domestic policy," changes which deserve a "public gesture of understanding from the United States." Rather, it is to avoid disarming ourselves, vis-à-vis liberals and conservatives who are so anxious to make the very best of any changes in South Africa, by taking the potential for a certain range of change seriously. It is to locate such changes as do emerge—as well as the many continuities that also exist— firmly on the grid of our growing understanding of the complex realities of South African capitalism. It is precisely in pursuit of this latter goal that, in the first two chapters, we seek both to delineate the chief characteristics of the organic crisis that has given rise to the tensions currently so evident within South Africa (chapter 1) and to explore some of the implications, present and future, of the paradoxical, even contradictory, package of unaccustomed reform *and* renewed repression which defines the "total strategy" as a response to that crisis (chapter 2).

There is another crucially important reason for approaching the question of ruling-class strategies in South Africa with as few preconceptions as possible: as Gramsci notes, the "terrain of the conjunctural" is the terrain upon which the "forces of opposition organize." Of course, deep-cutting "organic" developments have already shaped and reshaped the terrain of such struggle in crucial ways. One might mention revolutionary achievements elsewhere in the region—Mozambique, Angola, Zimbabwe—among many other factors. But most important has been the tempo and direction of South African capitalist development itself, development which has continued to demand the build-up of urban-dwelling Africans and, in concert, the build-up of an ever more dangerous and assertive, but ever more economically essential, black working class. The most novel dimensions of the South African state's "total strategy" are directed expressly toward defusing this volatile reality—the "urban problem" which, in the end, Prime Minister Verwoerd's original bantustan ploy has not really begun to touch in a fundamental way. Further, the attempted cooptation of elements from the urban black population which this involves—winning them to an "alliance with capitalism," as the *Financial Mail* put it—must certainly alter the terrain, affecting both the strategy and tactics of those who seek instead the total transformation of South Africa. It is one of several aspects of the picture which we must keep front and center as we attempt (in chapter 3) to identify and evaluate those classes from which a different kind of alliance, a revolutionary alliance, can ever more effectively emerge.

Fortunately, as noted at the outset of this introduction, the 1970s have amply demonstrated that it is not necessary merely to hypothesize the presence of revolutionary energy in South Africa: it is there. A more pressing matter—to be resolved by those engaged in significant practice within the country itself—is the discovery of the political format that will best focus that energy, and best consolidate a revolutionary class alliance. There is a long and deeply imbricated history of struggle against oppression in South Africa which has already structured to a considerable degree the range of possible nominees for the role; moreover, additional nominees are frequently forthcoming, both from South Africans and from others. The spectrum would include the several liberation movements, long since banned from

having an aboveground political presence, as well as the various
continuing organizational expressions of the Black Consciousness
movement, itself much banned. Even the highly compromised
Gatsha Buthelezi, chief minister of the Kwazulu bantustan,
claims to reach out from his Inkatha movement toward a South
Africa-wide political project. And then there are those, among
them several recent Trotskyist writers in particular, who urge
the construction of a novel "working-class party"—vastly different from the "petty-bourgeois, peasant-based national liberation movements" which are seen to have failed to deepen the
struggle into a socialist one elsewhere in the region.[5]

There are extraordinarily complex issues involved here,
not least the nature of the interplay betwen nationalist and socialist projects in South Africa to which the preceding sentence
alludes. Such issues are the focus of ongoing work on our part,
to be published in due course; here, in our final brief chapter 4,
we will have space only to hint at some tentative guidelines,
though guidelines which, however tentatively advanced, we
hope may be useful to the North American left as it seeks
to relate more positively to the South African struggle in the
years ahead. To anticipate, we will conclude that the national
liberation movement format remains, under South African conditions, a valid blueprint for socialist revolution, even though it
is a format within which the working class must become an
ever more important and self-conscious component; and that
the African National Congress of South Africa demands support as best providing of this format, although it seems likely
that the ANC which ultimately wins the struggle in South
Africa will be rather different from the movement as we know
it today. Not an entirely straightforward conclusion, needless
to say, but one which is strengthened by the fact that, as we
shall argue, the ANC is already changing as the terrain of
struggle alters in South Africa and as the pace of events picks up.

1. THE ORGANIC CRISIS

What are the key dimensions of the organic crisis of South Africa's racial capitalism to which we have alluded above? In this chapter we will explore the economic and political aspects of this crisis. But first it will be necessary both to specify the main components which, historically, have come to shape the racial capitalist system itself, and to identify those actors, on the shifting stage of South African capitalism, who play the most important contemporary roles.

I. The Logic of Racial Capitalism

The logic of racial capitalism? One thing that generations of liberal historians and economists in South Africa have sought to emphasize is precisely the *illogicality* of this system. Thus they have argued vigorously that "ideological factors" like racism and Afrikaner nationalism—inherited, perhaps, from the frontier experience of the Dutch/Afrikaner pioneer vis-à-vis the indigenous population or from recidivist memories of decades-long struggles against British hegemony—have warped the preferred rationality of capitalism. However, the testimony of recent Marxist scholarship confounds any such comfortable assumptions.[1] On the contrary, it has demonstrated the manner in which, under South African conditions, racial oppression and capitalist exploitation have come to feed on and reinforce one another. The key was the diamond- and gold-mining revolutions of the turn of the century when the political economy of race became, definitively, the political economy of a cheap labor supply.

Here the migrant labor system and the practices of tight control over the freedom of activity of Africans (e.g., hut taxes, further land expropriation and other methods to force them into the workplace, the compound system, the pass book and other mechanisms to police them in the "modern sector") were locked into place at the very heart of the economy. As Harold Wolpe and others have demonstrated, within the broad framework of "segregation" the African reserves—sustaining the migrants' families and providing a point of reference for their own security and welfare needs—subsidized South African enterprises, facilitating the holding-down of wages. And this fact has consistently made such enterprises, the mines and the white farms in particular, more profitable, even more viable, than they would otherwise have been. It is true that white workers have, upon occasion, moved to safeguard various job categories for themselves and have kept them from being "Africanized" at a cheaper rate for the job. But the various notorious examples of job reservation—the "job color bar"—which have sometimes brought labor and capital into conflict within the white polity have been much less important, historically, than what F. A. Johnstone has called the "exploitation color bar." This—the guarantor to capital of a cheap labor supply—has been the bottom line of the South African system.

"Afrikaner nationalism," many Marxists would argue, has been no more "irrational" a factor, but instead has encapsulated the demands of a fluctuating alliance of classes and class fractions produced on the terrain of South African capitalist development itself. Critical of Afrikaners like Generals Botha and Smuts who, soon after the Boer War, aligned themselves in power with British-based and local English mining capital, other political leaders chose to resist the free run of such capital and to defend the "national interest." At this stage, the notion of advancing Afrikanerdom's interests blended into a broader concept of (white) South African nationalism, and under General

Hertzog's leadership placed in power in the 1920s a ruling coalition of Afrikaner agrarian capital and the quite volatile white working class (with a dash of aspirant English industrial capital added in). Nonetheless, even if not yet the project of the more militant and narrowly Afrikaner nationalism which was to come, the expansion of the state sector—the mammoth Iron and Steel Corporation (ISCOR), for example—was soon seen as strengthening Afrikanerdom's hand and as complementing the private sector advances begun in the 1910s by Afrikaner capital through the cooperative movement, the National Press (a publishing venture), and the fledgling insurance giants Sanlam and Santam.

This nationalist project became much more prominent in the 1930s as the ideologues of the secretive and powerful Afrikaner Broederbond launched an increasingly successful cultural (including linguistic) revivalist movement, part of a broadgauged plan to mobilize Afrikaner "ethnic power" for political purposes. Even more important, argues Dan O'Meara, were a set of economic policies that began as a communal effort to help solve the problem of the "poor whites," pushed off the land by the increasing capitalization of agriculture, but came primarily to serve to advance the economic aspirations of an Afrikaner petty bourgeoisie with very bourgeois ambitions. Indeed, O'Meara has interpreted the chief cutting-edge of Afrikaner nationalism since the late 1920s to be precisely the class project of this latter element, a project which was intensified after the electoral victory of the Nationalist Party in 1948. Then came such developments as the speeding-up of the Afrikanerization of the public service and an ever more dramatically expanded economic role for the state, this latter also being used in support of the parallel advance of Afrikaners in the private sector.

Of course, one must avoid taking too reductionist a position. It would be a bold observer indeed who suggested that racism and Afrikaner nationalism did not have some "autonomous" resonance of their own beyond the economic-cum-class determinations which shape and structure their impact. Clearly, the communal nature of the Afrikaner project has had real meaning for such actors as Nationalist prime ministers D. F.

Malan and H. F. Verwoerd—as well as for many more humble adherents to the cause—and this has lent a drive and thrust to their undertakings which has made a tangible impact upon historical outcomes. It was not mere manipulation which made issues like South Africa's entry into World War II or republicanism such important talismen in South African politics. And it seems possible that ethnic interest—premised upon "Afrikaner identity"—may even today cut across class lines in ways that qualify the degree of flexibility open to the "crisis managers" of South African capitalism. Similarly, the ideology of white racism—though contingent rather than preordained in the nature of its links to capitalism and to the interests of that system's various classes—may not yield entirely gracefully to any proposed dismissal of it which might be suggested by the emerging imperatives of latter-day capitalist development.

There is another dimension of the situation—an eminently "rational" dimension at that—which must also be seen as breathing life into these latter variables. For there is a second kind of reductionism to be avoided, one which privileges economic calculation to the detriment of political calculation in explaining the motivation of the dominant classes. A capitalist system must not only exploit labor, it must also be preserved politically. Liberal capitalism, with its "free" labor market and collective bargaining system and its formally "open" democratic institutions, has been notoriously successful in this latter respect in many Western countries. In a racial capitalist system things are more complicated. Whatever its benefits to capitalists, the system is at particular risk because the reinforcement of class consciousness by racial consciousness among the dominated defines some particularly volatile and dangerous possibilities. It bears emphasizing, therefore, that the labor allocation mechanisms of the South African system—the pass laws, labor bureaus, and the like—have political as well as economic import; together with restrictions upon trade union and political organization and with a massive battery of security legislation, they have also served, historically, to *control* the African population. Thus they have not necessarily been wrong, those who have calculated that reinforcing the mechanisms of control and repression, rather than running the risk of innovative, "formative" action, of "reform," is the best bet for preserving those "certain limits" of the system that are essential. It is in this sense that the much discussed "laager mentality" of the Afrikaners, as well as various forms of last-ditch racism, can be seen to take their life, at least in part, from entirely sensible, if debatable, strategic calculations. Indeed, as noted earlier, these are matters over which even those in precisely the same objective class position might disagree.

These complexities having been noted, it bears emphasizing that the "political forces which are struggling to conserve and to defend the existing structure" (Gramsci)—their own line-up changing over time as South African capitalism has developed, of course—have faced the necessity of dealing with "organic crisis" before in South Africa. Some observers have seen the early 1920s as representing such a crisis, one marked by widespread labor unrest, both white and black, among other features. And certainly the aforementioned Pact government of 1924 did dampen down contradictions, consolidating the inclusion of the white working class as a junior partner in the privileges accruing from racial capitalism, for example. Moreover, the new bloc which the Pact government exemplified did help facilitate, in defiance of the most "multinational" segments of mining capital, the deepening of an indigenous process of accumulation and industrialization. Nonetheless, it is the situation of the 1940s which more aptly deserves the appellation of "organic crisis."

A number of trends coincided, most important the rapid escalation of black resistance to the exploitative racial capitalist system. This, in turn, was directly related to the continuing evolution of South African capitalism. There were two main features here. First, the overcrowded reserves had entered into precipitous economic decline and could no longer play quite the same role they had in subsidizing wages. Full, rather than qualified, proletarianization was afoot, meaning that Africans in larger numbers than ever before were being pushed to the towns and held there. Moreover, this coincided with a second process. In the wake of the protectionist policies established between the wars and of a boom—begun when South Africa abandoned the gold standard in 1933, but reinforced by the economic opportunities provided by the war—rapid economic growth highlighted by secondary industrialization was taking place. The fresh demands for African labor, including that of the semi-skilled and therefore more stabilized variety, meant that an active pull was also being exerted by the towns and by emergent industrial capital. It was these trends, then, which produced not only a vast—and ultimately irreversible—growth in the urbanized African population, but also a dramatic escalation of trade union organization and working-class militancy. When the latter process advanced so far as even to include migrant workers, and culminated in the extraordinary African mine workers' strike of 1946, South African ruling circles were shaken to the core.

As O'Meara has argued, "The violence of the state's response [to the mine workers' strike] not only indicated the degree to which it felt threatened, but foreshadowed the extreme repression after 1948."[2] But this hard line was not the only possible response to the crisis. There were other tangible cross-currents within the white community concerning the question of the best long-run solution to the urban-cum-working-class problem, and some liberal capitalist alternatives were already under discussion. Thus the reports of the several commissions (Smit, Fagan, and the like) appointed by the United Party in the 1940s to consider this problem reflected industrial capital's desire for a stabilized and semi-skilled labor force; accepting urban Africans as a given, these reports flirted with ways— modification of the pass laws, better education, even further trade union rights—to integrate them more tightly and smoothly into the capitalist system. It bears noting, however, that as regards any possible liberalizing/democratizing implications for the *political* sphere which might have been expected to follow from the emphasis upon the existence of an integrated economy, the commissioners invariably waffled—mumbling, at best, about the need for increased "consultation"—this being a failure of nerve that has beset South African liberalizers to the present day.

Moreover, such waffling was actually to be found embedded within the more strictly economic recommendations as well, the Fagan Commission opting for the migrant labor system even as it pressed its case for stabilization! In so doing, of course, it was merely striving to reflect the concerns of other fractions of capital—mining and agricultural—and the white working class. The former were nervous about the rising wage levels which liberalization might entail (levels industrial capital was better set to meet) and the implications for their own labor requirements of the drift to the towns; the latter were fearful of the increased job competition from underpaid Africans which was also implicit in liberalization. Yet, in the event, such waffling was not enough to stem the nervousness of all members of these various groups, and with the United Party's response to crisis so hesitant and contradictory, the way was open for the National Party to proffer its own solution.

The National Party project which underlay its narrow electoral victory in 1948 and its subsequent consolidation of power can be interpreted at several different levels, of course. What is unequivocal is that it offered a *hard* solution—the freezing of segregation into the institutions of apartheid rather than its liberalization—to racial capitalism's crisis. There followed tightened controls over the movement and activities of African labor, rigid separation of the races wherever possible, and fierce political repression (e.g., the Suppression of Communism Act). But whose class interests did this solution serve? Most overtly, no doubt, those of the main elements the Nationalist Party had grouped together into its winning coalition: the Afrikaner petty bourgeoisie, agrarian capital, the white working class. As noted earlier, the state now more aggressively pushed forward the interests of specifically Afrikaner capital—including both those of the petty bourgeoisie on the rise and of certain more developed bourgeois elements, especially in the Cape (Sanlam, *et al.*)—within the ranks of capital-in-general. With a tightening-up of "influx control" and a refining of the system of passes and of labor bureaus, the state facilitated a favorable allocation of labor—beyond the immediate pressures of the market—toward agriculture and other competitive spheres. And, in a related manner, reinforcement of the job color bar was presented as a reward to the white working class.

Not that the Nationalists' project even then can be interpreted as being merely the sum of such class interests. As hinted above, the nature of its racist and exclusivist-ethnic (Afrikaner nationalist) preoccupations lent this project much of its fire, its political focus and clout, its "extremism." Nonetheless, having done full justice to the complex interplay of class, racial, and national assertions which was present here, one may still doubt whether the outcome was really so very far out of line with the basic interests of the most developed (and essentially non-Afrikaner) sectors of capital. Of course, even after initial ultra-populist threats from the Nationalists—the nationalization of the gold mines, for example—had evaporated, there were some costs to be borne by such sectors: distortions introduced into an optimal allocation and utilization of labor by migrancy and by the highlighting of racial criteria in training and job definitions (problems which were never quite to disappear) and a measure of embarrassing pressure upon the growing number of multinational corporate participants in the apartheid economy from anti-apartheid forces at home.

There were also dangers. The hard line was merely sweeping under the rug—albeit with a very stiff and effective broom —the structural problems of the urban African and of the declining reserves. Yet in the short run it was effective, putting a lid on rising African political demands (a process which had culminated, by the early 1960s, in the banning of the leading African nationalist organizations) and, most important, disorganizing the African working class while driving down the wage bill. This latter dimension—the reinforcement of the exploitation color bar—meant rising profits, and as, on this basis, the South African economy settled into a long-term expansion, any potential contradictions within the camp of capital became muted. Small wonder that one Marxist analysis of the time could note that it was "naive utopianism to expect the forces of international capitalism, either directly or as mediated by various Western states, to risk a most profitable outlet for investments and exports for the sake of marginal improvements in the 'logic of the market.' "[3] The agonies of the United Party in the 1940s had already demonstrated the profound difficulties, under South African conditions, of conceiving, let alone mounting, an alternative project. Then, after 1940, capital found that apartheid worked; the bill would not come due for two decades.

That there should be such a bill is not surprising. For the dark side of the boom was present from the outset, racial capitalism's buttressing of both color bars, dictating that economic growth came to embody serious contradictions: limits on the size of the consumer market, a high rate of black unemployment, and, paradoxically, a shortage of skilled labor. These, it ultimately became evident, were not mere functions of the capitalist business cycle, but permanent structural phenomena with an adverse impact upon accumulation. Some brief elaboration of these weaknesses is in order here.

(1) The inclusion within the ruling Afrikaner coalition of a growing number of urbanized "poor whites" guaranteed them a privileged status in the labor market and channeled to them some small fraction of capital's rising profits. On this basis, the living standards of all white South Africans rose rapidly after 1948, providing ample demand in the 1950s and 1960s for the expanding consumer goods industries. From the late 1960s, however, the growing saturation of the white consumer market limited not only sales but also the ability of secondary industry to benefit from economies of scale. Since an expansion of the black consumer market was not then contemplated, this made more urgent the state's often reiterated, yet difficult to realize, call for an increase in manufacturing exports.

(2) A permanently high rate of black unemployment was, Legassick and Wolpe argue, an important condition of the postwar emergence of secondary industry. The large reserve army of the unemployed was crucial in facilitating the reinforcement of the exploitation color bar, allowing the "living wage" for blacks to be pegged at little more than the level of physical subsistence in the reserves, while compounding the difficulties of working-class organization (already restricted by harsh legislation). Yet, as even the very high growth rates of the 1960s failed to create sufficient jobs to absorb the growing labor force (partly because of a bias toward capital-intensive investment), unemployment rose steeply, reaching over 12 percent in 1970 and defining a looming political threat. As then-Prime Minister John Vorster noted: "The biggest danger in South Africa today is not terrorism, but unemployment."

(3) The freezing of the job color bar to protect white

workers perpetuated the "racist hierarchical social division of labor," as well as the related racial inequalities in wages and in education and training. Although white population growth (boosted by immigration) was sufficient to fill new skilled labor positions in the first, slower, phase of the expansion, shortages had already begun to appear in the early 1960s, reaching a figure of 95,655 in 1971. The result of these shortages, which occurred in secondary industries as well as in commerce and services, was lower productivity and less efficiency (i.e., higher costs), even though capital could neutralize such costs to some degree during the boom by ignoring the color bar or "floating it upward" (fragmenting and deskilling skilled jobs, moving low-paid blacks into the less-skilled tasks, and promoting the white to supervisor),[4] or by obtaining extra credit to pay for higher inventories.

Such weaknesses were to become of crucial importance. At the same time, other implications were of at least equal significance. Thus, when the bill did at last come due in the 1970s, the economic development of the apartheid years meant that the capitalist class to which it was presented had been substantially reshaped, and was different from the class once unable to agree on a strategy to meet the 1940s crisis. This point, too, requires elaboration.

The most obvious development is the much greater prominence of "Afrikaans-speaking" capital,[5] which "now probably has as much, if not more, in common with [its] English-speaking counterpart[s] . . . as with the blue-collar workers, teachers, and civil servants who have traditionally formed the power-base of the National Party" (*Financial Times,* February 29, 1980). As hinted earlier, underlying this new strength has been the establishment, since 1948, of numerous new parastatal corporations, managed by Afrikaners. The burgeoning state sector provided the groups clustered around the Nationalist project (particularly nascent Afrikaner capital) with the economic clout to direct the path of accumulation in their own interests, as distinct from the interests of foreign and local English capital. Besides ISCOR, the Industrial Development Corporation (IDC), and ESCOM (electricity), all brought forward from earlier periods, there are now also ARMSCOR (weapons), SASOL (oil-from-coal),

FOSKOR (phosphorus), and SAPPI (pulp and paper), among others. The advantageous conditions provided for all capital by apartheid, as well as the additional benefit of favorable consideration for Afrikaners in the award of the growing number of state contracts, have linked up with this increased state activity to allow Afrikaner capital—led by financial institutions which have mobilized Afrikaners' savings (the older Cape-based Sanlam and Santam insurance companies, and the Broederbond-sponsored Volkskas bank and FVB investment company)—to move into, and build up significant stakes in, industry, mining, and commerce.

Of course, this movement of the state into productive activity had other implications as well, not least the cost entailed in its being financed primarily by inflation. In this one particular, South Africa followed the pattern of many other capitalist economies of the time: from the 1950s, the monetary system was restructured to facilitate high levels of government borrowing at low interest rates, even though the new arrangements hampered the state's ability to control growth in credit extension by banks and in the money supply. Reinforced by rising prices in its major trading partners, the advanced capitalist countries, inflation became a structural feature in South Africa and this became extremely costly to capital from the early 1970s.

Yet whatever the longer run cost of expanded state economic activity to capital as a whole, or the medium-term benefits to less competitive Afrikaner capital, it must be emphasized that multinational and local "English" capital were also well served by such infrastructural development and state-subsidized production of producer goods inputs—just as they were well served by the hard-line labor policies of apartheid. Perhaps this fact is most graphically illustrated by the unchanging price of ISCOR steel between 1952 and 1970. More broadly, the industrial growth of the 1950s, premised on the extension of import substitution in, and growing markets for, consumer goods and heavy industrial inputs like iron and steel, helped further to lay the foundation for soaring profit rates during the 1960s boom. This, in turn, had implications for the make-up of the capitalist camp which were at least as significant as the expanded role of large-scale Afrikaner capital we have referred to above: on the one hand, the increased prominence of multi-national corporations, especially in manufacturing, and, on the other, the increased intermeshing and concentration of capitals, a trend which came to reinforce the economic power of a very small number of dominant corporations.

(1) In the first place, with very high profit rates practically guaranteed by the apartheid state's policies, and with a relatively advanced level of development, South Africa was a prime target for international capital when the latter, shifting gears, sought markets and production sites in suitable Third World countries for the high-technology, capital-intensive commodities whose production was the basis for postwar expansion in the advanced capitalist countries. After Sharpeville, when it was apparent that African resistance would be crushed (at least for the moment), foreign capital (American, British, West German, and Japanese most prominently) began to pour into manufacturing, helping to inflame and sustain the prolonged boom.[6] New industries were established—computers, synthetics—and existing ones expanded, modernized, their product range extended—chemicals, automobiles, electrical machinery, engineering, and others. The common denominators were sophisticated technology and capital intensity; the products were primarily producer goods, though some consumer durables were included. By the mid-1960s direct investment in manufacturing was the predominant form of foreign participation in the South African economy.

Several other points regarding foreign investment deserve mention, however. For example, until the 1950s most foreign investment (of any kind) had been indirect, involving, primarily, holdings of mining stocks. During the 1960s, foreign interest in mining continued but it now became more active and direct, as North American mining multinationals (AMAX, Newmont, Inco, Falconbridge) moved in, joining with local mining and state capital to develop new mines, South African mineral output was considerably diversified, the target being the vast resources of "strategic" minerals—chrome, platinum, copper, asbestos, and others—needed for Western industries (especially auto and steel). Moreover, Western banks increasingly became a part of the international mix of South African capitalism. As state spending rose in the early 1970s with a new wave of infrastructural projects and higher defense costs, portfolio investment—in the form of long-term loans from foreign banks to the South African state and its parastatals—increased substantially. This became ever more important in covering the trade deficit (historically one of the main functions of foreign investment in South Africa) since direct investment, though still growing, was now being financed primarily out of retained profits.

Of course, greater multinational participation did not lead to any cosmic change in South Africa's dependent and subordinate status within international capitalism. These aspects of South African reality had long been indexed by the country's lack of command over its own technology (particularly in industry) and, related to this, by the "Third World" pattern of the commodities making up its imports and exports. Indeed, if anything, such patterns were now reinforced, albeit at a higher level of economic development. Thus the multinationals' subsidiaries have merely adopted the technologies of their parent companies, and also explicitly restricted the exporting of their products from South Africa. Moreover, the search for markets for capital goods—another postwar thrust of international capitalism—further deepened dependence, a 1973 survey of manufacturers showing that three-quarters of them used over 90 percent foreign technology; for almost all it was cheaper to import technology than to develop it in South Africa. In consequence, machinery and industrial equipment make up about 75 percent of South Africa's imports. At the same time, the linking of technologies designed to benefit from economies of scale to the small South African market raises production costs and reduces the international competitiveness of industry; in 1973 only 14 percent of exports were manufactured goods, and most of this amount went to African countries. Significantly, such attributes of dependence were also to help shape the economic crisis of the 1970s.

(2) From the first years of the diamond- and goldfields, the commanding heights of the racial capitalist economy had been controlled by a relatively small number of corporations. Early on there were seven mining-finance houses controlling the entire gold-mining industry (and coordinating their activities

through a Chamber of Mines), and these houses were later to become involved in the beginnings of secondary industrialization between the wars as well. When, after 1945, the economy's base was broadened, the number of big corporations grew, but so did both the interconnections between them and their collective power relative to the large number of smaller firms. Many of the new investments of the 1960s and early 1970s were joint ventures between some combination of foreign, local private, and state capital (the latter through the IDC). The chemicals industry, for example, consists essentially of three companies: the state-owned SASOL; AE&CI, owned by Anglo American and Imperial Chemicals Industry of Britain; and Sentrachem, set up by FVB, the IDC, and British Petroleum. As we shall see, the consolidation and greater community of interest within big capital goes beyond purely economic calculation, shaping its response to the organic crisis and helping facilitate the translation of common economic needs into unified political strategy. However, it will be equally apparent that on the complicated South African terrain whose outlines we have begun to sketch in this section this translation cannot be, even then, an entirely easy or straightforward exercise.

II. New Conditions of Accumulation?

At the end of 1980, to be sure, "crisis" may seem the least appropriate description of conditions in the South African economy. The phenomenal rise in the price of gold, beginning eighteen months previously, meant a 7 percent growth rate, while such headlines in business pages as "Earnings Boost . . . Good News for Shareholders . . . Profits Still Rising" provided ample evidence of a boom atmosphere. This was indeed a dramatic recovery from capital's gloom during the second half of the 1970s when the economy went through a period labeled "the worst recession/depression since the 1930s." Yet the optimism may well be misplaced, even if the gold price rise has eliminated some of the symptoms of crisis and given an undoubted boost to accumulation. For this apparent boom does not really touch the underlying causes of the economy's earlier paralysis; higher gold prices cannot simply conjure away the structural contradictions which, as we have seen, characterize the accumulation process under racial capitalism and which were central to the development of the crisis of the 1970s in the first place. True, the timing of the latter (starting in mid-1974) was linked, on the one hand, to the general downturn of the international capitalist economy and, on the other, to black working-class action in Durban and elsewhere (although such action was itself related to the effects on this class of rising inflation and unemployment as economic difficulties grew). But it must also be underscored that as the "apartheid boom" began to tail off in the early 1970s and the pressures pushing the economy toward crisis built up, capital's ability to resist those pressures was undermined by growing inflation, skilled labor shortages, and balance of payments deficits.

The extent of the crisis can be illustrated by several different indices. The real growth rate, which averaged 5.7 percent annually in the 1960s, was negative in the first half of 1976, and zero in 1977; the volume of manufacturing output fell by about 6 percent from mid-1974 to mid-1975 and, after a small pickup, by even more during 1976-1977. Private sector investment in manufacturing began to drop from 1974, while total investment declined by about 13 percent between 1975 and 1977 as the state was forced to cut back spending on its projects. Slow growth meant that black unemployment rose even more quickly than during the 1960s, while the number of White, Coloured, and Asian jobless increased by 250 percent in the three years from January 1974. Meanwhile, there were mounting balance of payments difficulties, largely the result of the high import requirements of state expenditures on defense and investment projects (these also being a primary cause of rising inflation rates). Such difficulties were compounded by the fall in the gold price from early 1975 and reached a breaking point by the end of that year. A full 25 percent of foreign exchange reserves was lost during the first quarter of 1976, forcing the government to turn to the IMF for an emergency loan and to apply deflationary policies at home, thereby plunging the economy even further into crisis. The drying-up of foreign capital inflows in June of that year, after the start of the Soweto events, merely exacerbated this situation.

Of course, the impact of Soweto was much broader, deepening the economic crisis into organic crisis and indicating to some sectors of capital that the system's very existence was in jeopardy. In such a context it is not surprising that the economy's recovery—once it had bottomed out in late 1977—was extremely slow and hesitant, many firms remaining reluctant to invest during the following two years. Finally, the upward leap of the gold price boosted confidence and made more vigorous growth possible; now the government's senior economic adviser could assure the public and the business community that "the long-term secular trend of economic activity will probably be strongly upwards."[7] Yet the strategists of capital knew that things were really more complicated than that. Political uncertainty and slow economic recovery merely emphasized what had already become clear from the seriousness of the economic crisis itself: new conditions of accumulation were required, changes designed to facilitate both production *and* reproduction of the system. The business journal *Euromoney* summarized the situation in June 1979 by noting that "the high growth years of the 60's and 70's are over," and asking, "How can South Africa pull itself onto another high growth path?"

Achieving this latter goal by establishing new conditions of accumulation involves overcoming the major structural contradictions touched upon above and now to be explored more fully. For their persistence was a second, more specifically economic, reason for the sluggish recovery; just as they had hindered capital's ability to raise profitability so as to ward off crisis, so did they prove a drag on profitability after the economy had begun its upturn. Even in the midst of the gold boom such contradictions have remained prominent and led to considerable anguished hand-wringing within ruling circles, as the pages of the *Financial Mail* amply testify. Thus inflation, at 14 percent in 1980 and consistently over 10 percent since 1974, still threatens to run out of control; indeed a figure of 20 percent has been predicted for this year. And even though larger gold revenues may buy some relief from technological dependence—through substitution of capital goods presently imported—they cannot, in light of South Africa's position within the world capitalist economy, imply a permanent balance of payments surplus. Thus, in the last quarter of 1980, a combination of rising imports (due to the boom) and a (long-term?) dip in the gold price had already moved the current account back into deficit.

However, problems of inflation and in the balance of payments, intractable though they may be, are not the most serious that capital has to face in the 1980s. Overcoming the other structural problems—skilled labor shortages, the limits of the white consumer market, the high black unemployment rate —presents a much bigger challenge. Nor, since these relate directly to the situation of the volatile black working class, is overcoming them simply a matter of economic adjustment. It is also a political and ideological task, all these elements then being part and parcel of what the dominant classes themselves have come to call their "total strategy." In the remainder of this section we will consider only the narrowly economic logic lying behind such a strategy, reserving for the next section, and for the following chapter, an exploration of the full range of its "conserving" *and* "formative" dimensions.

Of course, "total strategy" is far too broad a label to apply to the response to crisis seen as appropriate by some sections of capital, the reference here being primarily, though not exclusively, to the smaller firms. Concerned about maintaining supplies of cheap labor, they emphasize a narrow definition of class defense rather than formative action, their hopes (and profits) being seen by them to rest on a further hardening of apartheid's hard line—on a decisive crushing of the black workers' newly rediscovered power. For these capitals, the great fear is that a transition to a more settled labor force, and to the higher wage bill this implies, would spell an end to their profitability. On the other hand, the embracing of a settled labor force, rejected as a solution in the 1940s, has been revived and become a central feature in the alternative strategy of a second and currently more powerful grouping within capital. Composed almost exclusively of big capital ("English," "Afrikaner," and foreign), its power resting on the increased centralization and concentration of capital since 1960 which we noted in the previous section, this grouping doubts the wisdom of the former elements' bald approaches. Even if not ready to drop completely the use of repression, its intent is to counter black working-class strength in a more subtle fashion. And it is, at the same time, ready to introduce those adjustments in the pattern of accumulation which the 1970s crisis suggested to be necessary, but which would be excluded by a straightforward reinforcing of the exploitation color bar. Thus, for this latter grouping, not only should black labor become firmly settled in the urban centers, but its living standard should be allowed to rise substantially by the granting of wage hikes and, simultaneously, by the inclusion of a broader range of commodities in the wage basket.

It will be apparent that any such enlarging of the black wage basket implies, in effect, a redefinition of the "historical and moral cost" of urban black labor which, until now, has been defined essentially on the basis of the physical necessities of existence in the bantustans. Of course, this latter definition began to fray at the edges during the 1970s as the black working class flexed its collective muscle; now, however, (some fraction of) capital itself is also attempting to intervene to alter it. Here one might note, for starters, Anglo American's recent urging that all mining houses raise black wages by 60 to 120 percent—because, as the *Financial Mail* (May 30, 1980) put it, of its "concern for workers"! Needless to say, the reason lies elsewhere, in part in a blatant attempt to buy off these same workers. But we can see that this ploy is also crucial to overcoming the limitations on economies of scale and on consumer demand—found to be so important both in the first phase of the 1970s crisis and in the period of partial recovery from it— imposed by the size of the white consumer market.

As one ideologue of commercial capital has put it, "Increasing black purchasing power is the only real answer to growth."[8] Not that these limits are equally constraining on all industries. They are somewhat less urgent, for example, for those industries which already supply a large black market— food, clothing, and other light industries; moreover, since these are industries whose average capital tends to be smaller, they are also the ones, mentioned above, which are least able to afford, and least enthusiastic about, a higher wage bill. In contrast, it is industries producing more durable consumer goods (again, big capital) which must become able to utilize economies of scale by expanding their markets. To take merely one example, the *FM* (March 23, 1979) sees that the "only real potential for expansion [of the domestic appliances industry] is the black market, but this depends on electrification of the urban townships"—which, not coincidentally, has now begun. General Motors' local chief executive expressed the interests of foreign capital succinctly and in similar terms (*Financial Mail*, June 27, 1980): "In the Western capitalist countries, population, and hence markets, are shrinking. The Third World is burgeoning in both numbers and infrastructure. In our small [sic] way, we are trying to influence the growth of the Third World component amid the population of this country. We need people to sell to and we intend to stay here."

This, then, is a crucial consideration for big capital. Yet having more people to sell to is only one side of the coin;* any redefinition of the market side of capital's activity must also pose questions for the production side. The immediate implication is that the achievement of economies of scale in production must take place in such a way as not merely to cover rising wage costs but also to raise profitability. And this means, in turn, that big capital's intention now must be to have rising labor productivity replace cheap labor as the basis of exploitation. As Harry Oppenheimer put this point as early as 1976:

> The increase in black wages reflects the beginning of a process, still actively continuing, of a change-over from a labour-intensive, low-wage, low-productivity economic system—typical of industrial development in its earliest stage—to the capital-intensive, high-wage, high-productivity system which characterizes the advanced industrialized countries.[9]

---

* It is worth noting one severe limit in particular on capital's ability to expand black purchasing power. This is the much more adverse impact of the rising inflation rate on the living standards of blacks as compared to whites. A recent study (in *Work in Progress* [Johannesburg], 17, April 1981) found that the increase in the price index for lower income groups during 1980 was over 20 percent, not the 14 percent figure for higher income groups cited above. Real wages for most urban blacks have in fact declined during the past three years, despite the higher money wages they have received. Urban black workers are thus in a situation of desperately trying to *maintain* living standards; any improvement remains a dream. We will return to this point later, when we consider the basis for the increasing militancy of black workers.

Indeed, it is from just such a perspective that low levels of productivity in South Africa (about the lowest among advanced and middle-level capitalist economies) have recently been "discovered" to be a problem. Thus in 1978-1979, only 16 percent of manufacturing output growth was marked down to productivity increases, although the average proportion in advanced capitalist economies is two-thirds. During the 1960s and 1970s, the rate of increase of labor productivity was fairly constant and at a low level. This reflected, in turn, the relative unprofitability for individual capitals of "deepening" their capital (introducing new technology to raise productivity) under conditions of a high rate of exploitation of cheap, disorganized labor: production costs could not have been lowered significantly, and the output increases would probably have remained unsold in the limited market available. Therefore, new technology was introduced when capital was simultaneously "widened" (capacity expanded and new jobs created by, for example, construction of an additional factory). However, if firms in the future respond to greater working-class pressure (and to the new "expanded market" gambit of capital-in-general) by allowing wages to rise to some degree, then they will be able to remain competitive and protect profits only by deepening their capital—introducing new technology which will, on the one hand, hold back the rise in the wage bill by eliminating part of the labor force ("Black wages have [already] risen enough to persuade many industrialists that machines are cheaper than men—and less militant" [*The Economist,* April 25, 1981]) and, on the other, increase the productivity of the remaining (higher wage) labor, thereby cutting production costs.[10]

This pattern for individual capitals does not translate directly when capital is taken as a whole. Here repeated introduction of the new labor-saving technology implies an even more rapid increase in the organic composition of capital, and consequent pressure on the profit rate, than was the case during the 1960s boom. But as is the case in advanced capitalist countries, this latter pressure could be more effectively countered than was the case under cheap labor conditions—*if* productivity can be raised sufficiently (particularly in the industries producing consumer goods and their inputs). If the rise in productivity in this sector is larger than the rise in real wages, then the reduction achieved in total production costs will be greater than the increase in capital's total wage bill across the economy.* In this way, profitability can be maintained, i.e., the share of the total income accruing to capital will be greater than that obtained by labor. This suggests a further complication, for capital will have to maintain a balance here, the achieving of which will no doubt preoccupy its strategists for years to come: it must not succumb to the ever present temptation to grab *all* of the increase in total income, but must allow real wages to rise to some degree so that its initial goal—expansion of the consumer market—is attained.

Yet whether for capital as a whole or for individual capitals, tremendous obstacles will need to be overcome before such general conditions of accumulation can finally be put in place. We have mentioned potential divisions within capital itself— between large and small capitals—as one possible obstacle, with small capitals much more sensitive to the appeal of maintaining a pool of cheap (and still migrant) labor. However, it may be that, in strictly economic terms, this is a contradiction which is not as antagonistic as at first appears. Big capital's goals do not necessarily involve a rejection of all aspects of the reserve-cum-bantustan system that guarantees a cheap labor supply; its continuing acceptance of it would merely involve embracing the necessity of separating, socially and economically, urban from rural blacks and focusing its economic strategy of socio-political cooptation, market expansion, and productivity increases on the former. And this does, in fact, seem to be a distinction which is already at the center of the reform initiative in South Africa, as we shall see. Much more controversial, perhaps, are diverse views as to the *political*—as distinct from the economic—merits

---

* In the terminology of Marxist economics, the extraction of *relative* surplus value will be increased, to become, in fact, the characteristic method of exploitation. We can note here, too, that in those industries producing production goods (machinery and raw materials), rising productivity directly counters the effects for capital as a whole of greater capital intensity. Lower production costs in these industries mean a limit to the rise in the organic composition of capital once the products are taken into use by their purchasers. The low level of development of the machinery and equipment industries in South Africa makes this point somewhat less important in this case, however.

of this drive toward a settled labor policy; but this is a debate to which we will also return.

No, there is another economic problem arising from the strategy sketched above which is much more serious for capital, although it is one which reinforces the necessity capital feels to settle an urban black working population. This is the familiar problem of shortages of skilled labor. Even under a continuation of old conditions such a shortage would have been severe; but if new technology is to be repeatedly introduced to raise productivity, the skill shortage suddenly becomes very severe indeed—especially, again, for big capital. Thus *Euromoney,* in answer to its own question cited above ("How can South Africa pull itself onto another high growth path?"), stated simply: "The problem of skilled labor has to be solved quickly." Similarly, Harry Oppenheimer complained in a 1978 interview that "Nationalist politics have made it impossible to make proper use of black labour. . . . Unless you keep the economy extremely small you can't man the skilled jobs with white people." And, during 1980, one speaker after another at the meetings of various business organizations (the Federated Chamber of Industries, for example) echoed these concerns, as did the governor of the Reserve Bank. Perhaps the extent of the problem can best be reflected by citing merely one statistic among the many which might be offered to dramatize a pattern that cuts right across the economy: although less than 0.1 percent of managers are currently blacks, it has been estimated that by 1987 whites will be able to fill only a little more than 40 percent of managerial and supervisory positions (*Financial Mail,* December 5, 1980). Obviously, in such a situation racially defined constraints on training, on job placement and the like come to seem, to important sectors of capital, much more restrictive than they have before.

As regards this issue then, but indeed as regards most of the issues raised in this section, more seems to be at stake than merely those "marginal improvements in the logic of the market" which were insufficient to move capital to develop a project distinct from that of the Nationalist government after 1948. Thus in identifying the outlines of capital's more urgently felt, present-day response to crisis, we see that it is this response which primarily explains the salience of the reform initiative both within and without the Nationalist Party in South Africa. However, the issue of a skilled labor shortage alerts us to one complication: even if it were to be successful in its own terms in breaching some of the structural contradictions and constraints upon accumulation, capital's initiatives may merely reinforce other contradictions. We will mention only two more, both familiar but of great importance. First, whatever success is attained in the current phase of import substitution, technological dependence will, once again, imply rising import bills as mechanization accelerates. Even worse, black unemployment will continue to climb as the economy becomes increasingly capital intensive. Despite occasional rhetorical flourishes about "labor-intensive investment" it seems probable that most sectors of capital now suspect the unemployment problem cannot be solved economically but only contained politically—displaced, that is, to the bantustans (a good reason big capital does not feel so very much at odds with some aspects of the bantustan policy). For, on one calculation, a thousand new jobs would have to be created *daily* for twenty years in order to eliminate the problem within the parameters of the present system!

Worsening inflation, higher unemployment, rising imports, and growing skilled labor shortages—once these continuing problems are spelled out, the gold boom loses much of its sheen. Undoubtedly capital's formative efforts vis-à-vis South Africa's structural contradictions are provided with much less space by the economy than it might wish. Yet we must conclude by reiterating that, for capital, formative efforts nonetheless remain the name of the game, involving, as we have seen, pressures for policies with respect to such items as the disposition of labor—its movement, training, job allocation, and institutional linkages to the system (e.g., trade unions)—and the instilling of new consumerist values, and possibilities, among blacks. And we must also add one final level of complication: these economic imperatives must play themselves out on the political terrain—the terrain where class, party, and ideology meet—and in present-day South Africa such "political" factors cut across any presumed "logic of capital" in extremely complex ways. To these further complexities we must now turn.

III. Political Crisis

We can move onto this political terrain by presenting in full the Oppenheimer statement from which we extracted his thoughts on skilled labor shortages several pages back; it is a particularly suggestive one:

> I think it presents itself, to us in the Anglo American Corporation in the first place, but perhaps to business in an ever widening circle, that Nationalist policies have made it impossible to make proper use of black labour. And . . . this is felt to be a danger in two ways: a danger because it is necessary in order to get the economic growth, to make use of black labour, because . . . unless you keep the economy extremely small you can't man the skilled jobs with white people. And on the other hand, it is felt that . . . if you are going to operate business successfully, you want to do so in a peaceful atmosphere, and the only way to have a peaceful atmosphere is to enable black people to do better jobs and to feel a part of the economic system. And I think it's because Nationalist policy . . . was felt to prevent these things happening that it was looked upon as a danger. I would think most of the business world looked on it as a rather long-term danger. I think probably we [Anglo American] tended to think of it . . . as a rather shorter term danger than many of the others did.[11]

Here spelled out quite explicitly are some of the main terms of capital's current attempt to revivify and guarantee capital accumulation. And note, in particular, the phrase "peaceful atmosphere": Oppenheimer's referent now becomes political and highlights (if slightly more obliquely than other of his statements) the growing challenge to racial capitalism springing from the dominated classes. This was a challenge—we have described it above as part of the deepening of economic crisis into organic crisis—brought to a boil in the 1970s by the considerable exertions of these classes and linked, in turn, to both the successes of capitalist development, and to its weaknesses.

To its successes, in that the trend toward an industrial economy and the growing concentration of an urban-centered, working-class black population—the baseline of trouble in the 1940s —has necessarily continued, despite the Canute-like protestations, and actions, of Verwoerd and his successors. To its weaknesses, in that the 1970s combination of high rates of black unemployment *and* of inflation helped stoke the resentment of this expanding urban population. The results were explosive: Durban, Soweto, and the like. Unfortunately, we cannot talk about everything at once; we shall have to analyze these events—from the bottom up, as it were—later, but it bears emphasizing here that they are the bottom line of the dominant classes' concern, more urgently demanding their response than even the economic imperatives we have been discussing. Moreover, the resuscitation of critical consciousness and political self-confidence on the part of blacks which these events exemplify is not readily reversible. The current boom is unlikely, therefore, to displace the need for "political crisis management" by the regime, whatever its economic implications might be.

Here lies their difficulty, however. For the second political dimension of the current crisis is precisely the inability of the dominant classes to hit upon a consistent and coordinated response to the many contradictions which face them. It is here, again, that the much vaunted discussion of reform has come to the fore. Bracket, for the moment, any full discussion of the many ambiguities that surround the substance of "reform," its scope and meaning, in present-day South Africa. Bracket, too, the question of whether, and for how long, any attempts at "formative" action by these classes to redefine the terrain of struggle can be expected to be successful. Taken even at face value, suggestions—from Prime Minister Botha, in particular—that changes might be in order that would serve to stabilize a more ,skilled black workforce or to safely institutionalize the black population's participation within South Africa's urban society have evoked reactions clearly revealing the multilayered tensions, hinted at in the introduction, within ruling circles.

The most visible of political events in the white community bear witness to this, these being highlighted in recent years by a struggle within the ruling National Party itself between the *verkramptes* (the "reactionaries," the hardest of hardliners on apartheid) and the *verligtes* (those deemed to be "enlightened" and reform-minded). Most recently, the 1981 election evidenced such tensions both within and without the party, as National Party nomination meetings in many instances were polarized around these emphases and as other parties pulled at the government from the left and, particularly, from the right. However, as Dan O'Meara has recently demonstrated,[12] the events of the searing Muldergate scandal of 1978—a scandal centering around the illegal manipulation of state funds and state influence, at home and abroad, in the service of Nationalist Party hegemony, which threatened to tear the party apart—had already encapsulated the jockeying for position between these two tendencies. The result: the defeat and departure from the Nationalist Party of Connie Mulder, *verkramp* heir-apparent to John Vorster's prime ministership, the discrediting of Vorster himself, and the emergence of Botha and his coterie of *verligtes*—themselves active in provoking exposure of the scandal in the first instance—to a position of ascendancy. Moreover, this struggle is one that has seemed as explicable in class terms as in the rather more obvious terms of intraparty intrigue.

For it is clear that the strengthening of the *verligte* position has been linked to the sea changes within the ranks of capital discussed in section I. It reflects the gravitation of the emergent Afrikaner bourgeoisie toward a clearer meeting-of-minds with the multinational corporations and with the most developed (and now formidably diversified) segments of South African-based mining capital (e.g., Anglo American). And this, in the context of the organic crisis, has meant a much stronger political basis for the "liberalization" of racial capitalism than existed in the 1940s. One dramatic index that something is afoot within the ranks of Afrikanerdom was the publication of a book, in the waning Vorster years, by A. D. Wassenaar, head of Afrikanerdom's most powerful corporate body, Sanlam. Entitled *The Assault on Private Enterprise: The Freeway to Communism* (Capetown, 1977), it lambasted the South African state for its continued paternalism and intervention in the private sector, and its refusal to let the logic of the market run. Reacting at least in part to the effect of high levels of state spending in deepening the economic crisis, Wassenaar left any implications which such a perspective might have for dealing with the race question more or less unstated. But as one of the earliest statements of the "free enterprise" ideology that has become so pervasive within the dominant classes' definition of reality, it is clear that it readily feeds into the kind of emerging economic project of big capital traced in section II.

Quentin Peel, in an article entitled "Why Business Wants Reform" (*Financial Times*, June 17, 1980), provides further evidence of this thrust. While he suggests that anti-apartheid campaigns overseas have been one important lever on business attitudes, he also marshalls considerable testimony to the fact that there is a powerful internal logic to change: "We are committed to those policies [the training and use of skilled black labor, radical improvements in black education] because enlightened business is totally opposed to discrimination *and because we need to achieve faster growth,*" says ,Reinald Hofmeyr, executive director of the Barlow-Rand group, South Africa's largest industrial group (emphasis added). "If you want to continue operating in stable conditions, you must do something to avoid a revolution," says the chief executive of a U.S. computer company. "We think we can cope with a faster rate of change. It is essential for business to take the lead," says an oil company executive. "Better wages mean less turnover," says the managing director of Metal Box of South Africa. It is this group that Botha speaks to (and for) when he waxes most eloquent—for instance, at an important meeting, symbolizing the new rapprochement between state/party and capital, which brought together the full cabinet and 250 prominent South African businessmen in late 1979—about the need for change and his government's commitment to it.

It should also be noted that Botha's reformist stance has its origins not only in his political base among Afrikaner capital, but also in his long-standing links with the military: he was Minister of Defense for many years (in which position, in fact, he earned a rather hawkish reputation). But the close fit between the stance of the military and that of the most advanced sections of capital has had a much stronger basis than that. For the military, for good reason, has been more aware than most of the seriousness of the African challenge, both regional and domestic, and of the fact that the crisis in South Africa is indeed organic. (Or, to put it in the jargon the military itself has

come to use, that the challenge to "survival" is "total": economic, political, and ideological.) In consequence, it has also
been gravitating to the position that only by curing certain of
the country's structural contradictions—albeit, once again,
"within certain limits"—will defense, let alone growth, of the
system be possible. Thus General Magnus Malan, chief of the
South African Defense Force (and recently appointed Minister
of Defense in Botha's cabinet) has explored the imperatives of
"survival" in numerous speeches in the past few years. While
emphasizing, significantly, that "free enterprise" and "economic
growth"—not Afrikanerdom and racial hegemony—are the core
of the system to be defended, he has assured his audiences that
the "SADF is ready to beat off any attack and although the
indications point to a considerable escalation in military operations, we are strong enough to withstand this onslaught." Yet he
knows that it is the volatility of the home front which increasingly defies any simple military solution and so concludes that,
"We must take into account the aspirations of our different
population groups. We must gain and keep their trust." As
he remarked on another occasion:

> Bullets kill bodies, not beliefs. I would like to remind you that
> the Portuguese did not lose the military battle in Angola and
> Mozambique [sic], but they lost the faith and trust of the in-
> habitants of those countries. The insurgent forces have no
> hope of success without the aid of the local population.[13]

Here, in the battle for "hearts and minds," the language of
reform is seen most clearly as being not only the language of
market rationality but also the language of counterinsurgency!

Glenn Moss, in a particularly trenchant discussion of the
"total strategy"[14] that has come to encapsulate the collective
foresight of this alliance of big capital and the military, has
suggested that what is occurring, in consequence, is the transformation of the National Party from a populist movement into
a party of the bourgeoisie. This is suggestive, yet it quickly becomes apparent that, under South African conditions, the populist cocoon of the now emerged Afrikaner bourgeoisie is not so
easily cast aside. Just as reform has its class basis, so does re-

sistance to reform. True, the white working class is declining in numbers and in influence (though those that remain are particularly resentful of any watering-down of racially defined job reservation or closed-shop agreements). More important, perhaps, is the fact that even the white "new petty bourgeoisie" which becomes more prominent as the white working class moves up the job ladder is by no means an obvious candidate for supporting reform. Indeed, this class—much of it employed by the state, and with a vested interest in the vast apparatus of apartheid—seems at least as likely to link up with the traditional petty bourgeoisie (the small farmers and the least developed of private sector entrepreneurs) in an alliance against any "concessions," against any capitalist-sanctioned advancement of the interests of Africans. Within the white community, such elements have the advantage of numbers and the 1981 South African election bears eloquent testimony to their continuing political clout.

The political consequences of these shifts and realignments in class alliances seem graphic, the deep split within the Nationalist Party having already been referred to. Thus *verkrampte* confronts *verligte* ("Botha and his pragmatists," as one *verkrampte* has contemptuously termed the latter); and to some extent, too, the Cape wing of the party—long the stronghold of the most developed sections of Afrikaner capital and political base for Botha—confronts the Transvaal—much more (though far from exclusively so) the center of petty-bourgeois/working-class interests and base for Andres Treurnicht, militant *verkrampte* rival to Botha inside the Nationalist Party. Indeed, so severe has been the political infighting that Botha, since assuming the prime ministership, has attempted to build an additional institutional base for his policies somewhat to the side of the arena of (whites-only) democratic participation and the conventional state apparatus. This has involved reorganizing the cabinet into six new cabinet committees, these in turn to be quite tightly controlled by the prime minister and his office's significantly expanded secretariat. Important, too, has been the direct inclusion of non-parliamentarians—military officers and businessmen (including many non-Nationalists) nominated by the prime minister—on such committees, including on the enormously powerful State Security Council. Increasing use is also being made of the commission of inquiry format to map out policy in crucial areas, allowing space for the reforming input of intellectuals and businessmen outside the confines of a state bureaucracy which is seen to have become deeply wedded—ideologically and by virtue of self-interest—to the structures of unregenerate apartheid. Moreover, the knife has been turned directly on that bureaucracy itself as considerable reshuffling has advanced the power of *verlig* elements within it and as the Public Service Commission, freshly mandated for the task by the appointment of a number of important businessmen, has set afoot the "rationalization" and "reduction" of the state system.

So aggressive has Botha been in this regard that some liberal critics have blanched at his authoritarianism (including the scope he has given for the vastly increased prominence of the military in the corridors of power), even while applauding the fact that this has seemed to represent a centralization of power in the interests of reform and business-approved commonsense! Yet the fact remains, of course, that Botha cannot simply ignore the white polity. There is a real fear of splitting the Nationalist Party irrevocably, and simultaneously a real constraint upon his freedom of maneuver which, as noted, the recent election revealed. Far from running a campaign which would place the calculus of reform at the center of his platform, Botha found himself pulled sharply to the right and encouraged to run a very hard-line campaign. We have already mentioned the Nationalist Party nomination meetings; in these the *verkramp* elements seem to have strengthened their hand (and therefore their parliamentary presence). And then there is Jaap Marais of the far-right Herstigte Nasionale Party, with his tart message that "the more you give the black man the more he takes" and that the government's "left-wing" policies mean "giving up, giving in, giving over, and eventually giving away our own country." Of course, the National Party retained its overwhelming parliamentary majority, but with its popular vote down from 65 to 55 percent. Quite clearly, Marais' message had its impact, with his party expanding its vote markedly—much more markedly than the Progressive Federal Party (the party of Harry Oppenheimer and others), with its liberal critique of government policies, though it, too, made some gains.

Noting these trends, the *Economist* (March 28, 1981) managed to find some solace in the fact that this right-left split is no longer so clearly communal, with more non-Afrikaners— including the white immigrants from Rhodesia and the Portuguese colonies—now with the Nationalist Party (and on its right wing) and "a small but significant number of Afrikaners, including a slice of the intellectual elite . . . disillusioned at the inadequacy of Botha's reforms . . . moving leftwards towards the PFP." One conclusion: "As group solidarity becomes less of a factor, and policies gain in importance, South Africa should, slowly, become more amenable to processes of rethinking." The other conclusion, less sanguine: "All this does not bode well for a bold reformist line after the election." Indeed, it is tempting to explain the apparent schizophrenia of Botha's policies in these electoral terms. Schizophrenia? Witness Joseph Lelyveld of the *New York Times* marvelling that

> at home [the South African government] authorizes black unions and harasses their leaders; it admits blacks to white universities and bars them from living near the campuses; it eases up on censorship of black authors and bans black newspapers; it promises a "new deal" for urban blacks, then proposes legislation that denies them access to the courts to defend the minimal rights they have; it acknowledges that its policy of developing independent black "homelands" has failed totally to produce economically viable states and pushes more of these tribal satrapies toward an independence that is likely to be equally meaningless.

Or Eric Marsden, writing in London's *Sunday Times* (January 25, 1981) of the period prior to this year's election campaign and juxtaposing the two Bothas:

> In the last two years Pieter Willem Botha has built up a fund of international goodwill such as no South African prime minister since General Smuts has enjoyed. Relaxation of petty apartheid restrictions, recognition of black trade unions and provision of greater educational and training opportunities

for blacks have led to widespread expectations of a genuine change towards multiracialism and social justice. Now, in a mere fortnight, much of this overseas credit has been frittered away—by the hard line taken at Geneva over Namibia, the introduction of the "fingerprint bill," a new wave of detentions, and the banning of two black newspapers in Soweto. Suddenly the clock seems to have been turned back.

The conclusion? Marsden feels confident that "the move towards reform has been checked only temporarily" by electoral calculations, while Lelyveld, following the 1981 election campaign closely, takes a more somber view: "The little Botha intends to do could never be enough for those who won't vote next week, but it may already be too much for those who will."

Reform if necessary, but not necessarily reform: this paradox is fundamental to contemporary South Africa. What bears emphasizing here is that the paradox cuts even deeper than the kind of electoral calculations we have just been highlighting (though these are real enough and, as seen, do serve as a focus for class struggle *within* the white community). For the contradictions mirrored in Botha's policy oscillations are ones which cut right across the reform camp itself and across most of the calculations of capitalist strategists in South Africa. Once again, any too neat a reduction of the reform debate either to a straightforward manifestation of the "logic of capital" or to an epiphenomenon of class alliances can tend to obscure our understanding of the precise nature of the incoherence which marks the dominant classes' response to crisis. We must return to some of the elements introduced at the outset of the chapter.

The reference here is not chiefly to those (relatively autonomous) ideological guarantors of the populist alliance— racism and Afrikaner nationalism—which framed the hard response to capitalist crisis after 1948, even if these are perhaps now more seriously in contradiction with capitalism's economic calculations than once they were. Rather the primary reference is to the political logic which we saw, in part, to underlie these variables, a "logic" which now focuses the fear that reform is really a Pandora's box. Structuring a program of economic expansion around the urban African fact, or attempting to coopt Africans by making available novel advantages, however limited: these are seen as ploys which, in sanctioning what ultimately must be uncontrollable forces, threaten to facilitate rather than preempt destruction of the system. Nor is such a fear confined to *verkrampte* circles. Even some of the most sophisticated actors in the capitalist camp, in spite of their eagerness to smooth production within the system, get nervous at the thought of jeopardizing the existing mode of *reproducing* that system in favor of a still hypothetical alternative. On the one hand, they cannot stand still: the crisis—economic, political, ideological—is much more serious and much less likely to be bullied into dormancy than in the 1940s. On the other hand, the passage from racial capitalism to liberal capitalism seems a particularly hazardous one. Or, to change the metaphor, it may be suggested that the dominant classes, mounted on the tiger of racial capitalism, now find that they can neither ride it altogether comfortably, nor easily dismount.

One great strength of the *verkrampte*/HNP position lies here, more perhaps than in any appeals to residual atavisms which might otherwise be thought to be their most important stocks-in-trade. Take Treurnicht's belief, as epitomized by the *Financial Mail*, that "apartheid is all or nothing: you can't keep the core of white supremacy alive if you start liberalizing around the edges." Or take the parallel view, advanced to coincide with the election campaign, of General Hendrik van den Bergh, Vorster's right-hand man prior to Muldergate as (then) head of the Bureau of State Security (BOSS). Describing South Africa as being in "a classic prerevolutionary situation," he warned the *Johannesburg Star* (as reported in the *Financial Times*, February 4, 1981) that

> the government's policies were leading to racial confrontation and black Majority rule. . . . [T]he attempts by the present government of Mr. P. W. Botha to remove racial discrimination and improve the quality of life of the black majority would lead inevitably to demands for political equality. . . . [H]e said the urban black population had always been the "achilles heel" of the ruling National Party's policy of separate development. Yet Mr. Botha is arousing a "steadily ris-

ing level of expectation" among blacks. "The systematic removal of discriminatory measures and other crash programmes
for improving the quality of life must inevitably lead to the
removal of the final form of discrimination—political discrimination."

Of course, Botha need scarcely "arouse" a steadily rising level
of expectation; that is there already. But these *verkramptes* are
not self-evidently mistaken in a number of their other premises.
Moreover, even though their harping on "white supremacy" is
significant, it must be emphasized that there is good reason for
capitalists much more color blind than Treurnicht to fear that
not only such "supremacy" but capitalist exploitation itself
might be swept away by any such drive for political equality.
Small wonder that the hard line continues to have its appeal,
even if the most vociferous of its advocates choose to admit the
existence of only one horn of the South African dilemma.

Verligtes are much more fully conscious of the dilemma
(the risks inherent in change set against the economic imperatives of reform and the political logic of counterinsurgency),
and are therefore more securely impaled upon its horns. We will
see this clearly when we turn to an analysis of the actual substance of reform in the following chapter and observe at closer
hand the paralysis, the lack of clear purpose, which is often
evident in the initiatives that concept embraces. And see, too,
the temptation, within the terms of the "total strategy," for the
government to fall back upon the repression side ("total control," in the sardonic phrase of one business journal) rather
than the reform side—the "conserve" rather than the "change"
side, as it were—of that strategy. Nor is this incoherence confined to the *verligtes* of the National Party who might, in any
case, be thought of as merely "sunshine liberals," still infected
themselves by strong residues of "white supremacy" and Afrikaner nationalism.

For it should not be assumed that either the strong pull
toward a novel strategy for capital-in-general which we explored
in section II, or the perspicacity of many of its most outspoken
leaders, has made even the most advanced sections of the business community an absolutely unequivocal force for dramatic

change. True, the latter do weigh importantly, now more than ever, in the political arena and in the policymaking field, and they have also managed to pull together to organize some reformist initiatives outside official channels: the activities of the Urban Foundation, with its well-heeled, corporate-funded programs, begun in 1977 to develop new urban housing schemes and training facilities for urban blacks, represent one well-known example. Nonetheless, the bourgeoisie's overall class interests can often founder on the rocks of the specific capitalist's individual calculations in the absence of a political leadership to focus (and enforce) its collective project. Given the disarray among the Nationalists, therefore, the government-business alliance has sometimes seemed more a case of the blind leading the blind than the guarantor of any very straightforward attempt to rectify capitalism's contradictions. In addition to far-seeing businessmen whom he met (as quoted above), Quentin Peel also met many who remained "very conservative" and others who were very much anchored in short-run perspectives. "You can't expect businessmen to encourage trade unions," wailed one British executive—this on the one hand while, on the other, the state's policy regarding such unions, for all the trumpeting of a movement away from the "bad old days" of suppressing black activity in this field, remains quite equivocal, as we shall see. Similarly, Elizabeth Schmidt has demonstrated that individual American firms tend to evade, where possible, even the rather bland reformist terms of the Sullivan principles on corporate conduct in South Africa which they themselves had earlier adopted—despite the fact that these principles might seem to represent a charter of (minor) change in their own (mutual) (long-run) enlightened self-interest.[15]

And then, inevitably, there is the political question; here a failure of nerve is even more likely. The Progressive Federal Party, very much a political voice of enlightened capitalism, may provide a final case in point of the ferocious cross-pressures that are at work within and without the South African white community. Thus Marsden, in the article cited above, noted that in the election the PFP launched "an all-out attack against the press bans, detentions, and the failure to accept the U.N.

terms on Namibia" and "is also challenging Botha to fulfill pledges of substantial reform." But its

> weakness is that it is opposed to majority rule, which [Alex] Boraine [PFP chairman] says would be disastrous and would mean "winner takes all." He believes that even radical African leaders such as Dr. Nthato Motlana would accept a power-sharing compromise; *but in Soweto the clamour for one man, one vote is growing louder by the day.* (Emphasis added.)

"One man [sic], one vote": this essential bottom line of liberal-capitalist strategy in successfully incorporating the mass of the population within its hegemonic framework elsewhere in the world is perhaps impossible for capitalism in South Africa, and in any case seems non-negotiable for the foreseeable future. Ultimately, this is the most fatal weakness of the reform strategy.

2. THE CONJUNCTURAL: TERRAIN OF DEFENSE

What, then, are the concrete strategies which are being mounted by the dominant classes, in the context of organic crisis, in order to defend the essential "limits" of the present South African system? It will be clear by now that we need fear neither these classes' omniscience nor their omnipotence in this regard; it would be mistaken—and also politically demobilizing—to over-estimate their ability to cure incurable contradictions in their own interests. But it would be equally unwise to overlook either their "incessant and persistent" efforts to do so, or the implications of those efforts. Even on the political front there is movement, despite the fact that the ruling-class game is still being played out primarily on the exhausted terrain of "separate development" (section I, below). More prominent are efforts which fall well short of deracialization, let alone democratization, of capitalism, but which, in focusing mainly on the crucial "urban question," are nonetheless of some substance. These involve moves which, in the words of the *Financial Mail,* "strike out, albeit extremely cautiously, in the direction of moderate adjustment and building up a black labour elite and middle class which will have a stake in stability and provide a counter to the process of radicalism." We will analyze further the economic, political, and ideological resonance of these moves in section II, while noting very clearly that the regime itself is by no means confident about such a "reform" strategy. For as we shall also see in this chapter, when we look at the build-up of the apparatus of repression and "security" which is the second term in the "total strategy" equation (section III), the state continues to wield a very big stick indeed.

I. The Politics of "Separate Development"

As seen, cheap labor provides the key to understanding South Africa's racial capitalism; in turn, the reserve system, underwriting labor migration, has provided the key to the availability of cheap labor. Apartheid—the hard solution— merely locked that system more firmly into place in the face of the strains induced by the further processes of capitalist development. Nonetheless, the architects of apartheid preferred not to leave the matter there. They soon felt the necessity, both at home and abroad, to seek to legitimate the inequitable distribution of land (87 percent set aside for 20 percent of the population, the whites) and the subordination of the African population which the reserve system entails in terms other than those of *baasskap,* unalloyed white supremacy. A new rationale—an initial foray into "formative" activity to alter the political and ideological terrain—emerged only slowly, from the mid-1950s on, and through the exertions of Dr. H. F. Verwoerd (first as Minister of Bantu Affairs and Development and later as Prime Minister) in particular.

(1) *The Bantustans.* Verwoerd's intention was to repackage racial distinctions (and racially defined discrepancies in power) in ethnic terms and thus present ethnic pluralism, national diversity, and "separate development" as an inspiring blueprint for the subcontinent: "We are trying to establish well-disposed little black neighboring states and to safeguard them from such dangers [e.g., "of joining up with foreign countries"] by being prepared to render all kinds of services to them."[1] As is well known, in the years following the first articulation of this policy the reserves were variously conceived and re-conceived— as "bantustans," "tribal homelands," "self-governing states,"

"emerging black states"—and granted an increasing measure of what was nonetheless still largely formal autonomy. Moreover, after Prime Minister Vorster accelerated the policy in the mid-1970s as part of his detente strategy vis-à-vis the rest of Africa, the whole process culminated in the possibility of the reserves gaining "independence," a route so far followed by four of the ten states-in-the-making designated, along tribal lines, by the Pretoria government. "Independence"—but of course the underlying economics of this development was never in doubt, as admitted from the outset by Verwoerd: "The Bantu homelands . . . may be areas which to a large extent, although the people live within their own areas and are governed there, are dependent on basic incomes earned in the adjoining white territory." Nor, for that matter, has the basic intention of the politics of separate development been concealed: it is "to form the basis of the maintenance of political power by whites in the so-called white country" (Gerrit Viljoen, chairman of the Broederbond, 1976). All Africans, urban and rural, are defined unilaterally as belonging to one or another of these units: "If our policy is taken to its logical conclusion as far as the Black people are concerned," said Connie Mulder in introducing the 1978 Bantu Homelands Citizenship Amendment Bill into parliament, "there will not be one Black man with South African citizenship"!

Whatever may have been their hopes of swaying international opinion by such patent sleight-of-hand, the dominant classes were not naive about the degree of acceptability to the vast mass of the African population of this kind of attempt to legitimate the system. True, there was some intention that the strategy of dividing (and thereby ruling) Africans along tribal lines, worked out over decades in the mining compounds and reserves, would be further reinforced by this device. Perhaps more importantly, there was the hope that Africans in the reserves might be encouraged in this way to focus their aspirations and their discontents locally, at the homeland level, rather than directing them toward the overall system of capitalist exploitation and racial oppression. But this latter possibility implied a corollary: in practice it meant facilitating the emergence of an African petty bourgeoisie—grounded in the staffing of the new administrative structures of the bantustans and in entrepreneurial advancement within the private sector—which could be expected to develop vested interests complementary to those of South African capital and the apartheid state and to act as a buffer between the latter and the mass of the dispossessed. It came to imply, in short, that at least as crucial as the attempt to undermine concerted resistance by splitting Africans regionally and ethnically is the attempt to do so *by further stratifying them along class lines.* Although governmental cooptation of quasi-traditional chiefly structures into its administrative network foreshadowed this ploy from very early days, on balance the initial tendency was to forestall the emergence of privileged classes of Africans in the reserves in order to reinforce the economic pressures upon all Africans to work in the "white" areas. But in the 1950s, as Molteno has pointed out, the strategy began to change: "The deliberate nurturing of a Black aspirant bourgeoisie formed part of a broader strategic recognition of the necessity to let loose at last the forces of class stratification in the Bantustans. The Bantustans strategy of class polarization is to be distinguished from the Reserve strategy of class levelling."[2]

The crystallization of an alliance between such privileged blacks and white powerwielders around the bantustan initiative will be seen below to be of considerable importance, but evaluated in any broader terms the record of that initiative is a feeble one. For example, those bantustans that have moved to "independence" remain virtually unrecognized by the international community—though here the Reagan administration's rumored invitation to Prime Minister Lucas Mangope of Bophuthatswana to visit the United States does stand as an ominous straw in the wind. Nor, as hinted, has the ploy convinced many Africans of its legitimacy or succeeded in validating ethnicity as the primary point of political reference for them. Thus the high-powered Quail Commission, appointed to investigate the wisdom of Ciskei's seeking independence (it recommended against such independence but went unheeded by ambitious Ciskeian elites), found 90 percent of all Xhosa-speaking blacks desiring one person, one vote in a unitary South Africa, this also being the goal, according to another poll, of 92 percent of Zulu speakers in Soweto. In no bantustans have the inhabitants opted for "freedom" in a free vote, and crudely authoritarian internal political structures are the rule. Moreover, these "little black neighboring states" are entirely unviable: the three which are already independent (Transkei, Bophuthatswana, and Venda, with Ciskei to join them in December 1981) receive an average of 75 percent of their revenues from South African subventions, and in the largest of these, the Transkei, only 15.2 percent of the labor force is internally employed. Indeed, overall, more than 70 percent of the homelands' "economically active" population is involved in the migrant-labor system, while the rate of homeland job creation fails to absorb more than 10 percent of those who are newly finding their way onto the job market. The result: vast rural slums, wracked by "poverty, ignorance, and disease."

This is a situation which the South African regime is, in the first instance, much quicker to worsen than to alleviate. Thus, at one level, where geographically feasible (in Kwazulu on the very outskirts of Durban, for example), it has moved to redraw bantustan borders so that even some of the more settled workforce are incorporated within them—as so-called commuters. More important, however, is the role, discussed above, of the bantustans as the repositories—the "dumping-grounds"—for the unemployed from the urban areas (and also from the white agricultural sector, where increased mechanization has undermined residues of labor tenancy, settled some workers but displaced considerable populations, and in many ways reinforced the need for merely seasonal migratory labor in this sector). Massive population removals of these unemployed, of the illegally urbanized "appendages" (i.e., families) of contract workers, and of others continue apace, this being still the ugliest of all aspects of apartheid. Indeed, as we shall see shortly, an attempt to tighten, not relax, the mechanisms of influx control to keep the unemployed locked into the reserves and to drive a wedge between the more settled elements of the urban workforce and the more migrant-cum-marginal elements is at the very core of the "reform" initiative. The result? Sheena Duncan, an outspoken liberal critic of the regime, suggests, as quoted in the text of a *Financial Mail* article, that "the small group of privileged urban blacks whose quality of life will undoubtedly improve 'may well become less urgent in their demands for political power and serve as the lid on the kettle of revolution for some years to come.' " This is a controversial reading of developments in the urban areas to which we will return. However, her attendant point is much less controversial: the price will be "dreadful human suffering in the homelands," and the less-privileged majority "will inevitably become more inclined to reject the capitalist system and to turn to other ideologies for support and rescue."[3] The *FM* (January 25, 1980) took the same point somewhat further: under the circumstances, chances are that

> South Africa by 1990 will not be an efficient white-dominated economy drawing its labour requirements from convenient labour reservoirs dignified as states. Instead the homelands will simply have replaced Mozambique, Angola, and Zimbabwe as buffer states, breeding grounds for conflict. The heralds are there already: witness the attack on the Soekmekaar police station [in Lebowa]. Pretoria's "solution" to racial turbulence (to which the Nationalists have been the main contributors) will have degenerated into a nightmare.

Basic contradictions inherent in South Africa's policies begin to surface here, of course. The regime may feel it has little alternative, economically and politically, but to use the bantustans as dumping grounds in this way, but it too has begun to realize the dangers in such a practice. True, its first instinct is to reinforce its bantustan allies—those political-cum-bureaucratic elites who now act as the willing gatekeepers of the labor bureau/influx-control system—in the most straightforward manner by strengthening them militarily, against their own people. The authorization of extremely repressive security legislation within the homelands, the extensive training programs offered local police, the proliferation of "Black Regional Units" and "independent" bantustan armies largely under the guidance of the South African Defense Force are all cases in point (although the SADF is also occasionally active throughout the homelands in "development efforts"—medical and educational, in particular—as part of its "hearts and minds" campaign). Nonetheless, there is some public admission of the fact that the bottom line of the problem is economic—even if there is relatively little the regime is prepared to do about it.

A first item which has seemed to spring from such an admission is the long-drawn-out charade of attempting to "develop" the reserves-cum-homelands as separate economies in their own right. As the 1950s Tomlinson Commission, appointed to draw up a blueprint for bantustan policy, put the point at the time, "Either the challenge [of facilitating such development] must be admitted, or the inevitable consequences of the integration of Bantu and European population groups must be endured." In fact, only a minuscule percentage of the financing Tomlinson projected to be necessary was ever forthcoming; in addition, incentives (cheap labor, government subsidy) to decentralize industry in the direction of the borders of the bantustans (or inside them) have never been deemed sufficiently economically attractive by South Africa's business community to enable that aspect of the policy to make a significant dent into bantustan unemployment. The activity of the (South African government-controlled) development corporation in the bantustans have come by and large to service the generally quite opportunistic endeavors of Afrikaner entrepreneurs (casinos are a current favorite) and the advances in the tertiary sector of African quasi-entrepreneurs (most of them state functionaries and politicians). A similar pattern has prevailed in the agricultural sector, where some agribusinesses (generally white owned, despite the apparent anomaly) have prospered and where, from "betterment" and rehabilitation (including land consolidation) schemes, much the same stratum of petty-bourgeois Africans as mentioned above has made gains. True, the current gold boom has encouraged a slightly accelerated effort to punch money into the bantustans, but along more or less the same lines as before. In the end, then, we return to the premise that these entities are simply not viable; indeed, even discussing them in such terms runs the risk of obscuring their essential role within the broader economy: as massive prison camps, of benefit only to their warders, both black and white.

The second, more recent, aspect of bantustan economics (and the attendant attempt at legitimation of the whole enterprise) represents a rather different tack—and a somewhat more surprising one. For, in the spirit of "reform," it involves a much franker admission than ever before that the creation of a series of viable little black neighboring economies (to underpin those "little black neighboring states") is a will-o'-the-wisp. One effect of this admission is some downplaying of the drive toward "consolidation" of the individual homelands. Such consolidation was to have pushed forward the linking-up of the latter's often much-divided component parts (Kwazulu, for example, is comprised of forty-four quite separate patches of territory) and the further purchasing/trading of white lands so as to reorder these homelands into more "logical" economic units; now any extreme version of this program is being deemed much too expensive as well as economically beside the point. Instead, the emphasis is increasingly upon the imperatives of integrated *regional* development and, as befits the renewed saliency of free-market ideology, upon the need for a free run for the private sector across the full sweep of South Africa in order to facilitate growth. A 1980 Bureau of Economic Research, Organization, and Development (BENSO) report delivered the rationale for this: "A solution to the problem of race relations in South Africa does not lie in the creation of a number of separate economies, but rather in economic cooperation and a system of separate political sovereignties." And the theme of economic cooperation was one that Botha hammered home at the Transvaal Nationalist Party Congress in late 1980 only hours after his rival, Treurnicht, had warned the delegates, in the words of one reporter, that "free markets would jeopardize the whole edifice of apartheid."

Of course, it is clear that the free market, however much unfettered, can provide no real solution to bantustan misery. Nonetheless, it is not surprising that the *Financial Mail* (a true believer in this kind of solution) was moved to crow that Botha's assertions demonstrate the failure of decentralization and "effectively overturn the grand Verwoerdian plan to restructure this country into a patchwork of independent states, each with its own reasonably viable economy." Not that all businessmen would necessarily agree with the *FM*'s further points that such an overturn removed "what little moral justification there is for influx control" (the latter being seen by that magazine as forestalling the free movement of factors of production), or that it "presages the need for a new political relationship between blacks and whites that takes into account the hard realities of economic life"; as we have seen, for many —and not merely for *verkramptes*—these extrapolations of the argument may seem a little too cavalier regarding the dangers which would also be inherent in such developments. And certainly Botha, in pushing the case for the economic logic of integration, has echoed BENSO's parallel retention of the classic Nationalist Party line of "separate political sovereignties" (while also holding very firmly indeed—as an investigation of the recommendations of the Riekert Commission in the next section will make clear—to influx control).

Thus Botha's solution has come to rest, politically, on the notion of a "constellation of states" for Southern Africa, a notion first unveiled with considerable pomp and circumstance, and to a very receptive audience, at the November 1979 summit meeting with businessmen mentioned in the previous chapter. This constellation is seen by Botha and his colleagues as, precisely, a means of reconciling "separate development" with a necessary reassembling of the pieces of a divided South Africa (while also following up on Vorster's earlier, and unsuccessful, detente initiative by seeking to draw into South Africa's economic net those other, more independent, states in the region which are included in Pretoria's definition of the proposed "constellation"). So far there have been few takers for this proposal of "economic cooperation," and few, at home or abroad, have been taken in by this latest attempt to legitimate South Africa's policies. But the pull toward such an emphasis is significant nonetheless.* Certainly it has gone far enough to

---

* A 1980 booklet on the constellation from the South African Foundation suggests the possibilities some have seen to be implicit in this governmental initiative. Thus Pretoria University's Professor J. J. Stadler summarizes its more manipulative side in the phrase "share political and diplomatic responsibility with the 'domestic group' to communicate outwards," while Deon Geldenhuys of the South African Institute for International Affairs, going further, states that "this process may involve an initial confederation of South Africa and the independent former homelands, perhaps ultimately leading to a federation. In this sense, a constellation could be regarded as a design to join together what apartheid has put asunder"!

move such an ally of Pretoria as Bophutatswana's Mangope to
attack the possible displacement of the priority of bantustan
consolidation and economic decentralization by reintegration
and regional cooperation as potentially prejudicial to those who,
like himself, have already opted for "independence."

Moreover, it has reinforced the reluctance to go into the
wilderness of independence on the part of those other bantustan
leaders who have not already done so, encouraging them instead
to talk more aggressively of such possibilities as "dual citizenship," various kinds of federalisms, and the like. And there are
even bolder proposals for reintegration, like those developed for
Natal by Dr. Jan Lombard on behalf of the South African
Sugar Association; as an alternative to the "consolidation" of
Kwazulu within that province, he looked to much more extensive economic interpenetration between Kwazulu and the rest
of Natal—and a future of power sharing. Of course, the idea
was rejected out of hand by the central government (though
warmly received by Kwazulu's Chief Minister Gatsha Buthelezi), but its surfacing did demonstrate clearly some of the
cross-pressures which the "reform" initiative encapsulates. For,
as Colin Eglin of the PFP has put it:

> Mr. Botha's strategy ends the myth that it is possible to frag-
> ment South Africa. It makes more urgent the need to start ne-
> gotiations on a new political dispensation for South Africa
> which is no longer to be divided. . . . [T]he government's deci-
> sion to abandon economic separate development in favour of
> multiracial; regional development has fundamental political
> and constitutional consequences. . . . And, as economic separa-
> tion is replaced by economic "cooperation," so the NP's com-
> mitment to political separation will have to give way to polit-
> ical cooperation and in due course the acceptance of the con-
> cept of political power sharing.

Needless to say, this is just the case that Mr. Treurnicht has
been trying to make, but from the right!

(2) *The Community Councils.* If there are complexities
for the government here, even more complicated has been the
continuing issue of the urban African. For this embodies a practical problem for ruling-class strategists that is not in any way

swept aside by the theoretical solution of homeland citizenship for all.* We noted earlier how unconvincing a device such "citizenship" is to most Africans. Now the government has had to attempt to suppress a report by its own Human Sciences Research Council which reveals how little rooted it is not merely attitudinally but in the concrete realities of everyday city life: 57 percent of the black men in those urban areas were born there, 80 percent have neither parents nor children in a homeland, 60 percent have not even visited a homeland in the preceding year, and so on. Nor did the relevant government department's initial response to these realities—recommending intensified media coverage to counteract declining interest in the bantustans and revival of a 1978 government report's idea of establishing political constituencies in urban areas to elect representatives to homeland governments, for example—seem very promising. Botha, too, is aware of the problem: questioned regarding Mulder's statement that someday there would be no black South Africans, he recently replied: "I cannot visualize a situation in my life time when we won't have black-skinned people in the Republic of South Africa" (*Johannesburg Star,* April 25, 1981). Moreover, responsive both to the economic imperatives which suggest the need to view the firmer settling in the cities of some significant proportion of these "black-skinned people" as a virtue rather than an evil, and more alert, perhaps, to the full range of political complexities of dealing effectively with the volatile urban African, he has sought devices other than the mere importation of homeland politics into the townships as a means of coping with the challenge.

Interestingly, these devices have close parallels to the bantustan strategy, though now adapted more specifically to the urban terrain. Particularly important in this regard is a variation on the bantustan theme of turning stratification within the African population to dominant-class advantage, of attempting to peel away a "privileged group of blacks in the urban areas" (as Sheena Duncan conceptualized the point) and to attach their

---

* This is in spite of the fact that the latter policy remains a source of considerable menace to every African, whether "settled" in the urban areas or not.

interests (and ideas) more firmly to the wheel of capitalism. We will explore this attempt shortly, but what may be noted here are the strict limits which are set to the possible political cooptation of such elements, whatever may be the possibilities of improving their lot economically. These are limits which, in fact, are even more firmly in place than in the case of the bantustans; as the *Financial Mail* (November 7, 1980) put it, "The government is assuming that having been given the keys to a limited economic kingdom, privileged blacks—let alone the others—will not ask for the political one as well."

Not that even then the parallel breaks down entirely. The *Financial Mail* (May 18, 1979) itself has recognized the extent to which government plans to devolve certain limited powers onto black community councils (and onto black trade unions) in the urban areas represent an "attempt to co-opt a small black leadership group to help it [the government] carry out its policies," noting that

> by and large this strategy has been successful as far as bantustans are concerned. Most homeland "governments" have gone along with administering key aspects of the labour system. . . . One effect of setting up governments and parliaments and civil services all over the show is to put the educated elite on to official payrolls, which is a good deal healthier than having them fomenting unrest. So well has this cooption policy worked that government is now gambling on applying it in the urban areas.

Beyond this, an attempt to simulate urban popular participation in the post-Soweto period was probably as important as "jobs-for-the-boys" in mounting such a novel departure. Thus, as early as 1977 the new Community Councils Act was presented as granting "self-government" to those with a more permanent status (that is, the "Section Tenners" in terms of the Bantu [Urban Areas] Consolidation Act, a category to be clarified below) in the black urban areas. And this year the relevant minister, Piet Koornhof, is introducing legislation to give such councils—now "town" and "village" councils—somewhat wider "municipal" powers over various social, economic, and law-and-order matters than originally envisaged. For those who chose to participate as councillors, control over "community guards" will give them "what amounts to private police forces" and, in addition, there are "powers of patronage over business undertakings, schools, new businesses, churches and the like" (*Financial Mail*, November 7, 1980). But, once again, the white government retains virtually unlimited dominance over the whole process, while the councils (black faces for white) are ceded such unenviable tasks as collecting—and raising—rents (this being all the more necessary since, in the words of the Riekert Commission, "black communities [must] bear to an increasing extent a greater part of the total burden in connection with the provision of services in their own community"!) In short, the ploy of "participation" is virtually negated from the outset, while the entire charade has the continuing premise of segregation as its most blatant feature.

"Formative" attempts—here an ounce of urban political participation—are always potentially two-edged swords for the dominant classes. Ironically, in the game of reform the latter stand to win most when they put themselves most at risk— precisely at the point, that is, where the attempt at cooptation could most easily collapse into significant concession. Similarly, when reform, in the formative sense, really is the name of the game, the popular forces must proceed with caution, choosing the moment when the level of class struggle suggests that using a particular institution can, in effect, turn it back against the government, and being wary of the moment when entry of some of their number into such an institution marks their abandonment of the struggle for genuine transformation. What seems clear is that, despite the foreshadowings of such a possibility, this is not yet the level of contestation represented by the government's community council ploy; it is simply too raw, too unrelenting, too risk free. Thus, while practice vis-à-vis the councils has varied from place to place, the Soweto result seems indicative of its general failure: straightforward boycott and a 6 percent poll in the 1978 council elections, elevation of David Thebahali (with 97 votes!), an unconvincing stooge, to chairmanship, and a recent decision to postpone elections another year in order to avoid the disruption resistance to them might cause.[4] Clearly, it is more credible leaders like Dr. Ntatho Motlana (of the Soweto Committee of Ten) whom the government would like to tempt aboard: witness, to take another example, the invitation extended to him, a year or two ago, to join one of the six newly formed regional advisory committees on blacks outside the bantustans. The reasons for his refusal of this and other "openings" underscore the hollowness of most of the government's initiatives, even in the eyes of all but the most opportunist of urban petty bourgeoisie (not to mention in the eyes of other urban elements—students, workers, and the like—who watch such leaders carefully and press upon them). In Motlana's words, "These changes have no meaning for black South Africans. They are there to serve the interests of the white tribe. . . . A common citizenship, common fatherland and shared power are what the blacks want. Otherwise we are talking at cross purposes."

(3) *The President's Council.* Paralleling the "community council" initiatives, though not yet very much more successful, have been governmental gestures toward pulling together at least some of the actors in urban areas into new kinds of centralized institutions, the recently formed President's Council being the most dramatic such innovation. Sparked, no doubt, by the involvement of both "Coloureds" and Indians in the new militancy of the 1970s—the "Black Consciousness" movement of the period had come to embrace both groups, and not merely Africans, within its definition of "black"—various forms of co-optation-by-representation of these groups-without-homelands were bruited about by the government. Specifically, the Schlebusch Commission suggested new institutional possibilities (including parallel parliaments and other variations on such themes) and, in particular, the creation of the abovementioned President's Council (replacing the South African senate) to further plan innovation in this regard. Of course, the "representatives" on this council from the Coloured and Indian communities are merely prime ministerial appointees (indeed, it has been boycotted by the PFP because it is so clearly manipulated in this way) and, in the event, no really representative figures from these two communities have come on board. Nor does there seem to be much doubt that, at this stage, any constitutional dispensation which the council comes up with will

leave the white parliament firmly in the driver's seat. Nonetheless, even the contemplation of some kind of multiracial decision-making and eventual representation—contrasting as it does with the NP's self-confident driving of the Coloureds out of national political institutions in the 1950s—is an index of the pressure the regime feels.

Africans were not invited onto the President's Council, "separate development" again being the stumbling block to any real innovation in this sphere. Still, there were some gestures here too, Botha originally proposing a "black council" to be structured parallel to the President's Council as part of the constitution-making process. Even the nonindependent homeland leaders refused to serve on this body, demanding a place on the President's Council itself—a step which, to the government, would have implied a tacit acceptance of the premise of a unified South Africa beyond anything it is currently prepared to concede. Nonetheless, some on the council still see this kind of extension of the multiracial concept as a possibility.[5] Take, for example, Bill Sutton (once a United Party member of parliament) who has said: "The President's Council must create a focus of interest in itself. It must forge a working relationship between the groups represented here—then reach out to other groups, in the homelands, the urban blacks, and so on. I would say there is still time for a negotiated settlement, and this council is the vehicle to bring it about."

Will the government feel able to go so far? For the moment the indications are strong that it will not, but we must remain aware that the philosophy of cooptation is strongly afoot within Afrikaner intellectual circles, and some "thinking about the unthinkable" is taking place. Witness the Afrikaans-language press. Thus, the Johannesburg daily *Beeld* on developments in Zimbabwe: "Whites in Rhodesia learned the lesson the hard way. . . . We are still strong in South Africa. From strength we must negotiate and reconcile." Or its influential editor, Tom Vosloo, acknowledging that the African National Congress, "the mother body of black organized politics in South Africa, might have the support of millions of blacks in the country" and going so far as to contemplate publicly the necessity of negotiations with even that organization (albeit while outlining the most restrictive of preconditions for any such negotiations) : "We should not live in a dream world that the *status quo*—a white government which talks for and on behalf of the whole country—can be upheld forever. May Ian Smith's notorious UDI rule of a 'thousand years' pull us back to reality." Or, finally, the equally prominent Dr. Willem de Klerk, editor of *Die Transvaler:*

> Hard, cold, equal negotiations are now on the agenda. . . . The whites in this country are increasingly sincerely predisposed to establish a new dispensation. A dispensation of human dignity for all. Removal of discrimination. Equal opportunities. Even a new look at the old bastions of separate development. The whites want consultation and discussion, constellation or confederation or however one wants to give joint responsibility to all national groups. The whites want to give their share of a meaningful compromise for a political settlement that will link us meaningfully as partners.

Rhetoric, much of this—but they are worried!

Of course, more predictably, liberal elements in the capitalist camp feel the need to advance even further along this line of march. Witness the *Rand Daily Mail*'s own response to the 1980 election in Zimbabwe:

> Every white South African should look to Rhodesia now to see the consequences of delay; of missing chances to do favourable deals while there is still time; of destroying the moderate black leaders by giving them nothing to show for their moderation except the deadly image of collaborators; and of polarizing the races and radicalizing the minds of the blacks until in the end there is a great nationalist upsurge for the man with the most extreme image.

In this regard, we have already seen the PFP's Colin Eglin emphasizing the logic of political negotiations which he sees to be attendant upon the increased recognition of the imperatives of economic integration. In much the same vein is the *Financial Mail*'s view that "eventually, if Botha means business he is going to have to stride ahead with reform that all can see and appreciate. Consultation must give way to negotiation. Negotiation must yield to election. Power will have to be meaningfully shared" (May 16, 1980). And then there is Oppenheimer's observation (*FM*, March 28, 1980) that "black politicians have always been playing power politics rather than protest politics [because] until recently the white government left them no way of playing power politics, except to aim at revolution." His hope: "I think that what is happening now is making it possible for black politicians to aim at power within an acceptable system and within a peaceful dispensation"!

Yet it is the general thrust and direction of this kind of argument rather than its precise content which is significant. For no very clear and precise strategy emerges from such liberal emphasis and, as noted at the end of the previous chapter, certainly not any embracing of the goal of "one person, one vote" (not any embracing, that is to say, of the apparently much-feared and much-rejected "Westminster system"). For many such liberals, too, there is the lure—the safety—of "separate development"; thus they have tended, in a great number of their statements, to accept the homelands as *faits accompli,* and on that basis to see them as possible building blocks for the federal or "consociational" solutions to South Africa's "constitutional problems" which are all they are prepared to contemplate under the rubric "power sharing." At the same time, they occasionally announce themselves open to the extension of the franchise at least to urban Africans (". . . 1 million or 2 million blacks with a non-bantustan franchise would lower the temperature of rising expectations . . . and, even if they were unanimously to vote socialist or liberal, which is unlikely, it would hardly endanger Afrikaner supremacy" [*Financial Mail,* September 14, 1979]). And they can even talk, from time to time, of having African political parties (including those which have been banned) among the participants in a (repeatedly proposed) "national convention" to discuss South Africa's future. Thus they twist and turn and, of course, in light of their outrageous hedging it is tempting to see any such proposal as a mere shell game. Tempting, but perhaps not quite correct:

like so much else afoot in contemporary South Africa, these
preoccupations do indicate the extreme contradictions which
wrack the racial capitalist system, and the desperate, if confused,
search which is underway for the means of preempting the revolutionary import of those contradictions.

Contradictions indeed: it has even been stated (*Financial
Mail,* July 4, 1980) that Botha sees the President's Council as
a step toward a national convention, and that he has said as
much privately to some black leaders. If this is the case, one
must assume that, at best, he is of two minds on the subject; and
that, in any event, he is even more wedded than are the liberals
to the premise that ethnic diversity/separate development, rather
than South African unity, must be the basis for any negotiations
which might be forthcoming. In consequence, it remains true
that very little stands on offer politically to the black population.
Not that anything short of one person, one vote would be a
legitimate outcome; but even from the point of view of those
urban black politicians who might otherwise seek to become the
agents of cooptation and legitimation there is little enough—
Oppenheimer's optimism in this respect thus seeming somewhat
premature. It remains a fairly uninviting and unpromising
prospect for the petty bourgeoisie to enter the political arena
on what are still overwhelmingly and unequivocally white
terms. More important, the terrain available makes it extremely
difficult for any such petty bourgeoisie, even were it so inclined,
to contemplate organizing and carrying the mass of the people
with it in a "transformist" manner into the camp of capital—
all the more so when one remembers just how mobilized and
politically conscious its possible popular constituency already is.
Needless to say, we have seen enough to know that we must be
alert for further innovation by the dominant classes in this
sphere. Yet the failure of those classes—despite their obvious
concern—to begin seriously to deracialize politics and to attempt
in that way to structure a political process compatible in the
long run with the continued reproduction of South African
capitalism remains noteworthy. Moreover, this is the aspect of
the situation which seems least likely to change formatively in
the near future.

II. The "Urban Question"

Riekert and Wiehahn: these two names, heads of state-appointed inquiries into the influx-control system and black trade unions respectively, have come to stand for the central core of ruling-class response to the organic crisis. Given the incoherent nature of the search for a global political formula (as discussed in the last section), their reports represent the most developed aspects, at this stage, of the "total strategy." Moreover, the gap on the political front makes even more crucial these particular "formative" efforts, directed as they are at the social and economic conditions of the urban black population—in the labor market, at the point of production, and in the townships. Innovations here become, in effect, some of the most important of those "keys to a limited economic kingdom" alluded to by the *Financial Mail* (above) as being a substitute for significant political advance.

Of course, the term "limited" is an entirely appropriate qualifier, state control still looming large in the lives of the (also limited) group of potentially privileged blacks concerned. Nor will handing over the "keys" be an entirely simple and straightforward exercise. Bracketing, on the one hand, the already discussed right-wing pressure to reinforce the hard line and, on the other, the opposition from below to dominant-class strategy, we will examine here this initiative's content and internal contradictions, as well as the structural barriers to its implementation, many of these being the ongoing legacy of apartheid. At the same time, we must return to Gramsci's (and Hall's) formulation to remind ourselves that one need not share the enthusiasm of most Western apologists for Wiehahn and Riekert in order to see that the strategy spelled out in their reports *is* formative, that, specifically, it is attempting to achieve a "new balance of forces" by shifting the weight of the urban black population in favor of the maintenance of capitalism. Only in the next chapter will we focus more directly on that population itself, to appraise the role that it has chosen to play in making its own history.

(1) *Riekert.*[6] The emphasis here is on the "Section Tenners," those blacks, in various classes, with rights to remain in

the urban areas on the basis of Section 10 of the Bantu (Urban Areas) Consolidation Act of 1946.* The bottom line of strategy vis-à-vis urban blacks—taking up most of the 1979 Riekert report—is the attempt to separate the working class into two fractions, a better-off group permanently settled in the urban areas, and the rest, *confined* to the homelands. Blacks with Section 10(1)(a) and (b) rights are to be regarded as "qualified" urban dwellers and no longer labeled "temporary sojourners" (as the apartheid glossary put it). Riekert recommended that substantial advantages in the labor market be granted to this group as compared with its current situation, although the proposal was hedged about with the predictable conditions that the group's size not be allowed to grow uncontrollably and that it be regulated to meet the requirements of both political stability and capital accumulation.

As hinted earlier, one side of the Riekert coin implies a considerable stepping up of influx control, a reinforcing of the long-standing attempt to reverse the flow of Africans who, increasingly unable to survive in the reserves, have accepted the risks of pass law arrest in return for access to the incredibly low wages of illegal city jobs. To counter their movement out of the reserves, Riekert recommended that the network of labor bureaus supervise even more closely all migrant employment contracts by making bureau validation a requirement. Linked with such tighter control is the imposition of heavy fines on employers of illegal workers (this being the recommendation which was most immediately implemented by the government). Such measures, it is hoped, will keep the unemployed and unemployable masses firmly locked into the reserves. At the same time, the number of contract workers allowed into the white areas is to be reduced as much as possible. These groups, together, make up the "disqualifieds," those with no hope of

---

* Section 10 (1) of the Bantu (Urban Areas) Consolidation Act prohibits Africans from remaining in urban areas for longer than seventy-two hours unless they are able to produce proof that they: (a) have resided since birth continuously in the area; or (b) have worked continuously in the area for the same employer for ten years, or have lived continuously (and legally) in the area for fifteen years; or (c) are dependents of men who qualify under (a) or (b); or (d) have been given permission to live and work in the area on contract.

gaining permanent urban status. They will continue to comprise the lower tier of the intended two-tier labor market. For them, Riekert contains no novelty, merely ever tighter control over their movement.

In contrast, conditions for the "qualifieds," who make up the upper tier, will theoretically be altered substantially and in the direction of the "free" labor market characteristic of a more advanced liberal capitalism; this is the other side of the Riekert coin, and of course the one most trumpeted abroad. Thus Riekert recommended several changes in the pass laws aimed at stabilizing the urban working class: "Qualified" Africans should receive a standing authorization to seek work, allowing them to change jobs independently of the labor bureaus, and they should also be able to bring their families to the cities, irrespective of the latter's status (though contingent upon housing being available). Movement between urban areas should be allowed, again contingent upon the availability of work and housing, this to allow unemployed but "qualified" blacks in smaller rural towns to take jobs in the industrial centers currently held by contract workers or "illegals." In addition, employers should be encouraged to hire "qualified" workers ahead of migrants, in part by making the authorization of the latter's employment contingent upon a lack of suitable "qualified" work-seekers. Finally, less savory to the "qualifieds" but no less essential in the eyes of Riekert, was the recommendation alluded to previously that the share of housing, transport, and services costs carried by "qualified" blacks be increased (as if these costs were not high enough already relative to wages); the intention here was to make a regular income essential, thus combatting what Riekert called the "work choosiness" of "qualified" blacks, their tendency to reject the jobs with the worst wages and working conditions, which were then filled by contract and illegal workers. The intended result of all this? The smooth operation of the scheme would mean a far greater job security for "qualified" blacks; unemployment would be related primarily to the cyclical trends of capital accumulation (as is white, Coloured, and Asian unemployment) rather than to the still rising secular trend of African unemployment (the burden of which would fall entirely upon the "lower tier" of the labor force); and job-market competition between "qualifieds" and "disqualifieds" would be exacerbated, thus further stratifying the workforce economically and dividing it politically.

It must be emphasized that the advantages intended for the "qualifieds" are not yet firmly on the statute book, the government having shown great indecision in translating most of Riekert's proposals into law. Draft legislation was finally published eighteen months after the report, but withdrawn for "review" three months later after coming under fire from big capital for not going far enough in eliminating influx control. Perhaps this indecision, in turn, reflects the considerable tension within the Riekert approach itself—as well as within the overall dominant-class strategy we have been exploring—between concessions to, and control over the movement of, "qualified" workers. Needless to say, any continuing controls make it all the less likely that the latter will be induced to perceive their interests as distinct from the "disqualifieds." For example, the government has made it clear that it is not yet ready to remove the "72-hour law," as Riekert has recommended. This notorious enactment makes it illegal for Africans without Section 10 rights to remain in an urban area for longer than 72 hours. It is the chief measure used to expel Africans who are illegally in the cities, the pass book examinations at train and bus stations and in township streets through which it is enforced resulting in thousands of arrests annually. In Riekert's view, the 72-hour law would become redundant since illegal Africans would be unable to obtain either a job or accommodation, and so would have no incentive to remain in the city. Its elimination was seen to be an extra benefit to the "qualifieds," relieving them of the harassment of the pass examination—while also downplaying, for international consumption, a particularly sordid aspect of authoritarian rule in South Africa. For the government, however, repression remains necessary (at least during the transition to Riekert's scheme); its White Paper on Riekert noted only that: "if the stricter application of the other [influx-control] elements . . . prove effective . . . the repeal of the 72-hour provision may be considered again."

Moreover, even if Riekert's scheme is fully enacted, his proposals suggest that expulsion measures must remain prominent, with the marginal change that residence and workplace, rather than the streetcorner, will become the key areas for the scrutiny of an African's *bona fides*. Such measures certainly will remain necessary, since past experience with the pass laws suggests that Riekert's tightening of influx controls is not likely to succeed in preventing urbanization. Capitalist development, as we have noted several times above, works to undermine any attempts to control the movement of labor on the scale it has reached in South Africa; indeed, this was one of the factors which made the Riekert report necessary. Since the ruling class will not, and cannot, develop the reserves adequately to eliminate unemployment there, and since many firms (especially the most marginal) will still seek to employ "illegals" so as to lower their wage bill, the resultant drive toward the cities must serve as a continuing drag on the crystallization of relative privilege in the labor market for the settled urban labor force.

Of even more immediate impact on the daily lives of the latter group will be the ongoing effort to expel "illegals" from the cities. As suggested, any eventual elimination of the 72-hour rule and street-pass examinations is likely to result in greater emphasis not only on workplace control (by means of the aforementioned fines upon employers) but particularly on residential control. Thus late-night pass raids on homes, already a much-hated feature of township life, are likely to become even more prominent, given the alacrity with which the 72-hour law is enforced; under the Riekert scheme it will be the same state apparatus (police and township administration boards)—much slower than the state's upper echelons to drop the old apartheid habits—which will be charged with controlling the presence of illegals in the townships. The necessity for continuing harassment and control of even the "qualifieds" in the Riekert scheme undermines, in this way, its own attempt to coopt them. Equally relevant is the shortage of housing in the black townships, the current wait for family units being a staggering nine years. As a result, even many qualified blacks are forced to rent space from families (often relatives) who have been allotted homes. But such subletting is illegal, so that night pass raids on homes may yield as many "qualified" as "illegal" victims, providing the former with no greater sense of a stake in the system than the latter. Moreover, the housing shortage has further, even more serious, ramifications for the Riekert scheme: some of the intended privileges of the "qualified" group are, as noted, contingent upon the availability of accommodation, and in its absence such privileges may well remain mere chimeras.

(2) *The Housing Question.* The lack of housing is thus a particularly likely place for the contradictions in the Riekert scheme to come bubbling up. Yet the implications of this shortage for the dominant classes' urban strategy go well beyond this, being of significant enough proportions to constitute a barrier to the strategy in its own right and one which, like the unemployment problem itself, seems impossible of resolution within the constraints of the present system.[7] Why is it so important? Because sufficient and adequate housing is a crucial component of any improvement in the living standard of the urban black population. In this way not only political cooptation but also capital's market requirements are tied to the need being met. Yet despite liberal urgings that part of the gold-mine tax bonanza be spent on housing, the state's own intervention remains framed by the apartheid model of token state expenditure on new housing (in 1968 a freeze, now lifted, was placed on urban housing construction), a model which is itself responsible in large measure for the present shortage.

Thus the 1979-1980 budget allocated only 73 million Rand to low-cost housing, enough for 12,500 units—though estimates of the likely backlog over the next two decades begin at 4 million units! In addition, as noted earlier, the devolution of limited powers to the township community councils (responsible for the provision of housing, services, and infrastructure) carried with it the condition that the townships continue to be self-financing, thereby effectively placing a very low ceiling on capital spending (including new house construction); of course, this did not relieve the councils of the need to raise rents to expand revenues in order to meet even the most minimal demands upon them, a move which, in turn, resulted in widespread rent strikes during 1980. But that is another, if closely related, story. Here we must ask why the earlier apartheid model is still alive and well. The answer is significant: provision of new housing on a vast scale would so dramatically under-

score the permanence of the urban African that even *verligtes*
—let alone *verkramptes*—get cold feet at the prospect; in effect,
all the tensions, and the risks, of reform can be seen to be encapsulated in this one issue.

It is true that the second prong of the apartheid state's
original housing policy—preventing the development of a private housing market in the urban townships—is slowly being
bent back. This has happened because of pressure from big
capital, as focused, in particular; through the activities of the
Urban Foundation (mentioned earlier). The foundation sees
the provision of housing as a major priority in improving the
"quality of life" of urban blacks; as leading Afrikaner capitalist and Urban Foundation founder Anton Rupert put the
point at the initial conference, "This would be a logical point
of departure for the foundation's efforts. Housing and its related
facilities after all represent the basis of family life and the real
foundation of a settled middle-class society." Thus, in the wake
of considerable lobbying, a regulation allowing blacks to hold
99-year leases (not, we may note, full home ownership) was introduced with great fanfare in April 1979; complementing this
is a Riekert proposal that private investors be permitted to develop housing for "sale" under the leasehold scheme.

A straw in the wind perhaps, though after a year of operation the leasehold scheme, even with financial assistance to
"buyers" from the foundation (in the form of low-interest
loans), had attracted a meager thirty customers.[8] The option
of obtaining housing via the private market is thus restricted,
for the time being, to the most middle class of blacks—the only
group which can afford it and the group for whom influx controls are least necessary—with the cost of a house remaining well
beyond the reach of urban black workers; by one calculation,
the monthly repayment on a loan to buy the cheapest existing
house would lower, to the point of malnutrition, the living
standard of a family earning the income level necessary to obtain the loan. Moreover, to the extent that, despite these limitations, a black housing market develops involving capitalists
motivated by profits and competition rather than the needs of
influx control, all the most familiar fears will surface within
ruling circles. For such a trend can only contribute further

to the undermining of influx control which, of course, requires
state supervision of housing allocation and township expansion.
Though this contradiction may not develop in the short, or even
medium, term, given the present state of the fledgling housing
market, the prospect does serve to drive home again the point
made by Treurnicht and others of his ilk: any lifting of apartheid's lid may well lead to loss of control over the process of
change and to what is, particularly from their stolid, hard-line
perspective, unacceptable risk.

Perhaps more realistic in relation to working-class housing
needs is the Riekert proposal that employers be permitted to buy
or build houses in the townships to accommodate their employ-
ees. This might have some alleviating effect on the shortage,
while also providing employers with some further means of
control over possible job actions by their workers and even a
possible means of circumventing some of the restrictions on
their hiring of cheaper migrant workers. But the costs involved
are likely to make most individual capitalists, accustomed as
they are to the subsidization derived from the use of cheap
migrant labor, balk—unless substantial incentives, such as tax
allowances, are offered. Meanwhile capital collectively, and
particularly big capital, is pushing other options in response to
the need for working-class housing. The emphasis here is on
keeping costs as low as possible by having urban blacks either
build their own houses ("site-and-service") or improve a basic
structure with whatever resources they have ("core housing").
The possibility is seen of introducing a private market even in
this type of housing, and the Urban Foundation has begun a
pilot site-and-service project.

But again the state is reluctant to allow these forms of
housing, insisting, with touching concern for black workers'
living conditions, that such schemes would result in "inferior
housing." The underlying reason for this attitude was disclosed
by the senior civil servant in the Department of Community
Development (sic): "When this [type of housing] was allowed
in the 1950's, it simply created squatter shanties. It cost us
millions to clear up the mess" (*Rand Daily Mail,* March 13,
1981). Translation (in the wake of the cruel bull-dozing of
Unibel, Modderdam, and other such "shantytowns," and the

removal of their residents back to the reserves): "If people can build their own houses, we can't control the allocation of housing and therefore can't control urbanization either." But this merely underscores the general point: solving the housing crisis, by whatever combination of approaches, seems likely to make Riekert-based influx control unworkable. Yet we have seen that the Riekert proposals will themselves be ineffectual and self-defeating unless the housing crisis is resolved. Such are the dilemmas posed by the needs of reform, dilemmas which, to repeat, help account for much of the indecision as to the value of Riekert's report and the delay in the implementation of many of its proposals.

(3) *Wiehahn*.[9] We must now turn to consider the Wiehahn Commission on black trade unions (also 1979), which forms a necessary complement to the Riekert Commission. Its proposals are intended to restructure the conditions of capital's domination over black labor at the point of production in the direction of more subtle methods of control than the customary approach of outright repression, using security legislation, of black worker action. As we shall see, the process of moving "formatively" toward a new system of domination is not much more tractable than is the Riekert scheme.

In fact, a shift of direction for the industrial relations system began several years before Wiehahn, as a response to the 1973 strikes. The changes then involved revamping the failed factory committee system and the granting to African workers of the technical legal right to strike (though its absence had never prevented them). As D. du Toit has noted, "the significance of the reforms [in 1973] was symptomatic rather than substantial . . . the government [resigning] itself to the impossibility of enforcing an absolute prohibition on strikes by African workers any longer."[10] In other words, naked repression could no longer be the name of the game. The limits of these reforms, and their overwhelming rejection by African workers, were unambiguously evidenced during the next few years as an independent (and formally "unregistered") African trade union movement, which had its origins in the 1973 strike, continued to grow in size and strength.

Banning the trade unions was therefore ruled out as an option when the Wiehahn Commission was set up in May 1977 to deal with the mounting threat posed, in the context of the organic crisis, by worker assertions. In the words of the Wiehahn report, banning "would undoubtedly have the effect of driving black trade unionism underground and uniting black workers . . . against the system of free enterprise." Thus Wiehahn's mandate was clear: the means had to be found to incorporate the black trade unions within the system, surrounding them with the "protective and stabilizing elements of [that] system . . . and its essential discipline and control." The crucial recommendation in this respect was that the legal definition of "employee" be extended to cover Africans, so that their unions could be officially registered if certain conditions were met.

The *Economist* (May 5, 1979), calling this proposal "a radical change . . . for South Africa's black labour force," stated further that "at the heart of the report is . . . full freedom of association . . . [which] in the South African context is a revolutionary concept." Such uncritical enthusiasm was, of course, wildly off the mark; a few examples quickly demonstrate the degree to which the proposal actually falls short of "full freedom of association." Thus several criteria for registration are laid down, including a ban on the registration of general workers' unions. Beyond this, and despite the commission's recommendations to the contrary, the state's subsequent enabling legislation prohibited the registration of nonracial unions, in this way refusing to extend even an illusory freedom of association. And the state's first instinct was to limit the legislation in another crucial respect, as regards the eligibility of migrant workers for union membership. The Wiehahn report itself had not recommended an outright ban, restricting itself to spelling out why (the supposed difficulty of organizing migrants) and how (the tactics of governmental supervisory bodies) unions should and could be discouraged from recruiting migrants. However, the definition of "employee" in the legislation included only Africans who were permanent urban residents in fixed (not contract) employment—effectively the "qualifieds" of the Riekert proposals. It was only after a storm of protest from black unions, as well as from liberal critics such as the

PFP, that a ministerial exemption was issued to include migrants in the definition (the fact that it was an "exemption" not incorporated into the legislation making possible their exclusion at some future date).

Registration of African unions means that they will be able to participate in the state-sponsored Industrial Council apparatus.* Highly structured and restrictive under South African law, this machinery's chief function has been to remove capital-labor conflicts from the potentially volatile context of the shop floor onto a terrain where legal trappings and the high level of bureaucratization implicit in it make conflicts more susceptible to control by a combination of coopted union leadership and employers. Heretofore this machinery—combining control and economic concession—has served in just this way to domesticate white, Coloured, and Asian unions and to hinder the development of a broad-based union movement cutting across racial lines. Now the state's intention seems to be to draw African unions onto the same terrain of "business unionism" and institutionalized conflict, looking to a situation here too in which bureaucratic leaderships retain their members' loyalties by winning economic gains. As seen, this is a scenario which could mesh neatly with both the broader political calculations and the economic requirements of the dominant classes. Moreover, if the strategy were to be executed confidently, then, as a result of concessions over wages and working conditions, the potential improvement in living standards might be substantial for those Africans included in the new dispensation. Nor should such improvements be discounted as irrelevant, since they would meet the needs of (some sections of) the African working class. Beyond this, there are the benefits for itself which a bureaucratized union leadership could derive. Consequently, there may be considerable temptations toward cooptation for African unions, and even some pressure from below in this direction.

Of course, it must be emphasized again that all this is

---

* There is an added complication: such participation remains subject to the approval of all current participants in a particular council. Thus white unions would seem to have an effective veto power over the admission of black unions to the bargaining table, and the implications of this fact could also prove to be significant.

hedged about with a network of controls with which the state intends to ensure the unions' incorporation into the system. Thus the registration system involves an unspecified period of "provisional registration" during which the state will evaluate a union's *bona fides* before registering it. Both provisional and full registration can be withdrawn at any time. Once registered, a union becomes subject to a variety of controls over its finances, constitution, and membership, to state-supervised compulsory industrial relations training for its leaders, and to a total ban on any connection with a political organization. An Industrial Court will arbitrate on all labor-related matters, while a tripartite National Manpower Commission will oversee the entire system. The National Party leadership rationalized to its own electorate—and to its own right wing—what must have appeared to them to be a startling and risky innovation:

> Twenty-seven black trade unions exist already and have a membership of some 70,000. They will now effectively be brought under the discipline and control of the law, and this will include a ban on political activities, a control over their membership, access to their financial statements and balance sheets, and control over their overseas funding.

Nor is it surprising, given the breadth of these restrictions, that many left critics of the Wiehahn proposals have argued (as one put it) that "state control over labour matters has not been relaxed. Indeed, it has been extended into areas which were previously uncontaminated by sophisticated and systematic state control."[11] Yet it is worth reminding ourselves that the apartheid state's approach—using security legislation to suppress African labor action—implied that there were, in fact, *no* such areas free of state control. Some degree of control is seen by capitalist classes everywhere to be a necessary complement to the granting of trade union rights. The continued use by the South African state of various measures of control should not, therefore, be focused on to the exclusion of consideration of the more novel elements in the Wiehahn proposals.

For it is these novel elements—the concessions and privileges, however limited, extended to African trade unions—

which could be the dominant classes' strongest card, and the success of the overall strategy in this sphere may be more closely related to the flexibility with which this card is played than to the rigid use of any system of controls. If they are to have any hope of preventing union activity from spilling over into outright opposition to capitalism, the most sophisticated strategists of capital must seek to give their "concessions" a basis in reality. We have mentioned the possible granting of advances in wages and working conditions and know that these are not totally at odds with the requirements of accumulation. But we must also emphasize that those unions which already have mass support or seek to gain it must also have some perceptible freedom of maneuver, freedom which allows them to organize, to negotiate contracts, and to represent workers in shop-floor conflicts. Only insofar as it can unite to pursue this kind of policy can the dominant classes have any expectation whatsoever that the pressures toward incorporation will prevail.

What this means is that the South African state is on the threshold of meaningful risk—which, as we saw, is the hallmark of a genuinely formative strategy—in the union sphere, closer to that threshold here certainly than we find them to be in the political sphere. So close, in fact, that we find it feasible to argue, in the next chapter, that the "space" which such changes in the industrial relations system open up may also provide the African working class with a real opportunity to make advances vis-à-vis the dominant classes which are more than merely economistic. Of course, this is precisely what right-wing opponents of reform argue is inevitable, a position in which they feel strengthened, no doubt, when confronted by the militant response from the black working class to the Wiehahn proposals and their subsequent implementation (e.g., over the questions of migrant labor inclusion and of racial exclusivity). Ironically, in some of their fears these right-wing elements find an echo among business interests, which do not feel that even a reformed industrial relations system can bear all the weight of a mobilized working class. As a *Manchester Guardian* reporter put it (December 12, 1980), "More and more employers are coming to the conclusion that the only way unions can be kept non-political is to give black South Africans other vehicles for effective political expression."

Yet for such business interests this merely strengthens their argument for parallel political change, rather than weakening their drive for labor reforms. For many elements of big capital continue to push back against the right, seeking, in fact, far greater flexibility in responding to the unions. The deputy director of the Federated Chamber of Industries has argued, for example, that by "trying to force [black unions] into the system, we give them good reason to remain out of it." In some cases companies have even moved beyond state policy, the giant Barlow-Rand Corporation stating in its recent in-company guidelines on labor that "until the government . . . makes the registration procedures more attractive to black unions, we are going to have to continue to negotiate with unregistered unions." Of course, as we might suspect from our explorations in chapter 1, not all businessmen, left to their own devices and without a firm, state-enforced class lead, are attempting such enlightened strategies. Many continue to fall back on "parallel unions" (utterly tame black structures firmly under the wing of white unions), in-company unions, and workers' councils. Yet these, the *Financial Mail* editorializes, will "reinforce, rather than obviate, the trends towards militancy," the magazine quoting approvingly in this context "labor experts" who speak of the "folly of encouraging weak unions, which would not enjoy the support of their members." Speaking, presumably, for the most "formatively" minded of the capitalist class, it concludes (January 18, 1980) that

> African trade unions are here to stay and the new awareness among Africans of their bargaining power will spread and strengthen, particularly where Africans hold more skilled jobs. This being the case . . . the ball is now in the hands of government and management—government needs to provide the framework for a more flexible industrial relations system, and management needs to be more open to good faith bargaining with strong, representative unions.

Yet even on the terrain of the business community, it is not clear which camp will prevail. How much more complicated, then, is the problem within the white community—and polity—taken as a whole.*

We thus return to the tug of war within the dominant classes regarding overall strategy. No doubt the inconsistency of state policy since the publication of the Wiehahn report faithfully mirrors these tensions, the Minister of Labour rattling his saber one week and urging employers to negotiate the next. The legislation which enacted the original proposals is now to be amended, less than two years later, to provide further inducements to unions to register while considerably stiffening the sanctions against those which nevertheless refuse to do so. In its eagerness to incorporate the independent black unions, the state allowed several of them to apply for registration on a nonracial basis during 1980, despite its earlier rejection of Wiehahn's proposal that nonracial unions be allowed. But in approving the applications in early 1981 the state lost its nerve and granted them on a racial basis only. Meanwhile, the response to many of the widespread strikes of the past two years—arrests of union leaders, expulsion of migrant strikers from the cities—has revealed not only a reluctance to drop the well-tried (if no longer so well-trusted) method of harsh repression in order to enter the uncharted waters of subtle cooptation, but also the difficulties of doing so.

----

* Another area which we have seen to be of considerable importance —and contradiction—is the issue of a skilled labor shortage, which big capital regards as the most serious barrier to accumulation over the next few years. Yet the state has found it difficult to structure any adequate solution here too, Wiehahn's recommendations being extremely limited and evoking merely "a long yawn," as the *Financial Mail* (June 20, 1980) put it. Most of the burden of training is to be left to the employers, so that cost factors are likely to lead to less comprehensive and shorter training for black skilled workers. As the white unions are quick to point out, this would contribute to the creation of a group of "second-class African artisans, super-operators," with lower skills and lower wages than white artisans. This in fact appears to be the general intent of the recommendations, which also suggested that state-run training facilities remain segregated racially and that many trades be examined to evaluate whether they should be officially "deskilled" and deemed to no longer require apprenticeship periods. Not surprisingly, white unions reacted against this potential undercutting, though they were forced, in the circumstances, to call for unified, nonsegregated training facilities in order "to maintain standards."

In short, as in many other spheres, the "total strategy's" attempt to restructure the situation of urban black workers has been less than total, revealing many gaps, coming up against stern barriers to implementation, still not quite across the threshold alluded to above. Though the underlying thrust of the attempt is of considerable significance, it must be concluded that the package thus far offered the working class is unlikely to be of enough substance—the "economic kingdom" too limited—for them to regard a "stake in the system" as very much more than an overused and exhausted cliché. Yet we can now grasp as well the essential irony in this: any such failure merely leaves the dominant classes back where they started—in crisis.

(4) *The Black "Middle Class."* We must turn now to examine the dominant classes' strategy in relation to the urban fractions of the black petty bourgeoisie, "traditional" (involved in entrepreneurial activity) and "new" (this category defined by educational qualifications and by employment in roles attendant upon capitalist activity, primarily within bureaucratic structures—teachers, medical workers, administrators, and managers). These are groups—a "stable black middle class with a meaningful stake in the free enterprise system," as one leading white business organization conceives them[12]—which we have already seen to be cast by the regime in the role of political leaders of the black urban population through the township community councils and the abortive black appendage to the President's Council. Here we will focus on those additional efforts to incorporate them into the system which have centered on removal of apartheid-based restrictions that have retarded their "normal" development. Of course, this is also a ploy intended to further stratify, along class lines, the urban black population in a manner parallel to the polarization of classes attendant upon bantustan policy; once again, divide and rule.

A first aspect here is encouragement of the further development of a black trader class. This has meant the lifting of a number of regulations limiting their ability to accumulate (for example, being allowed to own only one business). In addition, Riekert recommended that African employers be given a claim equal to that of other employers in relation to the allocation of labor supplies. Other legislative amendments have opened new market opportunities for this group; thus the authority granted to the community councils will have an economic payoff over and above its political implications, some of the township powers—allocation of trading sites, provision of some township services—promising a possible platform (albeit a small and flimsy one) for private accumulation by the small group of African traders collecting around them. Nonetheless, the importance of these adjustments should not be exaggerated: the actual potential for the development of an independent black capitalist fraction through these means is extremely limited.

More significant is the lifting of the prohibition on white firms operating in the townships by allowing them to become minority partners of African businessmen. We noted earlier the importance to capital of expanding the black consumer market, and firms in several sectors—retail trade, entertainment, and finance—are eager to move into the townships. Although such ventures offer black businessmen their only real hope of establishing a significant base for accumulation, they have sometimes expressed (probably well-placed) fears that they will become merely "front men" for white firms, while those who choose to remain independent will be swamped by the competition. Nor will most be able to afford this latter choice, the avenues open to African businessmen to raise capital being very limited indeed. Even in this respect, however, the dominant classes stepped in to play a more active role by establishing (in November 1980) a parastatal Small Business Development Corporation (SBDC). This was presented by its prime instigator, Anton Rupert, as a parallel initiative to the Bantustan Development Corporations; the pattern is closer to that of the Urban Foundation, however, with the private sector providing most of the initial capital—the state kicked in 50 million Rand—as well as the direction. The major role of the SBDC will be to guarantee low-interest commercial loans to African businessmen, although it also intends to support management training and infrastructural development to service township commerce.

The traditional petty bourgeoisie in the townships will thus grow under the tutelage of, and at the pleasure of, big capital,

so that its political support for the latter will be more or less
assured. Other elements of the urban black middle class will be
less easily incorporated, their nonentrepreneurial roles ruling
out any such straightforward buying off. Beyond their (extremely compromised) attempts to structure cooptative political
institutions, dominant-class efforts vis-à-vis the new petty bourgeoisie have focused on the social sphere (where any benefits
also affect African businessmen, of course). A primary concern
here is, once again, housing, and we have already witnessed the
efforts of the Urban Foundation to support the development of
the leasehold scheme and the growth of a private market in
(mainly middle-class) housing. It is worth underscoring that
this is viewed by government, as well as by businessmen, as a
further means of promoting class stratification; Piet Koornhof, Minister of Cooperation and Development ("Cooptation
and Development," as the *Financial Mail* once wryly put it),
has been quite explicit on this point: "The 99-year leasehold
scheme . . . may lead to the erection of many houses by the
private sector which may contribute to greater differentiation
in housing on social and economic lines. . . . This would be an
important factor in the creation of a black middle class" (*Rand
Daily Mail,* October 16, 1979).

Owning one's own (improved) home can only go so far,
however, toward satisfying budding middle-class aspirations if
that home remains restricted to a black township. Although
the government is retaining the Group Areas Act, which defines residential areas along radical lines, it is moving in a more
limited way to deracialize other laws, a process it calls the
"elimination of hurtful discrimination." One may wonder what
would be considered "non-hurtful discrimination" and note,
too, that none of the measures involved touch the fundamental
institutions of class domination and capital accumulation. Nevertheless, since these expressions of institutionalized racism do
provide some of the fuel for the petty bourgeoisie's nationalist
fire, the new initiatives have some significance as formative
efforts. And they often reflect familiar contradictions, too, as
evidenced by a recent suggestion from a senior civil servant that
middle-class blacks "be freed totally from influx control" (which

is not necessary for control of their movement or allocation of their labor, given their class position). As was quickly pointed out, this "freedom" would require some documentary proof of such privileged status, a case of "having to carry a pass to prove that [they] do not have to carry a pass" (*Financial Mail,* February 6, 1981). A more developed initiative in this respect is the ending of the "petty apartheid" of racial segregation in (some) social areas (restaurants, trains and buses, park benches, and the like). Though nominally benefiting all blacks (and always packaged internationally in this way), this actually further reinforces class polarization since only the middle class can afford to enjoy the newly opened hotels, restaurants, first-class trains, and the like in white areas. Such a growing gap between the cultures and lifestyles of the different black classes will no doubt be further widened as such facilities, directed toward class-defined markets, become more common in the townships themselves as part of their increasing commercialization.

Nonetheless, whatever the potential long-term implications of these developments in terms of class stratification and cooptation, the dominant classes' emphasis here is important ideologically in an even broader sense. To be sure, all "formative" efforts have some such resonance, but more explicitly ideological work—the "restructuring of the ideological discourse," in Hall's phrase—is also a necessary part of the attempted construction of the new conditions of domination. Thus the elimination of petty apartheid is much more than a fraudulent ploy directed primarily at foreign critics: it is intended to transform the way in which blacks perceive their domination. Until now the most immediate experience of domination and of the barriers to advancement for the African petty bourgeoisie has been racially defined: being black, they did not "belong." But a "stake in the system" for middle-class (and labor elite) blacks demands that they *do* "belong," and demands therefore a new inclusive ideology, a definition of "belonging" where the racial term is much less prominent. If this new definition is to succeed, overt racial discrimination has to be reduced and racial difference has to become a less antagonistic contradiction. Of course, there is also a complication here, one we glimpsed when looking at the complexities of white electoral politics in chapter 1. For such a redefinition as we have been discussing affects most sharply precisely those subordinate classes within the white community which had themselves been incorporated into the inner circle in terms of the earlier racist ideology. They are now forced to adjust their own sense of "belonging" and they resent the loss of their previous exclusivity relative to the newly incorporated classes. This may explain why much of the most heated white opposition to the reform strategy has focused on these apparently less important desegregating measures, rather than on changes in the fundamental institutions of apartheid. The most public display of hostility and contradiction between Botha and Treurnicht, for example, was the result of government moves to desegregate a national high school rugby tournament!

Not all of the dominant classes' ideological work touches such raw nerves. A second important front here is the cultivation of appropriate "middle-class values" among the urban black population, attempting to shape in this way their self-definition as a group. Significantly, this is likely to be relevant even as regards working-class blacks, who can be expected, after all, to have already imbibed a strong dose of capitalist culture by virtue of their very entry into the "modern" economy (at least to the extent that this has not been countered by alternative forms of ideological work). The major instrument here is the media, particularly the print media, which has expanded over the past few years by the addition of several mass-circulation magazines aimed at the black market.[13] As always when dealing with the media, care must be taken to avoid too instrumentalist an approach; nevertheless, it is worth noting that the Muldergate scandal revealed that at least two of these magazines were directly and surreptitiously financed by the state. Though their precise ideological mix varies (some, for example, stressing black consciousness in its most liberal incarnation), the general thrust is consumerist, sexist, explicitly opposed to violence (broadly defined to include most forms of protest), and depoliticizing of even the most political of issues: a story on an education protest describes (with horror) how the students enjoyed themselves in the "riot," a column calls for an end to "intertribal fighting" because it makes the writer "ashamed" to be black. The pages are filled with glossy ads, and there are regular features on the townships' equivalent of the "beautiful people."

For the dominant classes, the purpose of all this is twofold: to encourage political support for capitalism while demobilizing potential militancy *and* to facilitate the expansion of the black consumer market. Of course, as shown by the now-banned Soweto newspapers, *World* and its successor *Post* (both owned by the country's largest press chain), ideology is itself a terrain of struggle; even here the ruling-class institutions can be turned to their own ends by the dominated classes. Despite some ambiguities, both these papers played an invaluable role in maintaining the momentum for genuine change built up by the Soweto uprisings, reporting information about popular struggles in different parts of the country and serving to reinforce a tradition of resistance by linking past and present struggles through features discussing the African National Congress (ANC) and South African Congress of Trade Unions (SACTU) and the issues of the 1950s.

Needless to say, the banning of these papers suggests, once again, that there is a limit to just how much risk the regime is prepared to take in allowing the expression (the better to coopt) of real popular energies. Nonetheless, ideological restructuring remains important as a safety net for such risk as it does intend to shoulder; it becomes crucial to any attempt to keep such popular assertions as are countenanced firmly on the terrain of capitalism. Even then, however, it is not the bottom line; everyone within ruling circles, from liberal to *verkrampte,* knows just how much popular energy there is to be contained in South Africa—and how difficult it will be to do so. In case its strategy fails, in case ideological work falls short and the controls built into the reform strategy do not function, even the most liberal in South Africa are keeping a firm hand on the weapon they have been most accustomed to using to protect themselves: a massive military machine and repressive apparatus. We must now turn to a brief consideration of this.

III. The Big Stick: Police and Military Repression

The implementation of the hard-line option from the 1940s meant that coercion of the African population, long the dominant classes' chosen means of maintaining their rule, became more deeply etched than ever into the institutions of the state. The repressive nature of apartheid is perhaps its best-known feature (and deservedly so), so that this section will be limited merely to underlining the continuing prominence of this crucial aspect, even in the context of contemplation of a reform strategy.

Although our analysis of such reform has emphasized its formative and novel elements, we did suggest that the stabilization of an urban black labor force depended on the stepping-up of control over the "disqualified" section of the African population. The violent presence of the state has long been the defining feature of the daily lives of this group, and this will become even more the case in the future, particularly in the rural areas, given the intention of preventing any further urbanization. Beyond this kind of day-to-day control over the movements of the African population, the original hard-line option also implied a beefing-up of the apartheid state's policing function in a second area: the suppression of trade union and political organization. The most brutal instances of this suppression—police shootings of blacks engaged in demonstrations—have become landmarks of resistance: Witsieshoek in 1950, Sharpeville in 1960, Soweto in 1976. More frequent, however, has been the use of a thin veneer of legality—security legislation, the police, and court systems—to smash organized expressions of opposition. This was the means by which the mass protest of the 1950s and early 1960s was finally crushed.

Even while attempting to mount its reform strategy, the state has continued to use these wide-ranging legislative powers in an unrestrained fashion against a broad range of expressions of resistance. In the three years from 1977, for example, 743 people were charged in 216 trials under the 1967 Terrorism Act alone, this being an act in which "terrorism" is defined to include activities with only the remotest connection to politics, let alone violence. Other laws frequently used in trials since 1976 have been the Riotous Assemblies Act (used against participants in, and organizers of, mass demonstrations), the 1962 Sabotage Act (whose actual title, ominously bland, is the General Law Amendment Act), and the 1976 Internal Security Act which, in replacing the 1950 Suppression of Communism Act, made culpable not merely "furthering the aims of communism" (the latter defined *very* broadly), but "any activity endangering the security of the state." A formidable enough array, one might think, but in fact these comprise only a fraction of the battery of security laws available, none of which have been repealed despite the "reform" process.

In addition to charging the leaders of various organizations on the basis of these laws, the state has continued to act more directly, detaining leaders without charge, banning them, their organizations, and their publications. The best-known recent example of such action is the arrest and subsequent murder in detention of Black Consciousness leader Steve Biko in September 1977 and the banning, a month later, of nineteen Black Consciousness organizations; as of June 1980 there were at least 330 people in "preventive detention" of indefinite duration. Though the state may have felt many of such groups and individuals were uncooptable, so that it was not losing much by suppressing them, in other instances the use of repression has been in even more obvious contradiction with the attempt at reform and cooptation. Thus, in 1977 the entire Soweto Committee of Ten was arrested, this embodying precisely the petty-bourgeois leadership which had some support in the township and whom it was therefore essential to incorporate if the community council strategy was to have any chance of working! Moreover, as we have already noted, the state response to most strikes since the Wiehahn report has been to suppress them, rather than go some way to meet (and incorporate) the workers involved, as a reform strategy would suggest to be the appropriate response. This tactic reached its nadir in the strike by municipal workers in Johannesburg in July 1980, when over 1200 striking contract workers were "endorsed out" of the city, their passes invalidated, and the union leaders charged with sabotage.

Not that such incidents should be seen as mere aberrations from the "logic" of reform, cases of "old habits dying hard." On the contrary, the perception of growing popular pressure only ups the ante, cruelly underscoring the tensions within the camp of the dominant classes, and as often as not reinforcing the other, repressive side of their own "total strategy." We are back to the metaphor of "riding the tiger" of racial capitalism; it is late in the day for cooptation, difficult to move, both on limited fronts and more generally, to that threshold of risk which we have discussed without that risk appearing too great, without the temptation to insure that risk with continuing repression— but in a way that, ironically, can only strengthen the right's resistance to reform!

For the pressure is great, and growing, as we will have occasion to show clearly later. Nonetheless, perhaps the most dramatic index of this is the number of political trials (beginning even before June 1976) in which charges have included "furthering the aims" of the ANC (and, occasionally, the Pan-Africanist Congress). Individuals have been accused of recruiting others for guerrilla training and, even more often, of returning to South Africa intending to carry out acts of sabotage (or actually doing so). The frequency of such trials, and the reports of attacks on many state installations, are evidence of the liberation movement's much stronger presence on the ground during the latter half of the 1970s, a presence closely related to the liberation of Mozambique, Angola, and Zimbabwe on the very perimeter of South Africa. These developments have led the dominant classes to see the security requirements of their continued rule increasingly in military terms, though this has not implied any reduction in the policing activities discussed above. Glenn Moss, in his analysis of "total strategy" already referred to, points out that this latter notion, as a conceptualization of the dominant classes' strategy, was in any case originally developed by the military as a response to the "total war" which, they argued, South Africa was facing. As Magnus Malan expressed it as early as 1977: "South Africa is today . . . involved in total war. The war is not only an area for the soldier. Everyone is involved and has a role to play."[14]

Malan has also argued, on occasion, that "the problem is 80 percent political and only 20 percent military." We noted in the last chapter the increasing prominence, springing from that premise, of the military in the state's policymaking apparatus—this being symbolized by Malan's own appointment as Minister of Defense. But the inclusion of the military here and in other manifestations (the rural "hearts and minds" campaign, for example) of the formative efforts (the "80 percent of the problem") has by no means resulted in the neglect of the other, military, 20 percent. Indeed, Africans, on the receiving end, would be forgiven for thinking that, in present practice, the percentage is still the precise reverse. Thus South Africa has built, in a process which is ongoing, a massive military machine, bigger than any other defense force on the continent. This has been seen by some as "intended as much to assuage white fear about internal strife as [to] guard against outside aggression" (*Newsweek,* September 29, 1980). But even the most strident supporters of reform as the means to eliminate the chance of "internal strife" also support the military build-up in shrill and demagogic terms. As the *Financial Mail,* for example, editorialized (February 22, 1980): "Those who would disrupt our affairs [i.e., the Soviets] must realize that we have steel which we will use. Thus the signals SA sends out during the coming months and years must be strong enough and clear enough to alert communist sponsors of terrorism against SA to the heavy cost involved."

The military build-up has not been costless for South Africa, of course. As we noted in the previous chapter, the rapid growth of military spending (a more than seven-fold increase during the 1970s) was one central factor fueling inflation. As to the armaments program itself, Western arms manufacturers have received much of this spending, despite the UN's 1963 voluntary arms embargo and its mandatory embargo, begun in November 1977 (following the Biko murder and Black Consciousness bannings). But, ever fearful of its Western allies being forced to impose effective sanctions, the South African state has developed its own arms manufacturing capacity through its ARMSCOR parastatal, established in 1968. Using technology under license from its erstwhile suppliers, ARM-SCOR has grown to the point where it now supplies between 65 and 75 percent of South Africa's needs and also has a growing export component. South Africa is the southern hemisphere's largest arms producer, and ARMSCOR a significant actor in the economy, with nine subsidiaries and 800 private subcontractors, half of which are significantly dependent upon its contracts. A director of the ubiquitous Barlow-Rand Corporation (the company which we saw to have taken the lead in negotiating with unregistered unions) was seconded in 1979 to become ARMSCOR's chief executive, an appointment which captures neatly not only the links between big capital and the state but also the two aspects of the total strategy.

Together with the Defense Force's estimated 1979 manpower of 494,000, of which 180,000 is the standing operational force (up from figures of 154,000 and 42,000 in 1967), ARMSCOR's production and procurement activities have provided South Africa with what has been called (*Financial Times,* August 22, 1980) "a daunting panoply with which to counter threats to its security, whether they be riots at home, guerrillas infiltrating from Namibia or other neighboring states, battles with African armies or limited naval harassment from a hostile power such as the Soviet Union." Included in this "panoply" are a sophisticated airforce, over one hundred infantry battalions, and an artillery armed with advanced-design cannon, firing, it seems almost certain, shells with nuclear warheads (both the latter coming courtesy of the US-Canadian Space Research Corporation). Nor are such materials allowed to rust even if, to date, the use of South Africa's "defense" capacity has consisted primarily of offense—naked aggression against the front-line states, particularly Angola and Mozambique, which have been hosts to guerrillas and refugees from Namibia and South Africa (and, previously, Zimbabwe). This is a tactic which has had the general support of the dominant classes. As the *Financial Mail* (June 6, 1980) put it, echoing the sentiments of everyone from Treurnicht to the liberals of the PFP, after the ANC's dramatic raid on the Sasolburg plant: "On the one hand, there is the matter of *realpolitik:* you hit back as damn hard as you can at the ANC. (After all, they are going to hit *you* damn hard.) On the other, manage the change to a sane and secure society."

Yet, as we have seen in this chapter, "managing the change" may be more than is possible for the dominant classes, the much more likely prospect being the steady heating up of the guerrilla war within South Africa itself. Moreover, as *Newsweek* noted, "Despite its military supremacy, South Africa has been unable to win the one battle [in Namibia] it is now waging. . . . [This] suggests there are significant weak spots in the nation's defensive superstructure." Among those which are becoming most apparent are the unwillingness of increasing numbers of whites to serve in the military, and the strain the size of the standing army places on the economy, especially in view of the already short supply of skilled labor. ("Businessmen must realize we're fighting for our survival. . . . So their commitment must increase. This is a long-term problem, not short term. The sooner people realize that the better," so says Major-General Neil Webster, Defense Force Director of Resources.) This has led to recent attempts to recruit an increasing number of blacks, though without much success so far. In addition to these points, there is the strategic problem of the bantustans (to which we have already referred and must return in due course) and, connected to this, the realities of South Africa's long borders and coastline.

And, finally, there is the most crucial weakness of all: as acknowledged by *Newsweek,* it is that "Pretoria . . . may not be able to cope with an at-home insurgency by non-whites [sic] —unless the decision were made to arbitrarily turn the nation's cannons on at least 75 percent of the population." In other words, superior firepower can only hold back a popularly-based revolution for so long, no matter how hard the *Financial Mail* and others in ruling circles wish to "hit back" at the ANC. The *verkramptes* are not wrong: "reform" is difficult to mount, and exceedingly dangerous. The *verligtes* and liberals are not wrong either: the hard line cannot work. "The police are stretched thin; the army is engaged in a debilitating, no-win war in another country [Namibia]. And the thing P. W. Botha and his generals feared most, a 'fifth column' of social upheaval taking place behind the backs of the men who are defending the borders, seems in fact to be happening" (*Financial Mail,* June 27, 1980). We must now turn to consider, in the remainder of this text, the forces which underpin the prospect of a popularly-based revolution in South Africa.

3. TERRAIN OF REVOLUTION

In the previous chapters we saw how much the calculations and the actions of the dominant classes are premised on their sense that the dominated classes are in motion and that it is revolution which must be pre-empted. Indeed, class analysis is, to perhaps a surprising degree, a tool which they themselves have used in order to plot their strategies of defense. As a result, we have already been forced to present some kind of map of the African class structure, albeit through the prism of the dominant classes' concerns; moreover, we will have a further opportunity in this chapter to question just how available Africans—the "black labor elite" and "middle class" in particular—are for the sort of cooptative strategies which the dominant classes may have in store for them. However, as we now move to look at the class structure of the African population more directly, the center of gravity of our perspective will increasingly shift away from such matters and come to rest on the question of the availability of the classes so defined for the revolutionary project which seems so clearly to be on the agenda in South Africa. Among scholars and activists, as we shall see, different emphases are possible regarding such matters, especially on the question of the precise nature and extent of the undoubted centrality of the African working class to the country's revolutionary process. In this chapter we will focus on that class (in section II), on its objective determinations and on its subjective propensities (as revealed, most prominently, in the dramatic urban actions of the

145

past decade); we will also (section III) look at other classes, the petty bourgeoisie on the one hand, more "marginal," rurally rooted elements on the other, and begin to explore the possible range of roles (if any) for such actors within the revolutionary camp. But we must begin (section I) by situating such class analysis more broadly within the specific process of *proletarianization* that South Africa has witnessed, this being the key to defining the precise array of classes which now confronts us.

I. Proletarianization under Racial Capitalism

In fact, we have already seen that the defining feature of this process has been the centrality of *migrant labor,* a reality which once led Samir Amin to term much of the southern half of the continent the "Africa of the labor reserves." Lionel Cliffe has extended the point:

> The terms in which most of the African people of most of the areas of Southern and Central Africa have been integrated into the world economy has been through labour migration rather than the direct production of commodities. In all the countries immediately to the north of the Zambezi, as well as the well-known examples to the south, not only have large numbers of African men come as *gastarbeiter* in mines, farms and industries controlled by whites and run as capitalist production units, but the communities from which these migrants have come have become geared to the production and reproduction of this special form of exported labour power.[1]

As noted earlier, one of the major contributions of recent Marxist scholarship regarding Southern Africa has been to theorize further the ways in which this migrant labor system came to service the accumulation process there by shifting the costs of reproduction of labor power to the quasi-subsistence sector; a focusing on the "articulation" of diverse modes of production and on the creation of a "labor-exporting peasantry" has been an important key to this kind of analysis. Of course, such scholarship has also emphasized that, in South Africa itself, an eventual decline in the productive capacity of the reserves became an important variable in shaping the intensification of state control over the migrant labor system which a more formalized apartheid strategy represented from the 1940s; it has emphasized, too, the important role of changes in the nature of capital (as well as the changing balance between its various fractions) in this regard. The result: the imperatives of capital accumulation led from an initial emphasis upon the enforced recruitment of labor toward the development of more precise mechanisms of control and, importantly, distribution of labor (e.g., the labor bureaus and the consolidation of the system of "contract labor"—earmarking migrants for increasingly specific tasks and periods of time in the white areas—as well as many other features of the full-fledged apartheid system).[2] More recently, with economic crisis and with a more sophisticated and capital-intensive capitalism on the ground, both the consolidation of a stratum of somewhat better skilled Africans *and* the repulsion of "surplus" Africans from the cities have become more prominent features (though not, of course, completely displacing migrant labor as a continuingly important term in the labor supply equation).

This much by way of backdrop, but we must not lose sight of a third variable: the actions of the popular classes formed by the above processes have been of obvious relevance to defining the dynamics of South African capitalism and continue to be so. Witness the impact of the strike wave of the 1940s on the emergence of the apartheid system; in all probability it was a factor of at least equal importance to either the decay of the reserves or the changing imperatives of capital in that respect (and especially important in defining the political calculations which have had to inform the dominant classes' strategy ever since). We have ascribed similar importance—though this time in helping force "reform" onto the South African agenda—to the upsurge of popular action in the 1970s. We thus come to what are the most crucial aspects of this subject: the impact of the migrant labor system upon the process of *class formation* among Africans in South Africa and the impact of that process, in turn, upon propensities for *class action*.

These are complex issues, to say the least. A recent issue of the *Review of African Political Economy* (*RAPE*) suggests editorially that for students of the region a "common point of departure . . . is the recognition that any non-dogmatic understanding of the class struggle in South Africa must allow for the realities of migrant labour which throw up a class that does not fit easily into the categories of either 'proletarian' or 'peasant.' "[3] Perhaps true. But it may make more sense to begin by establishing the continuum of social locations which the migrant labor system has determined for Africans in South Africa rather than zeroing in on this ambiguous stratum from the outset. At one end of this continuum, then, are those most firmly settled as workers in the urban areas (with Section 10 rights and/or moving up the ladder of skilled labor), and also some of those most permanently employed on the white farms or as commuters (in spite of the fact that the latter reside in the bantustans). Such elements are, unequivocally, to be considered a proletariat—though it is also the case, as seen, that certain strategists of the dominant classes would like to think of them as a potential labor aristocracy!

At the other end of the continuum are those most rooted in the rural areas, especially, given the sweep and nature of the migrant labor system in South Africa, women (along with children and old people). A peasantry? To some degree, but probably much less to be considered so than in other parts of Southern Africa. For it is precisely Africans' rootedness in the land— the necessary underpinning of even a "labor-exporting peasantry"—which we have noted as being under severe siege from the further evolution (and physical degeneration) of the overcrowded reserves that has been attendant upon the development of capitalism in South Africa in this century. Slowly but surely, the balance has shifted from a case of rural production subsidizing wages to one where wages subsidize rural production: cattle holdings have shrunk for the vast majority in the countryside and plots, located on overgrazed and leeched soils, have become increasingly dwarflike into the bargain. More viable agricultural undertakings in the reserves tend to accrue, as we have seen, to agribusiness or to the petty-bourgeois wards of the bantustan states—and often in the wake of so-called land reforms which involve the further displacement of quasi-peasants from the land.

This (at least partial) collapse of the peasant pole of the continuum has other implications. For it suggests that the migrant labor class referred to by the *RAPE* editors cannot so easily be seen as hovering between peasant and proletarian locations. Indeed, this group, which comprises a substantial percentage of those who are "economically active" in the reserves, increasingly finds itself with no really viable fallback position in the economy there. Thus many of its members, officially regarded as contract labor, work permanently in the cities, living in bachelor hostels and renewing their contracts annually (by means of a convenient system—for employers—of "call-in cards" developed for this purpose). Migrant labor, yes—but their migration consists in fact of once-yearly three-week visits to their families, still trapped in the reserves. This group comprises a significant proportion of the urban workforce: by one calculation, half of the African workers in Durban at the time of the 1973 strikes were such "permanent migrants." And then there are the many others for whom even this status is impossible but who have found their only choice to be moving to the cities, without passes, in order to seek "illegal" work, regardless of the risk. For figures show that

> workers benefit from urban work even if they have to go to prison as a consequence. The figures range between a 702.7% improvement in living standards for a worker from Ciskei who works illegally in Pietermaritzburg for 9 months and then spends 3 months in prison, to 28.5% for a person from Bophutatswana who works illegally for 3 months and spends 9 months in prison. A person from Lebowa who works illegally in Johannesburg for 6 months and spends 6 months in prison improves his living standard by 170%.[4]

These seem sound reasons for seeing the second tier of workers—and perhaps even their family members in the reserves?—as having more firmly proletarian credentials. Beyond this, we have also seen that the dominant classes experience real difficulties in perfecting (and uniting behind) their own ostensible strategy of prying the upper tier of "qualifieds" away from such migrants; equally important (as will become apparent in the next section), the working class has not, for its own part, permitted itself so easily to be stratified on the job or divided politically in the townships. And what, finally, of those unemployed who are being expelled in vast numbers from the cities and the white farms. Increasingly, they cannot be allowed even the minimal pretense of peasant existence upon their removal to the reserves but instead are being piled up (alongside former residents of "black spots" and "squatters" who have been removed from the "white" areas) in barren "resettlement villages." It is tempting to see these unemployed, too, as members of the proletariat—at worst as members of the "industrial reserve army" but defined with reference to their (erstwhile) proletarian locations nonetheless.

There is something to this, certainly, and we have ourselves implied such a categorization in the preceding chapter. At the same time, we must beware of oversimplification, for the rural locating of women with families (there are, of course, other women who are part of the migrant labor contingent) and of the unemployed (even though they may lack firm agrarian roots) does make a difference. This is particularly the case at the level of political and ideological practice. Thus, in a suggestive article, Duncan Innes and Dan O'Meara have focused upon the way in which such women perform "reproductive labour" within the household and also directly produce some of the "product necessary for the reproduction of labour power" (this epitomizing the "feminization of agriculture," in another of their phrases). As they emphasize, this "bonding of women of proletarianized households, i.e., households for which the sale of labour power is the *sine qua non* of its reproduction, is not experienced by them at the points of capitalist production, but on the land itself," so that the "oppression of women is experienced as a problem of rural, rather than industrial, production." They then most immediately confront the bantustan state and its petty-bourgeois minions, and beyond that the apartheid state as mediated by such realities as the pass laws. This is a different experience of capitalist exploitation than, say, that of the migrant and helps explain the prominence of the ideology of African nationalism:

The common feature of the urban and rural experience . . . is not overt capital itself. Rather it is *the white man* and *his* oppressive system of apartheid (and particularly the pass laws) which can be seen to be responsible for both the urban and rural poverty and degradation of African proletarians of both sexes—and it is through such an understanding of *white* oppression that the struggle of women in the reserves and men at the point of production can be linked together.[5]

A similar sensitivity may be in order regarding the "reserve army," that term itself masking as many difficulties as it illuminates. For if the actors epitomized by the term are in fact being de-peasantized, there is some chance that they are also being *de-proletarianized*. Adequately expressive analytical categories are difficult to come by: "relative surplus population," the "sub-proletariat," the "marginalized" all have some resonance, as does Chris Allen's term the "outcasts" (though the possible use of the label "lumpenproletariat" for some of these people might be more controversial). And the enforced displacement *to the rural areas* of these people renders such terminological tangles—and the practical complexities they reflect—even more complicated. Certainly, one important reality is that, as in the case of rurally sited women, these "outcasts" are now most immediately confronted by bantustan structures *and* by the generalized (state) form of the oppressive system, rather than capital at the point of production. These may be other actors, then, for whom nationalism has at least as much resonance as "proletarian ideology" in any of its more restrictive expressions.

We must also return briefly to the "two-tier" workforce. There are difficulties for the regime in turning such stratification to its own account, but this is a danger to take seriously nonetheless. For stratification of the proletariat is an old story in South Africa, the incorporation of the white workers as a "labor aristocracy" (and political ally) into the van of capital being the most graphic case in point. Even Coloured and Asian workers have been "communally" privileged in certain respects under the law (as regards opportunities for unionization, for example),[6] and this has sometimes produced the tendency for them to distance themselves from African workers. How divisible is the African working class in this way?

We have several times alluded to the objective determinants of such stratification, and statistics are also available to reinforce the point. Thus C. E. W. Simkins and D. C. Hindson conclude their careful statistical survey with the observation that "within the working class there appears (in the period 1969-77) to have been a fairly rapid replacement of whites by other races, with the share of Africans increasing particularly rapidly in the semi-skilled and artisan classes."[7] And Legassick and Wolpe have pointed to other related processes of even more subtlety, such as the possible breakdown of mechanisms of redistribution via kinship linkages cutting across the resident worker/contract worker divide as a result both of legal restrictions and of the "individualization" of families that inflation and recession (and, we would add, consumerism) breed. As they note, "Whatever other factors were involved, this also may have been an element in the conflicts which occurred at moments in 1976 between hostel workers and township youth."[8]

Nonetheless, workplace links between strata can be forged, the dramatic industrial actions of recent years bearing witness to that fact. Equally important, the continuing repressive role of the state vis-à-vis all Africans and the state's reluctance—despite "reform"—to fully commit itself to action in the fields of housing, elementary education, and minimal unemployment insurance also focus attention upon that level of the oppressive system, in the cities as in the countryside. As Legassick and Wolpe continue their argument with reference to this latter point, "The lack of intervention by the state in these processes of redistribution created a common interest among large sectors of the African population in resisting the commonly experienced and *shared* effects on living standards. This common interest expresses itself in the form of African nationalism or of Black Consciousness." Moreover, these are ideological expressions which not only draw together various strata of the working class but also, in the former case, cut across those ethnic divisions which the regime seeks to reinforce and, in the latter case, across those communal distinctions (African, Coloured, Asian) which are equally subject to dominant class manipulation.

Potential class alliances sealed, at least in part, by more purely "political" ideologies! Yet Marxists who emphasize the proletarian determinations at the point of production of most Africans in South Africa sometimes seem uneasy that ideological expressions which reflect the contradictions between the oppressed people and the state (or blacks *versus* whites) are at least as prominent as ideologies which focus upon class contradictions more directly. This can be a misleading response. As Ernesto Laclau has demonstrated,[9] in any class society a whole range of ideology-producing contradictions cluster around the (real) distinction between the "people" on the one hand and the "power bloc" on the other. Somewhat more amorphous than class contradictions, the latter can nonetheless give rise to "popular-democratic ideologies" (in Laclau's phrase) of great resonance: populism, nationalism, feminism, black power. It is precisely by fastening upon and drawing-out the genuinely revolutionary potential of such assertions that a working-class project can become a broad, hegemonic force in the society, addressing itself creatively to that society's diversity and complexity.

By the same token, these other ideological dimensions can play back upon the working class and expand its own terms of reference. For there is always a danger that "proletarian ideology" can collapse (and/or be pushed) back into mere working-class corporatism (or even the more limited trade union consciousness of smaller but well-organized strata of the working class), and not really raise itself to the level of contestation for the state. This has been a particular danger under liberal capitalism, where the political arena (and the state) present themselves, and are too often accepted, as open and neutral arenas for pooling and mediating diverse "interests." In South Africa no such temptation is readily available, the state being still etched in white for all to see; moreover, this aspect of the situation is unlikely to change quickly, the political front still being, as we have seen, the one upon which the "reformers" have most difficulty in acting "formatively" and preemptively. It should come as no surprise then—and indeed must be welcomed—that "political" ideologies of nationalism, racial consciousness, and democratic self-assertion are so much a *complement* to proletarian consciousness. In fact, it may be that they are essential to linking up the very diverse components of that proletariat, and are thus a crucial term in the revolutionary equation in South Africa.

There are dangers in such a formulation, too, the most important being the precise reverse of what we have just been discussing. It is the danger that preoccupation with the field of popular-democratic contestation could have the negative effect of displacing the proletarian core of struggle which alone seems likely to guarantee a long-run revolutionary direction. There is a dialectical relationship—and a necessary simultaneity—between these two levels of conceptualizing, and acting politically upon, the South African terrain, a dialectic which will have to be self-consciously sustained by the movement for liberation. (Or, to put it in Laclau's terms, these nonclass contradictions must be articulated with proletarian ideology and practice in order to guarantee their revolutionary provenance.) But this point will become clearer as we move to explore one final class in the African camp: the petty bourgeoisie, both rural and urban, "traditional" and "new," which has bubbled to the surface above the continuum of increasingly proletarianized Africans upon which we have focused until now.

Though severely constrained in their growth by the restrictive practices of the white-dominated system, such elements have been present on the South African scene throughout this century. Moreover, we have already glimpsed the manner in which they have come to new prominence around the structures of the bantustans, glimpsed, too, something of their role in the urban areas; we will return to them in section III. Here, however, it is worth emphasizing that from early days the "new petty bourgeoisie" in particular has turned its skills and training to account in the field of "modern" politics in a way that, for better or worse, has far outweighed its numerical strength. We know from experience elsewhere in Africa that the role of such elements is never entirely predictable. Located as they are between more fundamental classes, dominant and dominated, their tendency to identify "upward" or "downward" varies with the circumstances. Of course, this ambiguity in the activities of the members of the petty bourgeoisie also has been reinforced in South Africa by the ubiquitous prominence of the color line within the armory of racial capitalism; this has continued to constrain their upward mobility, especially in the political realm, and has made some of them more aggressive proponents of change—and more active converts to the cause of "national liberation"—than they might otherwise have been.* Small wonder that they have increasingly been a target for cooptation by the dominant classes—to the extent, needless to say, that the latter feel willing and/or able to bend the system to accommodate such a group. All the more reason, too, in the context of "formative" action, realized and potential, by the dominant classes, that the petty bourgeoisie's current credentials as a class ally within the movement for liberation should be subject to the most searching scrutiny. If such a class were to be left alone to "articulate" popular-democratic assertions, the revolutionary potential of these latter would be certain to be blurred. Fortunately, as we shall now see, this is unlikely to happen.†

---

* This kind of trajectory has been followed even further by students and other youth who were particularly responsive to the Black Consciousness ideology in the 1970s and who from time to time play an important catalytic role in the townships. But this group is very difficult to categorize in class terms: certainly most students at the high school level are children of workers in the first instance, even if, at the same time, the pyramid of education begins to carry them toward petty-bourgeois locations.

† It would be useful to be able to complement this analysis of the "class map" with a statistical breakdown of the African population. The South African state does not maintain adequate official figures, however, and the degree of "illegal" movement and employment, as well as other problems, means that no coherent picture emerges from the estimates of various researchers. Nevertheless, it is worth including one such estimate to provide at least a general idea of the proportions between different strata of the working class. According to Jill Nattrass, of a total African workforce in 1970 (the last date for which census figures are available) of 5.9 million people, just under 60 percent worked in the urban areas. Of these, 44 percent were settled, 7 percent commuters, and 49 percent migrants—nearly 85 percent of the latter being men. Forty percent of the remaining two-fifths of the labor force were farmworkers in the white areas, and 60 percent (or a quarter of the entire labor force) in the reserves, though it is not clear how many of these were actually employed. Nor is it clear whether this last figure includes women whose husbands work in the cities, or black mineworkers, of whom there were 600,000 in 1979. See Jill Nattrass, "The Impact of the Riekert Commission's Recommendations on the 'Black States,'" *SALB* 5, no. 4 (November 1979).

II. The Mass Strike

The "class map" of the dominated sketched in the last section—and indeed in much of this entire text—underscores the crucial difference between South Africa and the rest of Southern Africa: the much more advanced stage of the proletarianization-cum-urbanization process which has been reached there. Clearly, this has significant implications for revolutionary strategy. To begin with, the cities, nodes of white economic power, present a broad range of potential targets for guerrilla attack, while the black populations in the townships can provide both the necessary logistical support *and* recruits for the guerrilla army. As we shall see below, the reserves are potentially fruitful arenas for guerrilla action as well, though some suggest that the state's defensive capacity may well prove more effective there than in the cities. Prominent U.S. journalist David Halberstam, in warning of "The Fire to Come in South Africa" (*Atlantic Monthly,* May 1980) has put the case for the urban terrain bluntly:

> Any highly industrialized society is vulnerable to urban guerrilla-terrorist [sic] attack. Transport? Every lorry on the highway is driven by a black. Access? A black man can go any place in Johannesburg as long as his pass is in order, he is dressed poorly and he is servile in manner. . . . Vulnerability? Every home is vulnerable, every skyscraper, every goldmine. A society which lives off black labor cannot exist in the foreseeable future without it. Where black labor goes, terrorists [sic] can go too.

This may exaggerate the possibilities somewhat, but the point is not lost on the liberation movement. Its strategists have placed great emphasis on the necessary role of armed struggle and have argued, in particular, that "guerrilla warfare can, and has been, waged successfully in every conceivable type of terrain,"[10] including urban ones. Indeed, many of the actions in recent years by Umkhonto we Sizwe, the armed wing of the ANC, have begun to exemplify such an approach—witness the attacks on police stations in Soweto and other townships, the blowing up of rail installations around the country, the destruction of an electrical power station in Durban.*

These and other incidents are signs that "the fire to come" will indeed involve the urban areas. Yet armed struggle can be only one part of the story there, the ANC itself stressing the necessity for "the active support of the mass of the people . . . [which] has to be won in all-round political mobilization which must accompany the military activities."[11] Of course, the question of the precise balance to be struck between armed struggle and mass "mobilization" poses questions for liberation movement strategists; to these we will return in the following chapter. Here our attention will be directed primarily to the "mass of the population" itself and start from an understanding that a second consequence of the more advanced stage of proletarianization/ urbanization reached in South Africa is the much greater weight of the urban classes, particularly the working class, within any revolutionary project mounted there. In fact, we have noted more than once the importance of the actions of this latter class over the course of the past decade in placing "reform" on the dominant classes' agenda. At the same time, and of even greater consequence, these actions have placed revolution firmly on the agenda of the dominated classes!

In the light of these latter realities, however, it is worth reflecting briefly on the concept of "mobilization" as used in the ANC formulation quoted above.† For that word can easily

---

* The *Financial Mail* (February 1, 1980), in a hysterical reaction to the Silverton bank siege, stated that "the prospect exists for Palestinian-style suicide squads and Baader-Meinhof type factions in the cities." This is simply rubbish: it is worth emphasizing that the ANC has never resorted to gratuitous violence that could legitimately be classed as "terrorism." *Pace* Halberstam, and the paranoia of most whites, homes are *not* potential targets. Nor are factories and mines, which are not just the source of capital's profits, but also of black workers' livelihoods.

† Of course it must be remembered that the *Strategy and Tactics* document from which this quotation is drawn was written in the late 1960s at a time when mass action was at a particularly low ebb point. Clearly the ideal balance to be struck within the dialectic of leadership and mass action will vary with circumstances. As we shall see below, the important concern now is not so much the specific formulations of *Strategy and Tactics* as the manner in which the ANC responds to the new terrain of struggle—and of dramatic working-class self assertion—which we are investigating in this section.

lead to an underestimation of the extent to which the working class is already carving out for itself its own role within the revolutionary project. Certainly the movement-cum-party has a crucial role to play; moreover, as suggested in the previous section, this may be particularly true, under South African conditions, of a *national* liberation movement. Yet working-class self-assertion of the kind we have been witnessing in South Africa in recent years may have as important an impact upon the movement as the movement has upon it. In short, there is a *dialectical* relationship here which the word "mobilization" does not quite catch. Moreover, on the progress of this dialectic depends not only the class nature of the South African liberation struggle, but also, in many respects, its very chance of success. To some of these issues, too, we will return in the next chapter; but a clearer understanding of "class self-assertion" has immediate implications for such questions as the appropriate response to various "reform" initiatives; these we must begin to look at here.

One final general point which can help in conceptualizing South Africa's urban terrain is in order, however. Clearly, a crucial aspect of the dialectic we have identified is the interplay between "spontaneous" or decentralized class actions (mounted outside the ambit and control of the liberation movement) and those actions conceived as part of the movement's explicit strategy. It was actions of the latter type which characterized the mass struggles of the 1950s; then the most common tactic used to draw workers, *qua* workers, into the political struggle was the "stay-at-home." Yet this kind of political general strike, called by the liberation movement for a particular day and (usually) intended to have a limited duration (one to three days), has been criticized retrospectively on a number of grounds.[12] It is argued, first, that by remaining in the townships, the workers became easier targets for police control and harassment. Even more crucially, the tactic is seen as an abandonment of the point of production as a site of struggle. This view is sometimes linked to a more sweeping criticism of the approach of SACTU (the South African Congress of Trade Unions, linked to the ANC within the Congress Alliance, a movement also including the Indian Congress, the Coloured

People's Congress, and the [white] Congress of Democrats) during that period: that it overemphasized political issues at the expense of economic struggles based on shop-floor organization. Or, putting the point less sweepingly, it has been argued that at the very least SACTU realized the need to establish a firm base on the shop floor too late, since political events—Sharpeville, followed by the stepping up of state repression and the necessary turn to more violent political struggle—soon eliminated, for a time, the conditions under which this would have been possible.

There is undeniably some substance to these criticisms, and indeed the working class of the 1970s has not ignored the lessons to be learned from that previous upsurge. Of even more significance here is the thrust of an argument advanced in the early part of this century by Rosa Luxemburg against the very definition of the "mass strike" which might be conceived as lying behind the adoption of the stay-at-home tactic. This is a conception which sees the "mass strike" as an isolated event, executed with order and discipline, organized by and under the control of the revolutionary movement. While certainly not denying the necessity for leadership and for a revolutionary organization, Luxemburg emphasized the crucial function of the "spontaneous," independent expressions of protest and struggle by the working class. This, in turn, led her to a conception of the mass strike as a multifarious phenomenon involving all kinds of actions, political and economic, and being, in sum, "the method of motion of the proletarian mass . . . the indication, the rallying idea, of a whole period of the class struggle lasting for years, perhaps for decades."[13] Whatever the truth about the 1950s, it is precisely this conception of the mass strike, with its emphasis on the role of working-class self-assertion within the dialectic referred to above, which seems best to summarize and theorize what has been happening during the past decade of working-class activity in South Africa.

Certainly it was spontaneity which was the most visible feature of the strike wave in Durban at the beginning of 1973 that ushered in this period.[14] During January and February of that year strikes spread from one factory to another throughout the entire industrial area centered on Durban, with the textile industry being the main focus. These strikes came after nearly a decade of the almost complete absence of worker organization and activity, so that they were, to borrow again from Luxemburg, "a complete revolution in miniature." The organization of the strike wave was entirely informal (though not leaderless), as workers discussed their experiences in the townships and elsewhere, and gains won by one group provoked imitation at other plants. Strike decisions and negotiations took place most often at mass meetings held outside the factory gates. As distinct from the stay-at-homes, the workers now remained close to the factories where their collective strength was greatest, and they refused to appoint leaders openly so that they could not then be arrested. The element of spontaneity was summarized by the comment of one worker in response to a question posed regarding agitation by, or intimidation from, outsiders: "I am not afraid, nobody told me to go on strike. This thing comes from God. How do you think I can live on 9 Rand [per week]?"

In fact, as suggested earlier, much of the basis for the workers' actions was to be found in the festering realities of economic crisis. Ninety percent of the strikes centered on wage demands, these being a reflection of the drop in living standards as inflation accelerated. Most of the strikes resulted in wage gains of between 15 and 25 percent, while in many factories increases were granted even before the workers actually struck. The workers accepted these increases, even though in many cases their original demands were far higher—for a doubling, or more, of wages. However, such high demands, which had little hope of being satisfied, were themselves seen by observers to be "a statement of rejection, an affirmation of the desire for a quite different society." Thus, despite their focus on point-of-production issues, the strikes can be seen to have had a political edge, a view reflected by the results of a post-strike survey of workers in and around Durban which showed them to be expressing as much dissatisfaction as before, despite their wage gains.

Moreover, the impact of this strike wave was profound, altering the balance of class power, at least at the point of production, decisively and permanently. As the *Standard Bank Re-*

view lamented in April 1973, "The days are past when employers could bargain with Bantu [sic] workers from a position of unchallenged strength." The spreading of strikes to other regions and industries over the next several years reinforced the new situation, and was, in addition, crucial in pushing the economy over the edge into economic crisis. From the perspective of the working class, the wage gains were important, but the primary legacy of this first round of strikes (a round which tailed off in 1976 but never quite died out) was an alteration in consciousness, a new sense of its own power and of its ability to challenge capital successfully. This new power was to be reflected, at least in part, in the revival of trade union organization among the black working class.

Thus, on the one hand, registered unions of white, Coloured, and Asian workers affiliated to the Trade Union Council of South Africa (TUCSA) began to set up "parallel" unions for African workers, though in most cases these were merely paper organizations. Far more important have been three separate groupings which began to organize "independent" unions: the Trade Union Advisory and Coordinating Council (TUACC), centered in Natal, the Western Province Workers' Advice Bureau (WPWAB), in Cape Town, and the Urban Training Project, based in Johannesburg. Their geographic separation was reinforced by some tactical differences in relation to methods of organizing, but they shared two common features which were important legacies of the Durban strikes. These were a firm commitment to union democracy and control by the membership (particularly true of TUACC and WPWAB), and a strong emphasis on shop-floor organization and economic issues.

The budding union movement growing out of these three organizations was essential in maintaining the momentum of the strike wave over the succeeding years and, as we shall see, it has been in the vanguard of the more recent wave of dramatic strikes. Nonetheless, it remains tiny—even by 1979 only 3 percent of African workers were unionized. Thus, even though 200,000 workers had been involved in strikes by mid-1976, and had thereby sharpened the class struggle considerably, the political challenge to the dominant classes was not adequate to transform economic crisis into organic crisis. Nor, from the perspective of the dominated classes, had it quite managed to introduce that "strong revolutionary ferment" which for Luxemburg was the hallmark of the period of mass strikes. The advance to this kind of threshold was instead the major achievement of the series of uprisings which spread right across the country in 1976-1977 but which is now encapsulated under the blanket term "Soweto."[15] Even though these ultimately lacked the focus and clout to pose the threat of actually toppling the South African state, the students who spawned them in the townships were able to make their considerable advances precisely because they did challenge that state—primarily on the basis of a "popular-democratic" nationalist ideology, though one which raised the distinct possibility, if only for a moment, of effectively incorporating workers into its challenge. Hence the importance of the sixteen-month period which began on June 16, 1976, with a demonstration by Soweto high school students against the use of Afrikaans in their schools. Passing through such developments as the dramatic marches into the heart of such "white" cities as Johannesburg and Cape Town and the stay-aways which began to draw in the working class, and ending only on October 19, 1977, with the savage bannings of Black Consciousness organizations, this period saw the presence, if still in embryonic form, of many of the features of Luxemburg's mass strike.

The initial demonstration in Soweto, and most of the subsequent activity there and elsewhere, was organized independently by high school students—even if much of the ideological groundwork had been laid by the organizations comprising the Black Consciousness movement and, as a practical example, by the workers' strikes of the preceding three years. What also became apparent, however, was how effective such ongoing mass struggles were in expanding the constituency for change, in winning people over to the revolutionary cause and facilitating the spilling over of their immediate concerns into a more generalized challenge to the existing order. Thus, the initial concern to eliminate Afrikaans as a medium of instruction in the schools soon grew, with the harsh state response, into a demand for scrapping the entire "Bantu education system," and ultimately into opposition to apartheid itself. Drawing in broader sections of the population, the Soweto Students' Representative Council (the body which took over the leadership in that township soon after the uprisings began) became, for a short time at least, an effective alternative power structure there. It had widespread legitimacy among the people, and even the police had little choice but to give it some acceptance; it was able to force the end of the puppet Urban Bantu Council (predecessor to the Community Council) and sponsor the establishment of the Committee of Ten as an independent representative body. True, this kind of broader political momentum could not be sustained merely by a student core, nor in any case did it spread to enough centers to be a potent national force. In consequence, students eventually reverted to slogans which focused on their more immediate concerns. But this was still a valuable learning experience, and a major step forward.

And then there were the stay-at-homes. This revival of an earlier ANC tactic also represented a further attempt by the students to generalize their struggle—quite specifically, in this case, to the working class.* Moreover, the first four stay-at-homes, in August and September 1976, were extremely successful in terms of the number of those who remained away from work (with the Cape Town action, significantly, having as marked success among Coloured as among African workers). They were crucial in drawing workers into the uprisings and, in the context of the more general mass actions already in train, were also conducive to consolidating elements of a revolutionary perspective for the workers involved. Yet at the same time it must be emphasized that a November stay-away call (as well as one in June 1977) produced a very much smaller response than

---

* Nor was the ANC link entirely a theoretical one: soon after the uprisings began, students did turn for advice to old ANC activists, veterans of earlier struggles and bearers of the tradition of resistance, who were still living in the townships. However, the precise role of the ANC in mounting the stay-at-homes remains unclear, some observers claiming that the first one was called jointly by the ANC and SSRC and others claimings that what transpired was simply an imitation of the old ANC tactic.

the earlier undertakings and that, from November, the uprising as a whole tailed off (though it was finally brought to heel only eleven months later, with the massive state crackdown of that time).

Here we return to the necessity of an interpenetration of class and "popular-democratic" ideologies (and practices), for it is apparent that, as in the 1950s, the thrust of the stay-at-homes was linked more emphatically to the latter impulse than to the former. Thus, when their demands were not fulfilled, the momentum of worker involvement could only have been maintained if some attempt had been made to link up the broader political issues with economic struggles. This was not done; indeed, even those strikes and other point-of-production confrontations going on simultaneously with the township actions were almost totally ignored by those involved in the latter. In consequence, the next eighteen months saw a lull in mass action, though one punctuated by the fierce defensive action by squatters at Crossroads Camp in Cape Town against their "removal" and by scattered strikes. Yet despite the ultimate failure of "Soweto," it had achieved the significant advances already noted and, in the process, substantially reinforced the legacy of the Durban strikes, their "mental sediment: the intellectual, cultural growth of the proletariat." In the next wave of the mass strike, beginning in mid-1979 and still going on, the two strands of consciousness—one focused on the workplace, the other on the polity—would be strongly in evidence and, more than ever, would be working in tandem.

The first signs of a resurgence of mass action came with the development in May 1979 of a national consumer boycott in support of a strike by African and Coloured workers at the Fatti's and Moni's pasta factory in Cape Town; although the striking workers did not initiate the boycott, it was carried out under their direction. Gaining widespread support—even that of black trader associations and other petty-bourgeois organizations—the boycott eventually forced the company to settle. Here already there was a hint of a working-class project drawing in other sectors and linking shop floor and community in a constructive fashion. This was merely the beginning, however; even before this strike was over, working-class action was underway in other centers. In Ladysmith (Natal), a fare hike sparked a bus boycott which spread across the province. Meanwhile, the Black Consciousness-oriented Port Elizabeth Black Civic Organization (PEBCO) had been drawn, immediately upon its formation, into shop-floor struggle when its president, Thozamile Botha, was fired from his job at Ford Motor Company because of his political activities. Workers at the plant, mostly PEBCO supporters, immediately downed tools. PEBCO played a central role in generating political and material support for the strikers in the community and across the country during the subsequent eight-week conflict, a conflict which ended in victory for the workers even though Botha himself was arrested immediately after the settlement.

Building on these foundations, working-class action mush-roomed into perhaps the most sustained and widespread outburst of protest yet seen in South Africa.[16] Certainly the official count of 175,000 "man-days" lost through industrial action during 1980 broke all records. Major wage disputes occurred, including those at the Frame cotton mills near Durban (scene of the initial 1973 strikes); across the entire Eastern Cape auto industry several months after the Ford strike; and most recently at the Anglo American-owned Sigma Motor Company in Pretoria. Moreover, many important battles to win recognition of independent unions from employers are being fought, in response to the Wiehahn legislation. Perhaps the most dramatic action to date in this respect was the July 1980 strike by 10,000 members of the month-old Black Municipal Workers' Union (BMWU) in Johannesburg, a strike brutally crushed by the police—as many others have been. Yet these examples are merely the tip of the iceberg, the number of strikes during the first six months of 1980 being double that of the entire previous year. The pages of journals which document labor action remain filled with reports of shop-floor disputes, these apparently breaking out on an almost daily basis.[17] Many of these do not involve a union, though independent unions have been connected to all the major strikes, and their membership has more than doubled during 1980 to about 7 percent of the African workforce.

But if point-of-production struggles are the most prominent, the full range of activity is far broader than that. In addition to industrial strikes, there have been classroom boycotts, rent strikes, consumer boycotts, mass demonstrations, even another stay-at-home. Each action has absorbed the strength of earlier ones, built on the degree of organization already achieved and then in turn stimulated others; together they have contributed to the formation of a true mass strike. Perhaps the most complete interaction between the various aspects of struggle has been reached in Cape Town, where the long campaign in support of the Fatti's and Moni's workers left a highly politicized atmosphere. Thus the first half of 1980 saw several actions mounted in quick succession in that city, these often overlapping in time as well as in organizational terms. A three-week classroom boycott by Coloured students was joined by African high school students. Then the workers in the city's red meat industry struck, demanding management recognition of their plant-based workers' committee, with this followed almost immediately by their call for community support via a consumer boycott. Fare increases provoked not only a bus boycott, called by a committee comprised of forty community-based organizations, but also strikes for higher wages in the clothing and construction industries. Resident associations were formed to fight against rent hikes. A stay-away called to commemorate June 16 attracted a 75 percent response, while street demonstrations by students were met with police fire.

If struggles in other cities were not as tumultuous as in Cape Town, they were no less significant. The residents of Zwide township in Port Elizabeth refused to pay rent for eight months, while African students there, despite facing a particularly vicious reaction from the state, boycotted classes and, with their fellows in Cape Town, stayed out long after the Coloureds had returned in both cities. In Johannesburg, Coloured and Indian schools were boycotted (though not those in Soweto); however, there were widespread rent strikes in the latter township, led in most cases by branches of the Soweto Civic Association, formed by the aforementioned Committee of Ten.

Moreover, rent strikes were organized in several Transvaal towns, as well as in Durban. And in Kwamashu township outside Durban students boycotted (only to be met, as we shall see, by verbal condemnation from Kwazulu Chief Minister Gatsha Buthelezi and physical attack from the "impis"—bands of stormtroopers—of his Inkatha movement!).

Thus, even if some of these community struggles did not link up directly with shop-floor strikes to quite the same degree as in the Ford strike or in Cape Town, there can be little doubt that the overall picture is one of the working class dramatically in motion. At the same time, the mass strike is, and must be, something more than a headlong rush forward by the working class. As already hinted, tactical questions are constantly being thrown up by the struggles themselves, and have to be responded to by the emergent organizations of the dominated classes. In this respect, the advances made beyond the "Soweto" period have been substantial, the Coloured schools' boycott in Cape Town providing an instructive case in point. This was organized by a Committee of 81 (comprised of a representative from each of the schools involved) which, even the *Financial Mail* (May 16, 1980) could note, was "more coherent than the other boycotters both in the demands and their organization."

The initial demands related to particular and immediate concerns in the schools, such as the autonomy of student councils and the poor maintenance of school buildings, but these very quickly spilled over into a more generalized attack on the entire system of "inferior racist education" and on apartheid itself. Yet the committee never collapsed its short-term demands and long-term goals into each other, even calling a temporary halt to the boycott at one point in order to provide time for their short-term demands to be met and for a breathing space in which to consolidate their own organization. The discipline of the entire body of boycotting students reflects the level of democracy attained on the committee. In addition, there has been continuing evidence of tactical agility: the boycott was not of the schools themselves but only of scheduled classes, the students then being able to use the school buildings as assembly points and in several schools—often with the assistance of their teachers—to mount alternative education programs for short periods.* Finally, the students were more aware than ever of the limitations of their acting alone, and of the necessity for worker assertions. This led them to forge firm links with workers (and parents!) by involving themselves in the latter's struggles. At one high point of the Cape Town events in late May 1980, hundreds of students—already boycotting classes—played a crucial role in organizing the red meat and bus boycotts, called within three days of each other.

Of course, despite the fact that recent student actions have spread across the country even more widely than in 1976, there remains unevenness in the level of consciousness achieved. We have emphasized above that this is no less a danger for the working class per se—in light of its "objective" stratification, its regional variations, and the fact that nine-tenths of the workers remain outside the union movement. Luxemburg herself was insistent upon the necessity for cooperation between unionized workers and other strata of the class:

> The plan of undertaking mass strikes as a serious political class action with organized workers only is absolutely hopeless. If the mass strike . . . and the mass struggle are to be successful they must become a real *people's movement,* that is, the widest sections of the proletariat must be drawn into the fight.

But the events traced above have begun to reveal, now concretely rather than hypothetically, the positive role which "popular-democratic ideologies" ("a real people's movement") can play in sealing such fissures. Thus the community actions—bus boycotts, rent strikes, and the like—mounted within the framework of the mass strike have taken an immediate political form while simultaneously mobilizing workers across the board in

---

* It is true, of course, that unity between Coloured and African students in the city could have been stronger, the latter having never been entirely integrated into the Committee of 81 and, as noted above, continuing to boycott classes long after Coloured students had resumed them. It is also worth noting parenthetically that such apparently greater militancy may have been a tactical error since the state's closing down of the schools deprived the students of meeting places, removed the focus of their organizing, and contributed to the breaking down of their solidarity. Difficult to judge, but this is typical of tactical dilemmas likely to recur on the complex terrain afforded by South Africa.

economic terms. The point was neatly captured in the comment of one bus boycotter in Natal in 1979: "We don't earn high wages, so every increase is another burden on our backs. We do not believe we should suffer because the government's racial policies make it difficult to buy petrol" (the rising oil prices being the rationale offered for these particular fare hikes). Indeed, when popular-democratic ideologies become infused with working-class concerns many workers for whom point-of-production strikes may not be a viable option are drawn into the mass strike. Nor is the fact that a large number of these actions have taken place under the immediate auspices of apparently petty-bourgeois organizations *necessarily* a danger. As we shall see in the next section, the momentum of the mass strike may actually be such that many of these organizations (and their leaderships) are themselves being pulled downward toward the working class and incorporated within its hegemonic project as they are forced to relate to that class and to articulate its concerns and its demands.[18]

We know that the government's "reform" initiatives represent a closely related and quite self-conscious attempt to exacerbate any fissures which may exist within the proletariat. The potentially divisive impact of such initiatives must therefore be countered. Yet at the same time their gaps and contradictions— they are, after all, the product of a system on the defensive— must be located and pried further open, where possible, to allow the new terrain so established to be turned to working-class advantage. As far as countering their divisive impact is concerned, the "popular-democratic" assertions already mentioned can be important, community actions like rent strikes drawing together precisely those strata—settled workers and migrants in hostels—that Riekert sought to drive apart.[19] Moreover, the vitality of such ideologies is such that it is tempting to bring them to bear at the point of production itself as a counter to Wiehahn's expressed purpose of depoliticizing and bureaucratizing unions. This point was made, perhaps with some chagrin, by Freddie Sauls, an official of the union pushed aside by the Ford workers when it expressed reservations about the wisdom of their striking over a "political" issue:

In any plant anywhere in South Africa you'd find that party

> political and community issues are far more important to
> workers than worker-related issues, as workers relate their
> exploitation as wage earners to their political oppression. . . .
> Bring the political situation that blacks are faced with into the
> industrial environment and no law is going to stop it; no in-
> dustrial relations procedure or strategy is going to stop it.[20]

Though this is an overstatement, the Ford strike itself did drive
home the underlying point dramatically. Moreover, there can be
little doubt that the politicization of events there frightened the
dominant classes and pushed them much further onto the defensive on the trade union front. As the *Financial Mail* (November 23, 1979) noted during the strike:

> "There's a Ford in your future," runs the old slogan. . . .
> Many an employer might [now] be pondering its ironic truth.
> . . . For whatever the outcome of the last fortnight's unrest,
> it may well have marked a turning point in SA labour rela-
> tions—just as the Durban strikes did in 1973.

And certainly a generalization of the approach which emerged
at Ford would raise the overall level of worker militancy in
dramatic fashion.

Yet it also carries us back to a familiar danger, that of
blurring the centrality of the production process—and the socialist thrust which could spring from a clear understanding of this
dimension—to workers' struggles in the factories. It is important,
then, that there has been an additional, even more widespread,
response to the Wiehahn dispensation besides this "political"
unionism. That this should be the case is not surprising, of
course, since shop-floor organization and quite concrete economic
issues have been the focus of the independent union movement
since its beginnings. Moreover, in the three years prior to 1979
repeated requests by members of independent unions that employers negotiate with them were fobbed off with the reply,
"Wait for Wiehahn." Then, when that report was published,
many employers' first impulse (as we noted in the preceding
chapter) was to deal with tame in-company or parallel unions.
The demands of many workers have therefore come to focus on
the issue of employer recognition of *their* organizations, whether
unions or plant-based committees, and many of the resulting
conflicts have involved strike action.

Still, it was the issue of registration—state recognition now being possible for the first time for unions with African members—which required the most immediate response, post-Wiehahn. And the discussion of how best to deal with this issue divided the independent unions, with sharp tactical differences rising to the surface. On the one side, opposing registration, were the Cape Town-based unions—the WPGWU and the African Food and Canning Workers (a SACTU affiliate during the 1950s and the organizer of the Fatti's and Moni's strike)—and, emerging somewhat later, the BMWU and the East London-based South African Allied Workers' Union (SAAWU) (the latter's roots lying partially within the Black Consciousness movement). The view of these unions combined principle with tactical considerations, but their general argument rested on three points: the new system did not allow freedom of association and is intended to introduce new divisions within the working class (particularly between migrant and settled workers); the various state controls included in the registration package make internal union democracy and membership control impossible; participation in the industrial council machinery is not an advantage, but a trap to remove the unions from the sphere of shop-floor issues. In consequence, these unions have regarded their only weapon—whether against employers, parallel unions, or the state—to be their organized shop-floor presence and this, they have felt, would be sapped by registration.

As Bob Fine has cogently argued, this view may accept too readily the state's own position—that its control over the unions is assured, once the latter register—while failing to take seriously enough the possible benefits of registration, particularly the relief it could offer from the threat of state repression. Certainly FOSATU* has stressed this latter point, while also suggesting a belief that the state's policy does indeed reveal gaps and con-

---

* The Federation of South African Trade Unions (FOSATU) was formed in April 1979 by a linking up of TUACC, some unions in the Consultative Committee of Black Trade Unions (CCOBTU) which was linked to the UTP, and some Coloured unions which had disaffiliated from TUCSA. It emphasizes nonracial industrial unionism, strong shop-floor organization based on a shop steward structure, and independent working-class organization. Another central, the Council of Unions of South Africa (CUSA), was formed in September 1980 by the rump of the Consultative Committee.

tradictions in the system which should be exploited rather than rejected out of hand. Arguing that registration would increase their chances of forcing individual employers to negotiate with them, FOSATU activists feel confident that attendant controls will not necessarily be so powerful as to prevent them from maintaining their internal democratic processes and forward momentum, and they are confident, too, that registration need not compel them to participate on the Industrial Councils. Moreover, they feel this is the best way to counter the threat mounted by parallel unions on the terrain of registration; with the assistance of employers the latter might otherwise gain support, even if only temporarily, from black workers by winning real material gains, thus blunting the independent unions' claim to centrality.

To be sure, some have seen the difference over the approach to registration as related to somewhat different general approaches to organization, noting that FOSATU has on occasion counseled workers against striking where it has felt there to be little chance of victory. This has sometimes been to that union central's considerable cost, as in the Ford strike when they badly underestimated the strength of feeling among the workers. Conversely, the leadership in the other camp has been more inclined to allow worker militancy its head. Emphasis upon such a distinction has even given rise to the suspicion that FOSATU's approach may imply *too narrow* a shop-floor focus—the reverse side of the coin we have been examining—and thus run the risk of itself collapsing into economism, business unionism, and cooptation. It is therefore important to note that FOSATU, while continuing to fight for recognition from employers on a plant-by-plant basis, has actually sought registration for its affiliated unions by attaching two very crucial conditions to its applications: that the union be allowed to remain nonracial and that the category of provisional registration be scrapped. As already noted, their demand for nonracial registration was refused and these unions have rejected the racially premised certificates offered them. They thus remain unregistered and the jury still out on the tactical debate among the unions. Nonetheless, the FOSATU position—posing tough questions as to the tactics to be adopted on a shifting terrain—remains worthy of serious consideration. And this may prove to be even more true as the state, in crisis, continues to struggle to redefine its approach to trade unions, now offering some further concessions if also some familiarly pugnacious threats.[21]

In any case, it bears emphasizing that the shared features of the two tendencies within the independent trade union movement are more important than any tactical differences. Both have been involved in a number of major strikes, and the rapid growth of their combined memberships has far outstripped that of the parallel unions. They are therefore a particularly important manifestation of the emergence of a strong working-class project in recent years, a period which has affirmed that "the urban proletariat is now the soul of the revolution." As Luxemburg continued this statement:

> In order to carry through a direct political struggle as a mass, the proletariat must first be assembled as a mass, and for this purpose they must come out of factory and workshop, mine and foundry [and, we might add, township and school!], must overcome the decay to which they are condemned by the yoke of capitalism. The mass strike is the first natural, impulsive form of every great revolutionary struggle of the proletariat.

It is just this "first natural impulsive form" which we have now seen to be an accurate description of the situation in contemporary South Africa, constituting a giant step forward, being already the positive obverse of the crisis in South Africa and bearing the promise of a very different future for that country. Yet we need not romanticize. Though potent, such an "impulsive" thrust forward is not nearly coherent enough in its striking power, not completely hegemonic in its understanding or its aspirations, and certainly not fully self-conscious of the socialist implications of its assertions. We return by this route to the dialectic between working class and movement-cum-party with which we began this section and now sense more strongly than ever its absolutely crucial nature. We will consider this issue further in our final chapter. However, we must first turn our attention to a related matter, to a consideration of the availability of other social forces—rural and urban—as potential "class allies" for the working class within the framework of that hegemonic revolutionary project which is beginning to emerge.

III. Classes and Alliances

As seen, the assertions of the urban working class during the past decade have already had the strength to draw together that class's various strata into a common struggle on the shop floor and to interpenetrate effectively with closely related popular struggles in the townships. Moreover, there seems little doubt that the migrant labor system carries much of this message back into the reserves; so, too, does the flow of people who are pushed back by "removal" of the unemployed and of "squatters" (not least, in the latter category, those women who have tried to move to the cities "illegally" to join their husbands and thereby restore some semblance of family life to the African condition). In fact, in this way the entire migrant labor system becomes a kind of Trojan horse moving inside the enemy camp, circulating rising consciousness even as it circulates labor power. And this is true not only of the link between city and reserve, but also, one suspects, of the link between reserve and "white" farming area, that large, desperately exploitative, but most difficult to reach of all terrains of struggle in South Africa.

Of course, as we suggested at the outset of this chapter, a sense of grievance scarcely need be imported into the reserves from the "outside," even if the circulatory process just referred to may help to expand and generalize it. Grievance aplenty focuses upon the bantustan state structures and upon the broader apartheid system which encapsulates them. Indeed, in a previous chapter we found observers like Sheena Duncan and the *Financial Mail* suggesting that, as the latter reiterated the point on other occasions (May 18, 1979, February 1, 1980),

the real problem for the government is likely to come from the rural areas. . . . Huge pools of unemployed, resentful people in the Bantustans, who see themselves now formally excluded from the system, are likely to be fertile recruiting

grounds for insurgents. . . . There will be safer bases for re-
treat among the thousands of dispossessed people in the countryside, than in the suburbs. . . . [G]radual escalation of [in-
surgency] rather than urban revolution seems the most likely
long-term scenario.

One can strongly disagree, on the basis of the evidence adduced
in the previous section, with the overestimation of the system's
capacity to deflect urban militancy implied by such formulae
without, however, questioning their authors' reading of the
situation in the rural areas. Nor is it merely that social conditions are ripe for such guerrilla activity; so too are the logistics.
As Michael Hough, a "strategic specialist" at Pretoria University, has noted, "The bantustans form a horseshoe around
white urban areas, making them excellent springboards for
guerrilla operations." Moreover, "under international and local
pressures, future independent [sic] homeland governments might
be forced to turn a blind eye to incursions through their terri-
tories."[22]

Hough cites the specific example of Bophuthatswana: "[It]
is so fragmented that it is very difficult to control its borders.
Without influx control in Bophuthatswana there is little record
of movement in the area." And indeed the 1979 Pietermaritz-
burg treason trial of captured ANC freedom fighters documents
such a passage of guerrillas toward the urban areas, certainly
in far greater numbers than those who had been captured and,
as other evidence suggests, with effective support networks established among the populace along the way. But the terrain of
struggle offered directly by the reserves themselves also bears
noting, and indeed has been important from an early period as
"primary resistance" to imperial expansion shaded into the first
stirrings of the South African revolution. From the late 1940s
to the early 1960s, in particular, significant resistance both to
the government's attempted recasting and reinvigoration of
chiefly rule (as "Bantu Authorities") and to agricultural "betterment" sprang up in places like Witzieshoek, Marico, Sekhuk-
huneland, and Pondoland, a history well documented in Govan
Mbeki's *South Africa: The Peasants' Revolt*. True, Colin Bundy
and others have argued more recently that broader political
movements in South Africa were less successful than they might

have been in relating to these stirrings: the All-African Convention, a Trotskyist political organization of the 1940s and 1950s which did take an early interest, never quite linked up its rural activities with urban struggle, while ANC began only rather belatedly, in the period leading up to its banning, to take a real lead in this aspect of the struggle. But real possibilities were demonstrated nonetheless.[23]

Of course, the need to develop further the politics of mobilization and coordination of rural political action is no less pressing now than in the 1950s—although it is also the case, as we have seen, that the terrain has shifted somewhat. To a greater degree than is presently the case, the social basis of the resistance referred to above was still "peasant"—"the dying wail of a class over whom the wave of progress [?] was about to roll," in Barrington Moore's memorable phrase. Given the failure of that resistance to stay the wave of racial capitalism, we find that now it is the assertions of the proletarianized-cum-marginalized of the reserves that must be emphasized (marginalization referring, in the words of one South African author, "to the process of exclusion from direct economic participation, to the gross under-employment of women, to the phenomenal rates of youth unemployment"[24]). They are those who "hang around the factories and labour offices of Umtata and Butterworth [in the Transkei] hoping for jobs and begging food from the lunches of middle-class children" (although a handful do find work and thus become the seeds of an in-bantustan proletariat of a different kind). They are those left to rot in such "resettlement villages" as Dimbaza, Glenmore, and Winterveld, those starving on the land and, in Transkei, for example, those "nearly 1.5 million people (equivalent to more than half the total number of permanent Transkei residents) who passed through the region's prisons in the year ending March 1980, an increase of 34 percent over the previous year's figures." They are those who are "unlikely [to find their] conditions very much improved by the Transkei government's recent desire to export women domestic workers to West Germany."[25] They are those, in short, who provide the backdrop for South African Minister of Labor Fanie Botha's remark, "If we don't create sufficient jobs we will perish in the revolution of the unemployed."

There is always the danger that the intense and grinding social distemper which the above items reflect (and which are duplicated again and again throughout the bantustans) will merely turn the pressure inward, that crime and banditry or the (always potentially violent) squabbling between various villages or "factions" will become the order of the day. And certainly the new elites of the bantustans are more than happy to stir this sort of pot, manipulating ethnic slogans and various kinds of patronage, while also hoping to ensnare (and limit) people within an exclusively bantustan political process on this mystified basis. Yet despite evidence of some such developments, the sustaining of a significant level of popular resistance is still the most prominent feature. This is dramatized in such specific instances as the burning to the ground of the proposed Bophuthatswana Legislative Assembly in a mass demonstration the year before that reserve's "independence," the various physical attacks by large crowds on such bantustan chief ministers as Bophuthatswana's Mangope, Venda's Mpephu, and Ciskei's Sebe, the resistance in Lebowa of the Batlokwa to further removals (the latter being part of South Africa's attempt to "rationalize" the borders of that bantustan), and of the still-landed Matlala to high-handed governmental methods of agricultural "betterment" and administration.[26] But Barbara Rogers' useful study of the bantustans, in giving a detailed rundown of numerous such events, documents a quite general pattern of unrest, electoral boycott, and "attacks upon bantustan officials, vehicles, and buildings." Moreover, in observing the important role that students and other youth have played in many of these latter actions, Rogers cites a particularly significant observation from the *Rand Daily Mail*:

> There is little doubt a cardinal fact was the feeling among African youth that the homeland governments are part and parcel of the apartheid system. Hence a blow against a homeland government is seen as a blow against apartheid.

In short, Duncan and the *Financial Mail* are correct in finding tinder aplenty in the rural areas (including the bantustans' own quasi-urban centers), this in spite of the undoubted difficulties of organizing and focusing the diverse energies involved. Of course, one suspects that underground political work is already beginning to provide even more of the direction such energies will require. Moreover, in the present conjuncture this does seem to be a particularly necessary response, given the dominant classes' own self-conscious attempt to shift the terrain of struggle by reinforcing the two-tier labor market and deporting more and more of its contradictions and political problems—insofar as possible—to the reserves. The liberation movement need scarcely fear the jejune charge of undertaking a "flight from the cities" if it moves effectively to organize the nationalist-cum-proletarian struggle on such promising terrain.[27]

At the same time, it must be stressed that the revolutionary process on so diverse a social landscape as South Africa offers is likely to involve a complex interplay of coordinated and "spontaneous" (or, at least, highly decentralized) activities. Therefore it may also be that much of this tinder—in the reserves, but also on the white farms—will be most well and truly lit as part of a more general conflagration. Perhaps some foreshadowing of this was provided by the resonance which the 1976 events in the cities found in many of the homelands. In the coming confrontation, this same pattern could prove crucial in helping spread the South African defense force (and its black henchmen) even thinner on the ground, and in further demoralizing the white population. Whatever may be the most likely scenario, we can see that Marx's famous dictum regarding rural struggle—"the proletarian revolution obtains that chorus without which its solo song in all peasant nations becomes a swan song"—has to be modified in order to fit the greater complexities of the process of proletarianization in South Africa. Nonetheless, there can be little doubt that a rural "chorus" will be of considerable importance in South Africa's future.

Not surprisingly, the petty bourgeoisies of the bantustans have, by and large, placed themselves in firm alliance with the South African state in attempting to preempt any such developments. The aforementioned 1979 treason trial is immediately instructive here as regards the role they play vis-à-vis the liberation movements: "An interesting feature of the trial," writes *Work in Progress,* "has revolved around activity in the so-called 'independent' Bantustan, Bophuthatswana. Prisoners have been handed over by the Bantustan administration to the South African police without even the formality of extradition proceedings, and activities within Bophuthatswana have been charged as acts against the South African state. The close cooperation between the South African police and the Bophuthatswanan home guard in patrolling borders is also of interest."[28] No "blind eye to incursions" here. But the role played vis-à-vis the actual residents of such homelands is equally revealing, the on-again, off-again "emergency" in the Transkei being especially so. Such has been the pattern of repression in this latter territory that, when queried about the arrests made during one period of unrest in 1980, the sinister Commissioner of Police, Brigadier Martin Ngceba, said, "It is impossible to keep track of the numbers." Small wonder that this should be the case, given President Mantanzima's philosophy of rule as expressed on the occasion of the installation of the new Mpondo Paramount Chief in 1980:

> [He] said that the Pondos had learned their lesson during the 1960 Eastern Pondoland rebellion and he expressed the hope that it would not happen again. He advised the new Paramount "to employ the only way understood by black people and that is the stick." He said black people did not understand the philosophy of consultation and their problems were solved by use of the stick. He concluded: "The government of Transkei is stable because it deals with any problem as it sees fit. Our Security Act has looked after this country and many people will get hurt by associating with subversive elements."[29]

One final example of the "Papa Doc" atmosphere of these statelets must stand for the many more which could be cited. As Barbara Rogers has written:

> Another hazard for those not cooperating with the Ciskei government is the "Green Berets," a group of thugs who have attacked a number of people and beaten them up with their knobkieries. . . . In their most concerted action they attacked students in the streets and in boys' and girls' hostels; the action is thought to have been in retaliation for attacks on the cars of [Chief Minister] Sebe's family and his Minis-

ters. The Green Berets were seen to have arrived in official Ciskei government cars, one of them driven by Sebe's brother. Sebe denied that they had any connection with his government, but said they would probably be turned into a "home guard" after training by the South African police.

We have already sketched a profile of the black "beneficiaries" of this kind of bantustan "independence," the group Roger Southall has identified for the Transkei but suggested to be characteristic of them all: "A considerable number of chiefs, politicians and bureaucrats, and a group of petty traders and businessmen," Africans who "do not have the support of the mass of the population" but are nonetheless "finding opportunities of wealth, influence, and—in their own terms— prestige, which are available to them nowhere else in the Republic."[30] Some have stressed that this still leaves room for significant splits to surface within the petty bourgeoisie—premised on such underlying realities as the competition for the limited resources and opportunities actually available for purposes of cooptation within the narrow confines of the bantustans or, more positively, on a critical reaction to the gross corruption, authoritarianism, and subservience to apartheid of specific sets of power wielders. Such possibilities could easily be overstated, but in the Transkei, for example, the Democratic Progressive Party (and its several precursors), as well as newspapers like *Isaziso* (now banned),, have been—when given, for brief periods, some slight room for maneuver—foci for significant criticism of the Mantanzima regime.

Although sub-ethnic rivalries have not always been absent from such in-fighting, the Transkei opposition has also been a vector for the injection of broader political currents into the public arena: Hector Ncogazi's Black Consciousness-related critique of "independence" and Chief Sabata Dalindyebo's wellknown (and widely popular) affinity for the politics of the African National Congress are cases in point. Indeed Sabata, driven into exile, has now formally aligned himself with the ANC, as have some of his lieutenants. This speaks well for the continuing visibility and credibility of the ANC in the area, and also for the possibility that political cross currents in the bantustans can be played upon deftly to expand the constituency for liberation. Of course, there is also the danger of being dragged down to the level of the petty-bourgeois political game, or of merely ingesting reformism around some lowest common denominator of nationalist assertion. Clearly, this is very tricky terrain indeed—in terms of class struggle both without *and within* the liberation movement—and in any case no substitute 'or the sort of grass-roots revolutionary work in the homelands alluded to earlier.

One particularly unlikely recruit to the liberation movement—although the ANC did once meet with him several years ago—is the ubiquitous Chief Minister of Kwazulu, Getsha Buthelezi. It is tempting to see Buthelezi as just another bantustan leader. Around him clusters an all-too-familiar band of petty-bourgeois hustlers, and he is effusively committed to capitalism, given to quoting Harry Oppenheimer and Milton Friedman on the virtues of the "free enterprise system," and arguing, for example, that "each occasion when a black man manages to be in a position to establish any business is an auspicious occasion, not only for himself or his family, but also for the entire black community . . . [striking] a blow for us in the liberation struggle now being waged by blacks."[31] Although he has sought to recruit support among Zulus working in next-door Durban and in Johannesburg, he quickly rid himself of his Minister of Labor, Barney Dladla, when the latter began more effectively to press the grievances of such workers in the early 1970s; in fact, Buthelezi has little resonance in the important Durban union movement. He has also shown no qualms about playing the ethnic card, often wrapping himself in tradition and tribal symbolism in his attempt to entrench himself politically. Moreover, he wields power ruthlessly within his own fiefdom, squeezing out opposition parties, manipulating patronage, smashing student protesters when they mounted successful school boycotts in the sprawling Kwamashu township in 1980, and calling for the formation of "vigilante groups" to protect property and to keep dissidents in their place. Finally, after some initial attempts to associate himself with the mantle of the ANC, he has now distanced himself from any such affinities, while repudiating the notion of armed struggle in very strong terms.

Yet Buthelezi *is* different—a point which becomes clearer when he is located with reference to the "reform" debate within ruling circles. For if Mantanzima and his ilk are bantustan leaders after the *verkramptes'* own hearts, then Buthelezi plays to the liberals (with the *verligtes*—caught between—still not quite decided about him but, significantly, allowing him ample room to maneuver). Thus he has refused categorically to play the "independence" game and talks of a unitary South Africa—though he does hint that he may be open to "consociational" solutions and (as seen) to Lombard-like power-sharing for Natal. He seeks, despite his ethnic fallback position, to operate politically on a national plane, claiming more often now a South Africa-wide national-cum-racial liberating vocation, seeking to build up a coalition of like-minded movements—including the business-minded Coloured Labour Party and the Indian Reform Party—into the Black Alliance, and threatening to move into urban politics to contest for seats on the community councils (in Soweto, for example). He knows, too, that a credible "middle-class" leadership must be able to package the people and deliver them inside a reform dispensation if that middle class, and the system as a whole, is to be safeguarded. Hence his (admittedly now rather shopworn) populist approach and his attempt to build a quasi-grassroots organization in the form of his Inkatha movement (in fact, more a ward-heeler's delight—with para-military overtones—than anything else, but distinctive among homeland political institutions nonetheless). And, finally, he has chosen his white constituency carefully, with an investor's eye to the long haul. It is precisely big capital, local and international (Inkatha offices now grace both London and Bonn), the Progressive Federal Party (through an "on-going liaison committee with the PFP and Inkatha"), and, no doubt, the Nationalist Party *verligtes*—when they are ready for him—to whom he speaks. For this is what makes Buthelezi tick, and distinguishes him: he seeks to place himself on offer as the guarantor of "reform," as an insurance policy against the risks entailed in the shift from racial to liberal capitalism, as a man for all "national conventions" and all "power-sharing schemes," as, in the words of an *Argus* (Cape Town) newspaper headline, the "Key to White Hopes."

Of course, even if the dominant classes were to make him an offer he couldn't refuse, it seems more than likely that he could not deliver—probably not even in his own strife-ridden Kwazulu, certainly not across the full sweep of the bantustans, and especially not in the urban areas. The cities already have petty-bourgeois actors of their own, in any case. As we have seen, those Africans who are active in the private sector—their number still "extremely small" but "increasing," and their "role . . . purposely destined to grow," according to Roger Southall—are quite firmly tied into the circuits of white capital.[32] Moreover, aware of their own interests, they are eager to embrace the role allotted to them by "reform": "to serve as a bulwark to [i.e., against] any political uprising in this country," as Richard Maponya, a prominent Soweto businessman, put it a number of years ago. Sam Motsuenyane, president of the National African Federated Chambers of Commerce (NAFCOC) (and one-time guest at a Jimmy Carter prayer breakfast), has been equally forthright: "Ownership of property by Blacks . . . is an essential element in the development of Capitalism which is denied the Black people of South Africa. I cannot see how Blacks can develop a love for Capitalism if they are not allowed to become capitalists themselves and share equitably in the wealth of their country." Now, with the door slightly more ajar than previously, such elements are keen to seize the opportunities offered by the Urban Foundation and by legislative change. As described in 1980 by spokesman Moses Maubane, new assistant general manager of the African Bank, NAFCOC's "five-year development plan" looks to increased financial backing and expertise from both the white business community and government, especially in helping to launch black industrial undertakings (*Financial Mail,* March 28, 1980). To be sure, there is some in-fighting within the organization, and over one issue in particular, that of "separate development." Certain businessmen in both the townships and the bantustans (the latter also represented in NAFCOC, through regional Chambers) seek strong protection from white business; others have been inclined to go along with the logic of big capital's entry (including in the commercial field) into black areas, though simultaneously seeking certain safeguards for themselves (in terms of guarantees of partnership arrangements and the like). In fact, it is the latter group which has carried the day, thus announcing themselves, like Buthelezi, to be on offer to support, from the black side, any further liberal redefinitions of South African capitalism which may be forthcoming.

Nor can they quite stop there. If any urban group is being provided with—and, as we now see, claiming—the keys to the economic kingdom, it is Motsuenyane and his cronies. Yet even they are not comfortable with second-class citizenship (let alone with the threat of their having to assume bantustan citizenship); besides, they can feel the breath of the mass of the township population on their necks. In consequence, Motsuenyane has felt moved to speak out publicly for "one man, one vote," and has also been among those supporting the recent campaign for the release of ANC leader Nelson Mandela from Robben Island. Clearly, such businessmen realize how much more must be done not only to realize their own ambitions but also for there to be any chance at all of sucking other strata of the urban black population into the system on something less than revolutionary, anti-capitalist terms. Moreover, the other wing of the black "middle class," the "new petty bourgeoisie" (rapidly growing too, according to Simkins and Hindson's figures), finds itself buffeted by even more powerful crosscurrents in this regard.

As suggested earlier, this class must be seen, in the first instance, as being the political ally of the proletariat on the level of a shared nationalist-cum-racial project. The limitations of this are real enough: Anna Starcke's instructive interview in her book *Survival* with Dr. Ntatho Motlana, chairman of the Soweto Committee of Ten, finds him "despising" Communism, disavowing revolution, praising "free enterprise" (albeit within a "partially planned economy"), and manifesting his most impassioned resentments over such items as the level of salaries for black professionals and the discomfort of living in Soweto ("I earn enough to move anywhere. But I am trapped.").[33] At the same time, this group is more likely to be politically visible than its entrepreneurial counterparts and thus finds itself under considerable pressure from its fellow blacks not to collaborate, and indeed to go even further in the direction of opposition. In the heat of Soweto, with the students on the march, it was the pressure of the "severe generation gap between older, more cooperative blacks—community councillors, businessmen, teachers, and nurses—and black youth which sees its best chance in a revolution" that was important in this respect (*Financial Mail,* February 1, 1980). Common adherence to the powerful (if somewhat amorphous) ideology of Black Consciousness provided a ground for some petty-bourgeois elements to close that gap at least partially and to find roles for themselves in the struggle; it was under such auspices, for example, that Motlana found himself at the helm of the Committee of Ten as it was thrust forward, more or less spontaneously, by events in 1977. And it is the dynamic of the "mass strike," as analyzed in the previous section, which has continued to keep pressure focused upon the petty bourgeoisie.

Thus, this class is pulled in two directions, and some of its members have already made their separate peace with the reforming state (even though, as we have seen, the reforms are still quite modest). But many others have moved to deepen their populism (ideological maturing under pressure from the popular classes being what Cabral had in mind when he suggested that some members of the petty bourgeoisie could commit "class suicide"). In so doing they have continued to link up with the more *déclassé* youth/student group and, together with them, to move toward a greater emphasis upon the workers as the crucial class basis for social transformation. The Black Consciousness organizations, banned in 1977, had already begun to grow in this direction, of course, but a radicalization of their cultural/ national preoccupations (e.g., black pride) via class analysis has been an even more marked feature of the new groups which have sprung up under the Black Consciousness umbrella: the Azanian Peoples' Organization, the Azanian Students' Organization, the Congress of South African Students, the National Indian Congress, and the like.[34] Even somewhat more "establishment" organizations like the Committee of Ten/Soweto Civic Association have played an important part in sustaining aboveground political opposition to the South African government's schemes; there is a world of difference between the heartfelt denunciations by Motlana and Bishop Desmond Tutu of this year's vicious South African assault on ANC houses inside

Mozambique and the bloodthirsty barking, on the same occasion, of the most "left" of white parties, the PFP. And a considerable difference, too, between the activities of such leaders and the sophisticated quasi-collaborationist approach of a Gatsha Buthelezi.

True, not all of these political groups have found the organizational keys to grounding themselves firmly in a working-class constituency that, for a period under the leadership of Thozamile Botha, the Port Elizabeth Black Community Organization did. Yet the prominent participation of such elements in the rent strikes and other township actions recounted earlier is tangible evidence of the further maturing of the Black Consciousness impulse toward involvement with much more concrete popular demands. Moreover, an additional dimension is the growing pull of the ANC upon the group which has guided this impulse (and upon both its petty-bourgeois and its youth/student components). We will return to this theme in our final chapter, but here it can be noted how many of the "Soweto generation," upon leaving the country, found their way into the ANC in exile—to return, in many instances, as guerrillas and underground cadres. An impressive array of senior leaders has also so aligned themselves in exile: Barney Pityana, one of the original theorists of Black Consciousness, Mankekolo Mahlangu of the Committee of Ten and the Azanian Peoples' Organization, Thozamile Botha himself. Even more important, the ANC connection on the ground is now a much more live (if not quite open) issue within the full range of organizations mentioned above, and the ANC, in its turn, is much more inclined to reach out toward them.

Obviously this is all primarily to the good. On the one hand, it implies the further generalization and politicization of the struggle inside the country; on the other, it begins to internalize within the ANC forces freshly defined on the immediate terrain of struggle. A cautionary note may be in order, however. A recent pamphlet from the Catholic Institute of International Relations summarizes some of these developments by saying that the "ANC is thus entering the 1980's giving an increased emphasis to armed struggle and a multi-class unified movement, and it has cut back on earlier drives for worker organization."[35] And then there is ANC theorist Joe Slovo's proposition that "objectively speaking . . . the immediate fate of the black middle classes is linked much more with that of the black workers and peasants than with their equivalents across the colour line."[36] To be fair, this latter formula was advanced a number of years ago, but it represents, nonetheless, a potentially dangerous overstatement of the prospects for "class suicide," especially on the current terrain of possible reform and cooptation. In sum, we are back to the concerns regarding class alliances and ideology with which we began this chapter. Insofar as the Catholic emphasis is accurate, and Slovo's proposition still operative within the liberation movement, there are questions to be raised regarding the link of that movement to the "mass strike," the nature of the current "articulation" between nationalism and class struggle, and the future of socialism in South Africa.

4. THE FORCES OF OPPOSITION ORGANIZE

Our chief purpose in this short volume has been to present the components of the present crisis in South Africa, an organic crisis—economic, political, and ideological—only minimally qualified by the current gold boom. We find the camp of the dominant classes rife with contradictions, even though in terms of sheer power such classes are scarcely a spent force and in terms of "formative" action they may still have a trick or two up their sleeves. And, on the other side, we find the dominated classes in motion to an unprecedented degree, provided with unique opportunities—the dominant classes themselves are aware of this—but also faced with dramatic challenges. To undertake an exhaustive analysis of the range of political implications which spring from the situation so outlined would require a manuscript at least as long as the present one; we shall leave such a task for another occasion. Instead, we will strike a more exploratory note, attempting, briefly, to codify some of those challenges which will indeed be posed for the dominated classes—and for those political actors, the African National Congress of South Africa in particular, who seek to focus the energies of such classes for revolutionary purposes—on the terrain now offered them. We will then conclude with a brief comment on some of the possible implications of our argument for the practice of those concerned to support the South African struggle in North America.

I. The African National Congress of South Africa

The history of the development of the struggle against racial capitalism in South Africa already exemplifies many of the contradictory elements which define the challenge currently confronting the revolutionary movement. Thus, the stirrings of African nationalism which first found their focus in the African National Congress at its founding in 1912 were primarily petty bourgeois in provenance and notably reformist. More militant undertakings, predominantly working-class based, found expression outside the ANC, most distinctively in the dramatic, albeit shortlived and ultimately highly compromised, assertions of the Industrial and Commercial Workers' Union (ICU), under the leadership of Clements Kadalie. It was only in the 1940s that the national movement and the working-class struggle began to link up more effectively as, in the wake of the unprecedented strikes of those years, the ANC set down firm roots among the people, and, under pressure from its own Youth League, radicalized its perceptions of South African society.

This radicalization had two strands, however, one drawing the movement toward a more proletarian line—the increased prominence of the South African Communist Party within the ranks of the resistance making some contribution here—and the other toward a more exclusivist and militantly African nationalist-cum-racial line—an increasingly salient (and apparently successful) political perspective throughout much of the continent at that time. The consolidation by the ANC of a populist politics during the 1950s held these two strands together and facilitated the mounting of such impressive mass actions against the increasingly hardline Nationalist regime as anti-pass law demonstrations, boycotts, stay-at-homes, and the entire Defiance Campaign. But the meshing of such strands was an uneasy one, nonetheless. The positioning of the South African Congress of Trade Unions within the Congress Alliance underscored the workers' role but, as seen in chapter 3, at some risk of hyper-politicizing that involvement as part of a "mass movement" without fully consolidating workers' class practice at the point of production.

Linked to this was the danger that emphasis upon expanding the (pan-class) coalition of resistance might tend to over-privilege nationalist assertions at the expense of socialist ones, even the *Freedom Charter* of the mid-1950s, in some ways an impressive advance, remaining in the last analysis fairly ambiguous in this regard. How much this was merely a tactical calculation (wise or otherwise), how much an index of continuing petty-bourgeois hegemony within the movement, is still subject to debate. Moreover, one must take note of the attendant difficulties which arose in specifying the terms of the nationalist assertion itself. Certainly some Africans within the Congress Alliance (which, as will be remembered, included Indian, Coloured, and white groups as well) felt that the nationalist aspirations of the vast majority of the population (the Africans) had been watered down by overemphasizing the process of multiracial coalition building (and, in addition, by overemphasizing the "communism" of "white" leftists!). Much of the subsequent activity of this group—it split from the ANC to form the Pan Africanist Congress (PAC) in 1959—had a self-serving air about it (and its racial "radicalism" was certainly the very opposite of being socialist). Nonetheless, this unwelcome development hinted at the difficulties of enabling the strong, almost inevitable, surge of African nationalist (and racially triggered) resistance to racial capitalism to contribute to, rather than undermine, the mounting of a more broadly revolutionary project. In short, it became clear that under South African conditions, the nationalist/racial card would have to be played just as deftly as the proletarian card.

The ANC (still very much larger and more central than the PAC, in spite of the split) seemed to be undergoing a useful learning experience here, but unfortunately the process of learning on the ground was cut short by the fierce, early 1960s crackdown mounted by the South African state. This represented another lesson in any case. For so implacable was the enemy in South Africa that more than mass demonstrations were now seen to be in order; a fully effective approach would have to include a military cutting edge. In the meantime, the populism of defiance had suffered a severe defeat, both physically and psychologically: after a brief flurry of underground activity, the nationalist movements found many of their strongest leaders on Robben Island and most of the rest in exile. There the PAC, after a career of considerable opportunism, was slowly but surely to fall apart (despite recent efforts by John Pokela and others to pull it back together again). The ANC began much more effectively to lay the groundwork for military activity, but it suffered as well; never entirely absent inside the country during the 1960s and early 1970s, the movement was still considerably distanced from the scene there and the exile condition took its toll.

The movement did consolidate its links abroad, not only in Eastern Europe, the chief source of military equipment and training, and among the Western network of Communist parties, but also in much of Africa, and among many Western trade union, church, independent left, and even governmental (e.g., Scandinavian) circles. And this would prove to be important. But it was also difficult to avoid a certain flabbiness (petty-bourgeois tendencies?) setting in, as well as a measure of bureaucratization. Moreover, this latter danger in particular was strengthened by a freezing, outside the forcing-house of popularly rooted politics, of the relationship between the South African Communist Party (SACP) and the ANC. Of course, the precise nature of the link between these two bodies is not known outside fairly narrow circles, but it is close. Nor, in exile, has the SACP been one of the more "open" and independent of Communist parties; any revolutionary socialist who is not greatly enamored of Soviet definitions of reality must experience a certain unease in reading the SACP's *African Communist,* for example, or indeed in reading some of the ANC's own publications. Moreover, the saliency of external linkages and military assistance (contrasted, for many years, with the relative unavailability of a popular context for struggle)—as well as the enviable success of straightforward guerrilla undertakings elsewhere in the region (though on terrain very different physically and socially from that afforded by South Africa)—meant that the ANC's definition of the struggle ran some risk of being reduced to a too narrowly militarist one.

However, what is ultimately more striking than this range of potential weaknesses is the fact that the ANC had managed to stay sufficiently in shape to be ready to act when "organic crisis" struck in the 1970s (and when developments in Angola, Mozambique, and Zimbabwe moved the front line closer to home). It is true that, as worker and student assertions of the period began once again to place proletarian action and aggressive nationalism (Black Consciousness) firmly on the South African agenda inside the country in ways that we have outlined above, the ANC—if by no means absent—was not the most central of actors. Nor can it even now pretend to encompass the full range of "progressive forces" which are at large on the side of resistance. Nonetheless, in the past five years the movement has confounded its critics by demonstrating itself to be the political entity likely to field and to focus the broadest spectrum of revolutionary energies defined by organic crisis, and the most likely to facilitate the "mass strike" in becoming a truly hegemonic project. Certainly, it has attracted the best of those new recruits who have had to leave the country, and inside South Africa its political resonance is growing stronger every day. Thus even the London-based *African Confidential,* a conservative but often well-informed Africa news service, now writes (October 1, 1980) that "as the paramount exile movement, the ANC is gaining ground. The probability is that one day Botha or his successor will have to talk to it."

Why should the ANC have this kind of "gravitational pull" on the South African revolution? One important reason is its military capacity, which is now increasingly relevant, and seen to be so by those gravitating toward it. The ANC has prepared for this necessary level of struggle and is also equipped for it like no other group; here the absolutely crucial nature of the links established with the Eastern bloc reveals itself, whatever the attendant costs. Engagements with the South African Defense Force have become much more commonplace; the names of Rustenburg, Zeerust, Thabazimbi, Silverton, and Booysens spring to mind, as do recent reports of whites abandoning farms all along the Transvaal's northern borders because of the guerrilla presence. Moreover, it is clear that the numerous trials in the past few years involving charges for moving and caching explosives, arms, and leaflets are merely the tip of the iceberg of actions underway. And then there are the dramatic acts of sabotage: the well-guarded Sasolburg oil storage facilities last year, the pylons and other installations near Durban in April. Still not a major military threat, but full of promise to the mass of Africans—and challenging enough, even by 1978, to elicit from the head of the security police the admission that "South Africa [is] in a state of war" and that "an estimated 4,000 blacks [mostly members of the ANC] are currently undergoing training"; and, from Jimmy Kruger, then Minister of Police, the frustrated cry: "The ANC is everywhere"![1] The sophistication of some of these sabotage and military actions also argues the existence of a more than casual infrastructure of support for the guerrillas. One must suspect that a broad underground network, geared to political and military purposes, is in the process of formation, contacting people and groups and drawing them into the wider circle of resistance.

A second factor, less tangible but equally important, is the movement's hard-earned *legitimacy,* its centrality within the long history of resistance and, in particular, within the vast popular struggles of the 1950s. Such resonance is partly symbolic, and attractive enough on that basis alone. But this history is also quite concretely of the present moment too, as, for example, in the very persons of the many still on the ground in South Africa who were deeply and directly touched by the ANC experience. The resurfacing of an old ANC/SACTU militant like Oscar Mpetha at the center of strike action in the Western Cape—and now as an object of considerable state harassment—is a visible case in point of what is a much more widespread reality; complemented by such newly trained underground cadres as are now being put into place, the activity of these people begins to make association with the ANC tradition as much a real choice for others as a symbolic one! To this must be added the important fact that the ANC's history is now a much more *recognizable* one to some inside the country— worker or student—than it was perhaps five years ago in the first flush of the Soweto events. Then, momentarily, the situation seemed entirely new, the past a failure, the ANC a bit quaint. Now, however, in the cold light of repression and on-going struggle, various familiar problems have resurfaced as the preoccupations of the newly arrived generation of activists as well. If recognition of the need for sustained and serious military activity is relevant to this maturing process, so too is a growing recognition of the need to blend diversity and spontaneity with coordination and coherent leadership, military action with popular action, Black Consciousness with class consciousness, nationalism with socialism. Yet the attempt to deal with precisely such linkages—even if it has produced a record marked by failures as well as by successes—has been at the heart of the theory and practice of the ANC over the years.* Small wonder that, as the 1980s dawn, the new generation begins to find a home there.

Moreover, even though the ANC has not back-tracked at all on its multiracial principles, its blending of that theme with African nationalism is, if anything, less self-conscious and more self-confident than it was during the Congress Alliance period of the 1950s. The opening of the ANC to membership from all races in 1969 was probably an index of this, even if it did cause a certain (very limited) backlash within the movement (and the eventual departure of a handful of members to start a micro-movement, the "ANC-Nationalist"). Some of the more demagogic Black Consciousness types may still echo PAC's racist critique of the ANC, but this seems to be no great barrier to entry; moreover, the ANC itself has profited from Black Consciousness's strong emphasis upon *black* unity, this having defined a much stronger basis for involvement in the struggle by Coloureds and Asians.

There is, however, a left critique of the ANC that is intellectually much more serious than any such race-baiting posture. Not that the ANC has stood still on the proletarian-cum-

---

* A deeper understanding of the complexity of the South African revolution has also helped to further undermine the credibility of the PAC, seen initially by some Black Consciousness militants as a more natural historical point of reference than the ANC because of the racial question; moreover, the PAC, in disarray (despite occasional forays into the country), can provide no real answer on the military front. In addition, the Black Consciousness movement in exile has not offered a credible expansion of its frame of reference for purposes of sustained struggle, collapsing into a particularly rhetorical brand of ultra-leftism on the one hand (the London-based variant), and living off the international churches' dole on the other (the Holland-based variant).

socialist front, its *Strategy and Tactics* document, adopted in 1969, moving well beyond the *Freedom Charter* in underscoring the importance of the "large and well-developed working class whose class consciousness and independent expressions of the working people—their political organs and trade unions—are very much part of the liberation front." Although

> the national character of the struggle must therefore dominate our approach . . . our nationalism must not be confused with chauvinism or narrow nationalism of a previous epoch. It must not be confused with the classical drive by an elitist group among the oppressed people to gain ascendancy so that they can replace the oppressor in the exploitation of the mass. . . . This perspective of a speedy progression from formal liberation to genuine and lasting emancipation is made more real by the existence in our country of a large and growing working class whose class consciousness complements national consciousness.[2]

Nonetheless, critics have argued that this apparent privileging of the proletarian moment in the struggle remains as much rhetorical as real, and they are uneasy, too, that it is the SACP which, as chief "political organ" of the working class, seems to be looked upon as a guarantor of such "genuine emancipation."

Within the ANC this position has found most open expression in a recent critique by Robert Petersen, former editor of SACTU's newspaper *Workers' Unity,* Martin Legassick, a distinguished historian of South Africa, and others (all subsequently expelled).[3] Like some others on the left (of even more exotic hue), they have seen petty-bourgeois tendencies within the ANC being merely reinforced by Communist Party influence and Communist Party-style bureaucratic methods of work, thus undermining revolutionary possibilities. Indeed, for Petersen, Legassick, and company this is the bottom line of their critique and it premises their charges that the ANC remains too unresponsive to the semi-spontaneous and proto-revolutionary assertions of the proletariat and that, in any case, the ANC (and SACTU, the original target of their criticism) is not as active in underground political and trade union work among the masses as it should be (and might claim to be). A further corollary of their case is that, under such circumstances, "militarism" continues to be too tempting a method of work, the movement (at best) overemphasizing the "detonator" effect of guerrilla action rather than—again—mobilizing the masses to politico-economic action (or even eventual armed action of their own).

These kind of perspectives have led some Marxist analysts of South Africa to write off the ANC and to advocate various new initiatives: a working-class party here, a radicalized Black Consciousness movement there.[4] More closely in touch with the meaning of developments in South Africa, Petersen and Legassick recognize the centrality of the ANC, its gravitational pull. They therefore advocate creation within the ANC of a Marxist Workers' Tendency and now, from outside the movement, push this position. In fact, they tend to go much further and argue that the ANC that is crystallizing in the new cells forming within the country can, must, and will come to focus a proletarian-based socialist line in a way that the superstructure of the movement—those in exile, however active—cannot. The military undertakings of the latter are bound to be important, but so are the working-class-grounded assertions of the former, and ultimately, with victory, those inside will have to argue the toss with those from outside!

Of course, such people are important, if at all, for the arguments they present rather than for the (almost negligible) political weight they have. And there is much about their position that is entirely too schematic and one-sided.* They tend to overestimate the spontaneous clarity of proletarian revolutionary consciousness at the price of underestimating the possible hegemonic contributions of a more broadly nationalist project (in deepening the struggles in the rural areas, transcending the debilitating legacy of ethnicity, neutralizing many potentially dangerous petty-bourgeois elements *and* broadening the understanding of the workers themselves); they also underestimate

---

* Serious questions have also been raised regarding the wisdom of the *tactics* adopted by the Petersen/Legassick group in order to propagate their views, but this subject is outside the scope of the present discussion.

the possible danger, inherent in the advocacy of a much harder, more schematically proletarian line, of handing over the highly charged nationalist-cum-racial card to PAC remnants and/or the more demagogic wing of the Black Consciousness movement referred to above. Equally important, they downgrade much too sharply the value of the existing movement's experience and expertise to the new revolutionary forces which are emerging and miss, too, the extent to which a process of clarification of the movement's goals and strategy can cut right across the ANC, inside and outside the country (and perhaps even into the SACP itself), as it becomes once again firmly rooted in the South African class struggle on the ground.

Yet the central question which they raise is not a foolish one. Ruth First, an articulate writer and activist who is much more firmly within the ANC camp, has herself argued that any residue of "phase theory" within the liberation movement—national liberation first, socialism later—is bound to be misleading, politically and intellectually:

> I do not see any such thing as "pure" national or "pure" class oppression/exploitation. The national and the class struggle are not part of some natural order of succession, but take place coterminously. This is because workers are exploited as workers and also as members of a nationally oppressed group, and not even their national demands can be met without the destruction of the capitalist order. It is because national demands cannot be met under capitalism that the proletariat is the essential leader of the South African revolution and the struggle for national liberation, given this political leadership—*which has, I agree, to be asserted*—will at the same time be part of the struggle for socialism.[5] (Emphasis added)

An important formulation, yet First's proviso—that proletarian leadership is not automatic but must "be asserted"—may be even more so, especially in a situation where "reform" just might begin to meet some of the more narrowly "nationalist" demands of at least some strata of the black population (and even further elicit any "petty-bourgeois tendencies" which linger within the ANC itself). Thus the Catholic Institute of International Relations (CIIR) may feel entirely comfortable with its perception that the ANC has "cut back on earlier drives for worker organization," that its "programme for a united front acknowledges the important role of a non-racial middle-class leadership," and that its strong current emphasis upon the *Freedom Charter* (rather than the *Strategy and Tactics?*) finds it putting "forward a programme for the whole nation appealing to a wide spectrum of opinion in its emphasis on democracy and egalitarianism."[6] The revolutionary socialist will look for signs that adoption of such tactics does not imply a watering-down of the socialist impulse in South Africa (and that, in addition, any such "socialism" as is intended will have more popularly based revolutionary content than the severe limits of Communist Party orthodoxy have all too often dictated elsewhere).*

Of course, so strong is the attraction of "phase theory" and populist imagery that such formulations may seem to some to be putting the cart before the horse in an ultra-left fashion. Yet First's proviso remains important, for the extent to which proletarian leadership is asserted will have a profound impact upon the nature of a future liberated South Africa. Of even more immediate importance—in light of the energies, and the revolutionary potential, which we have seen the "mass strike" to embody—it affects the revolutionary prospect itself. The strength of such proletarian exertions, as directed both against capital at the point of production and, in the townships and the reserves, against capital's state, need to be magnified, not domesticated, by any movement that claims to provide them with leadership. And if, in turn, this is to be achieved, it may well require that such a movement be undergoing its own "revolution within the revolution" in order to strengthen such possibilities. One thinks of the debates and tensions within Mozambique's FRELIMO

---

* Ironically, the CIIR position is the precise obverse of that of Petersen and Legassick, though both view the ANC as a "revitalized" movement, and indeed as a potentially hegemonic one. Thus the Catholic authors see forces inside the country as taming the radicalism of those outside, while Petersen *et al.* see developments inside as beginning to outflank the outside leadership and pull the situation leftward! Obviously this reflects both very different views of the degree of radicalism represented by the SACP and different emphases regarding the key factors at work within South Africa (petty bourgeoisie vs. workers, nationalism vs. class consciousness). The differences in themselves provide an interesting commentary on the complexity of the dialectic at play in South Africa.

in the late-1960s as that liberation movement came more and more to reflect within itself the class realities of the social terrain upon which it was struggling. Although in South Africa the baseline of class action is much more "proletarian" than "peasant," it need imply no criticism to say that the ANC is now being accorded a similar opportunity to grow.

Nor, as should be obvious, is the process of growth starting at ground zero. The South African working class does not have to be discovered *de novo* by the ANC; despite the critics, there is a long history of working-class-oriented preoccupations at both ideological and organizational (e.g., SACTU) levels.[7] Indeed, the proletariat is strongly legitimated by the ANC in terms of a quite self-conscious, Marxist-oriented class analysis, and to such an extent that it cannot be denied status as a contender for hegemony within the movement if the case for this is effectively pressed. Of course, it may be that the direct linkage with the workers at the point of production is one of the aspects of the ANC's grounding inside the country which is least adequately developed at the moment (although even the truth of this proposition varies from area to area, depending, at least in part, on the extent of SACTU's previous presence). Nor is it an entirely straightforward exercise to determine what the most effective possible interplay between ANC/SACTU and the wide range of worker-based initiatives already in train might begin to look like for revolutionary purposes; certainly such is the pace of events that the full sweep of initiatives detailed in the previous chapter is unlikely to be neatly integrated into, or coordinated by, the movement at any very early date.* What can be affirmed, however, is that the working class is already part of that broad and active constituency which was mentioned earlier as underwriting the renewed prominence of the ANC and for which the widespread support for the Free Mandela campaign may be taken as a symbol. Just as the ANC can be seen to provide the political context within which the general run of revolutionary energies in South Africa is likely to come

---

* In any case, this may not necessarily be such a negative thing since it could have the positive effect of strengthening the hand of the working class vis-à-vis the political leadership in the longer run. But this is a controversial issue which we will not explore further here.

together most dramatically, so too does it provide a possible context for the proletarian core of those energies—and the potential socialist charge which it undoubtedly bears—to find increasingly effective expression.

For—once again, despite the critics—there is nothing entirely predictable about the ANC's response. To visit, these days, an ANC office in Africa is a very different, and much more exciting, experience than such a visit in the 1960s. The fact of being in touch with fresh possibilities, and aware of the need to respond to them, has begun, visibly, to bring a new kind of concreteness to the movement's activities and an openness to its analyses. As stated earlier, we will not attempt to foresee here what kind of balances between military and popular action, between township/reserve and workplace focus, between hegemonic nationalism and socialist core, are likely to epitomize the most positive resolution of the political processes ongoing within the movement; indeed, providing detailed possible scenarios for the dynamics of the class struggle either as directed against South Africa's dominant classes or as advanced within the ANC itself lies well outside our provenance and competence. Nonetheless, one conclusion does seem warranted. Just as the ANC is at the center of things, so the center of things is increasingly within the ANC: the continuing dialectic between this movement and the considerable revolutionary energies at play within the society has become the single most important process at work in South Africa's political economy. Not that there is any room for jejune optimism. The crisis in South Africa is still a long way from being resolved in favor of the popular classes, or in socialist terms. Nonetheless, the struggle is joined as never before.

II. The North American Front

As we conclude our writing, the newspapers of May 30 provide an ominous coda to our work. Confidential U.S. Department of State documents, leaked to the press, underscore the new willingness of the Reagan administration to work toward ending, in the words of one of the documents, South Africa's "polecat status in the world and to restore its place as a legitimate and important regional actor with whom we can cooperate pragmatically." There is no need to romanticize the Carter administration's record on South Africa—largely rhetorical and, by the end, not even that—to see that the Reagan team's determination to conceive the issue as being primarily one of "Communist penetration" promises even worse. Not that these documents come as a surprise; they are in tune with the general ethos of "Reaganism" and, more immediately, with Reagan's candid reply to a Walter Cronkite question regarding South Africa in March: "Can we abandon a country that has stood beside us in every war we have ever fought? A country that, strategically, is essential to the free world in its production of minerals that we all must have?" Or with Alexander Haig's toast to South African Foreign Minister Roelof Botha on May 14: "Let this be the new beginning of mutual trust and confidence between the United States and South Africa—old friends . . . who are getting together again."[8]

For Senator Jesse Helms, a *verkrampte* if ever there was one, this is all that need be said on the matter. For others there is a qualification, however. Even President Reagan expects "a sincere and honest effort" (his words during the Cronkite interview) on South Africa's part to solve its "racial problems"— if he is to be able to sell with full effect this new, more up-front, special relationship. Yet such an "effort" will not be hard to find for those with eyes to see, the basis for discerning it having already been laid down in a smooth article in *Foreign Affairs* (Winter 1980-81) by Dr. Chester Crocker, now Assistant Secretary of State-designate for Africa in the Reagan administration.[9] Surveying some of the same ground as we have covered, the State Department's new resident *verligte*—looking all the while to so sensible a goal as "amelioration," rather than to any such "escapist" notion as "full political participation"—finds not crisis but, instead, "fluidity and pragmatism" in South Africa's white politics, and "increasingly confident experimentation" from blacks like Gatsha Buthelezi!

Is the bucket of reform "half full or half empty," as Crocker phrases the question; there are no prizes for guessing his answer. Of course, as we have seen, there continues to be a good case for saying the bucket is even less than half empty, given the difficulties the dominant classes are having in pulling together their "reform" program. Certainly the racist dimensions of South Africa's system of capitalist exploitation are a legitimate and useful target for attack by supporters of the South African struggle in North America, and will remain so for some time to come. But it is also important to affirm that Crocker is, in any case, drawing water at a poisoned well, at the well of—precisely—capitalist exploitation. If, as and when racial capitalism "reforms" and "liberalizes" itself, inherited anti-apartheid slogans, however true and honorable, will only go part way toward counteracting the Reagans and Crockers and proving that such trends do not represent any "sincere and honest effort." To go further, the North American anti-apartheid movement will have to know more about the dynamics of South African capitalism per se and the place within that system of racism on the one hand and "reform" on the other; it is to the development of such an understanding that we have sought to contribute in this text.

Such an understanding also will be crucial to deepening our grasp of, and support for, the liberation struggle. Without denying the contribution of consciousness of racial oppression to the intensification of that struggle in South Africa, its class underpinnings are certainly as apparent—and will be all the more so to the extent that South African capitalism does manage to further stratify the African population and coopt some of its members. Yet even in advance of a full flowering of the latter changes, the confrontation of the dominated classes with capital has become more salient with each gearing up of the "mass strike." In consequence, any North American presentation of the South African situation which blurs this revolutionary thrust—the "articulation" of nationalism with the proletarian project—must seem more misleading and counterproductive than ever, no matter how much it may be the product of liberal good intentions. Of course, the preceding section has suggested reasons for our remaining sensitive to complexities, even contradictions, within the camp of liberation. Yet to the Reagans and the Crockers (or, indeed, the Carters and the Andrew Youngs) who, in a demagogic manner, counterpose misleadingly negative images of "violence" and "revolution" and "Soviet support" to their own flaccid schemes for South Africa we must answer firmly: "Revolution is what the revolution in South Africa is all about!" Overt support for South Africans in these terms—for the full range of militant activities on the ground and for the African National Congress as it increasingly focuses that militancy—must become every bit as important to the anti-apartheid movement in Canada and the United States as are principled denunciations of the racial capitalist system itself.

NOTES

Introduction

1. Stuart Hall, "Moving Right," *Socialist Review* 55 (1981).
2. Phil Jones, "The Thatcher Experiment," in *Politics and Power 2* (London, 1980).
3. Judy Seidman, *Face-Lift Apartheid: South Africa After Soweto* (London, 1980).
4. Centre of African Studies, *South Africa: Is Botha's Total Strategy a Programme of Reform?* (Analysis No. 3) (Maputo, October 1980).
5. Alex Callinicos and John Rogers, *Southern Africa After Soweto* (London, 1977).

Chapter 1

1. Work on the relationship between racial oppression and capitalist exploitation by Harold Wolpe, F. A. Johnstone, Martin Legassick, and Stanley Greenberg (among others) has been essential to our writing of this section, as has Dan O'Meara's work on Afrikaner nationalism. Greenberg's *Race and State in Capitalist Development* (New Haven, 1980) provides a useful recent bibliography.
2. Dan O'Meara, "The 1946 African Mineworkers' Strike in the Political Economy of South Africa," *Journal of Commonwealth and Comparative Politics* 13, no. 2 (July 1975).
3. Giovanni Arrighi and John S. Saul, *Essays on the Political Economy of Africa* (London and New York, 1973), p. 58.
4. Rob Davies, "Capital Restructuring and the Modification of the Racial Division of Labour," *Journal of Southern African Studies* (JSAS) 5, no. 2 (April 1979), and R. First, J. Steele, and C. Gurney, *The South African Connection* (Harmondsworth, 1973), ch. 4.
5. See Herman Giliomée, "The Afrikaner Economic Advance," in H. Adam and H. Giliomée, *Ethnic Power Mobilized* (New Haven, 1979).
6. See R. First, et al., *The South African Connection* and J. Suckling, R. Weiss, and D. Innes, *The Economic Factor* (Uppsala, 1975), as well as various recent works by Ann Seidman and Neva Seidman Makgetla.

7. G.P.C. de Kock, "The New South African Business Cycle and Its Implications for Monetary Policy," *South African Journal of Economics* 48, no. 4 (December 1980).
8. Raymond Parsons, Executive Director of the Associated Chambers of Commerce (ASSOCOM), quoted in *Euromoney* (June 1979).
9. Quoted in Judy Seidman, *Face-Lift Apartheid*, p. 12.
10. For related if rather different arguments on these issues see the important paper by Dan O'Meara, " 'Muldergate,' the Politics of Afrikaner Nationalism and the Crisis of the Capitalist State in South Africa," seminar paper presented at the University of Dar es Salaam, November 1980 (mimeo).
11. As quoted in B. Hackland, "The Economic and Political Context of the Growth of the PFP in South Africa, 1959-78," *JSAS* 7, no. 1 (October 1980).
12. O'Meara, " 'Muldergate.' "
13. Quoted in Glenn Moss, "Total Strategy," in *Work in Progress* (Johannesburg) 11 (February 1980).
14. Ibid.
15. Elizabeth Schmidt, *Decoding Corporate Camouflage: U.S. Business Support for Apartheid* (Washington, D.C., 1980).

Chapter 2

1. This and subsequent quotations in this paragraph, as well as background information essential to the writing of this section, are from Barbara Rogers, *Divide and Rule: South Africa's Bantustans* (London, 1980).
2. Frank Molteno, "The Historical Significance of the Bantustan Strategy," *Social Dynamics* (Cape Town) 3, no. 2 (1977): 25.
3. *Financial Mail*, May 18, 1979, and also Sheena Duncan, "The Effects of the Riekert Report on the African Population," *South African Labour Bulletin (SALB)* (Durban) 5, no. 4 (1979).
4. See J. Seidman, *Face-Lift Apartheid*, a useful source throughout the writing of this section and of the chapter generally.
5. In addition, the idea has even been floated of finding some "special political dispensation"—"city-state" status has been mentioned—for incorporating urban blacks into the "constellation" (*Sunday Times*, March 15, 1981).
6. See "Focus on Riekert," *SALB* 5, no. 4 (1979); National Union of South African Students (NUSAS), *Riekert—Don't Worry, Everything's OK* (Cape Town, n.d.); and D. Hindson, "The Role of the Labour Bureaux in the South African State's Urban Policy, with particular reference to the Riekert Commission's recommendations," African Studies Institute, University of the Witwatersrand, 1980.
7. As a leading banker admitted in 1977, "South Africa could go bankrupt in an attempt to meet the demand for low cost housing for all" (quoted in Development Studies Group, *Control* (Johannesburg, n.d.).
8. Of course, the Urban Foundation housing allocation for 1970-1980 was only Rand 5 million, 25 percent of its total budget.

9. See "Focus on Wiehahn," *SALB* 5, no. 2 (1979); NUSAS, *Wiehahn: Exploring the Contradictions* (Cape Town, n.d.); and Bob Fine, "Trade Unions and the Question of Legality in South Africa," unpub. ms.
10. D. du Toit, *Capital and Labour in South Africa* (London and Boston, 1981), p. 334.
11. NUSAS, *Wiehahn*, p. 14.
12. From a summary of a meeting of the Associated Chambers of Commerce (ASSOCOM) in *African Business,* quoted by Roger Southall in his informative article, "African Capitalism in Contemporary South Africa," *JSAS* 7, no. 1 (October 1980).
13. See "Consciousness, Class Struggle and 'Black' Periodicals in South Africa," *Work in Progress* 9 (August 1979).
14. Quoted in International Defense and Aid Fund (IDAF), *The Apartheid War Machine* (London, 1980), p. 5; we have drawn heavily upon this useful pamphlet in this section. See also SSD, *Repression in South Africa* (Cape Town, n.d.); Glenn Moss, *The Wheels Turn: South African Political Trials, 1976-79* (Geneva and London, n.d.), and sections on "Trials" and "The Courts" in various recent issues of *Work in Progress*.

Chapter 3

1. Lionel Cliffe, "Labour Migration and Peasant Differentiation: Zambian Experiences," *The Journal of Peasant Studies* 5, no. 3 (April 1978): 326, which also quotes Samir Amin.
2. See Harold Wolpe, "Capitalism and Cheap Labour-Power in South Africa: From Segregation to Apartheid," *Economy and Society* 1, no. 4 (November 1972), and related literature.
3. "Editorial," *Review of African Political Economy* (*RAPE*) 11 (January-April 1978).
4. From research by Jan Lange as summarized by Sheena Duncan in *SALB* 5, no. 4 (1978): 72; also Institute for Industrial Education (IIE), *The Durban Strikes 1973* (Durban, 1974).
5. D. Innes and D. O'Meara, "Class Formation and Ideology: The Transkei Region," *RAPE* 7 (1976): 82-83; important writing on women in South Africa can also be found in several recent issues of *Africa Perspective* (Braamfontein), for example no. 15 (Autumn 1980).
6. See Dave Lewis, "Registered Trade Unions and Western Cape Workers," in Eddie Webster, ed., *Essays in Southern Africa Labour History*, Ravan Labour Studies 1 (Johannesburg, 1978).
7. C.E.W. Simkins and D.C. Hindson, "The Division of Labour in South Africa, 1969-1977," *Social Dynamics* 5, no. 2 (1979): 11.
8. M. Legassick and H. Wolpe, "The Bantustans and Capital Accumulation in South Africa," *RAPE* 7 (1976): 105.
9. Ernesto Laclau, *Politics and Ideology in Marxist Theory* (London, 1977), chs. 3 and 4.

10. Joe Slovo, "South Africa—No Middle Road," in B. Davidson, J. Slovo, and A. Wilkinson, *Southern Africa: The New Politics of Revolution* (Harmondsworth, 1976), p. 199.

11. *Strategy and Tactics of the African National Congress,* reprinted in *ANC Speaks: Documents and Statements of the African National Congress, 1955-1976* (London, 1977), p. 179.

12. For important discussions, see Eddie Webster, "Stay-Aways and the Black Working Class Since the Second World War—The Evaluation of a Strategy," unpub. ms., 1980, and Rob Lambert, "Political Unionism in South Africa: A Review of E. Feit's *Workers Without Weapons: SACTU and the Organisation of African Workers," SALB* 6, nos. 2-3 (September 1980).

13. These and subsequent quotes are from Rosa Luxemburg, *The Mass Strike, The Political Party and the Trade Unions* (New York, 1971); of great assistance in applying Luxemburg's work has been the interpretation in Norman Geras, *The Legacy of Rosa Luxemburg* (London, 1976).

14. The next two paragraphs, including the quotations, are drawn mainly from IIE, *The Durban Strikes.*

15. On the "Soweto" events, see especially Baruch Hirson, *Year of Fire, Year of Ash. The Soweto Revolt: Roots of a Revolution?* (London, 1979); John Kane-Berman, *South Africa: The Method in the Madness* (London, 1979); and Alan Brooks and Jeremy Brickhill, *Whirlwind Before the Storm* (London, 1980).

16. Much detail about all the actions during 1979-1981 can be found in various numbers of Barry Streek, ed., *South African Pressclips* (Houtbay), especially the special supplements on the independent trade union movement in 1979-1980, on the rent struggle of 1980, and on the nationwide school boycotts in 1980.

17. See various issues of *Work in Progress,* and, for additional analytical and descriptive material on particular strikes, various issues of *SALB.*

18. Thus many community actions have been led by such organizations as the Soweto Civic Association and the Azanian People's Organization; interestingly, the latter organization recently stated its major demand to be the repossession of the land, with the black working class identified as the "machine" which can achieve this (*Financial Mail,* January 30, 1981).

19. Ironically this is in part a result of another Riekert recommendation noted above—that townships be self-financing. In most cases the rent increases then necessitated have been applied indiscriminately to both strata of the working class!

20. "Interview with Freddie Sauls, Secretary of NUMARWOSA," *SALB* 6, no. 2-3 (September 1980): 64.

21. For statements from the WPGWU and FOSATU on the registration issue, see *SALB* 5, no. 4 (November 1979), and 5, no. 6-7 (March 1980). See also Martin Nicol, "Legislation, Registration, Emasculation," in the latter issue of *SALB,* and Fine, "Trade Unions and the Question of Legality in South Africa."

22. As quoted in *Financial Mail,* January 19, 1979.

23. See Govan Mbeki, *South Africa: The Peasants' Revolt* (Harmondsworth, 1964) and Colin Bundy, "Land and Liberation: The Agrarian

Question and the South African Liberation Movement," seminar paper, Institute of Commonwealth Studies, London, October 30, 1980.

24. "Winterveld," *Work in Progress* 10 (November 1979); see also G. Maré, "Marginalization Theory and Contemporary South Africa," *Africa Perspective—Dissertation No. 1* (Johannesburg, 1979).

25. Quotations from "Four Years On: Transkei Since Independence," *Work in Progress* 14 (September 1980).

26. See the articles on the Batlokwa and the Matlala resistance in ibid. 12 (April 1980).

27. Callinicos and Rogers, *Southern Africa After Soweto*, p. 200.

28. "The Treason Trial: 'Never on Our Knees,'" *Work in Progress* 10 (November 1979).

29. *Daily Dispatch* (Durban), March 13, 1980, as quoted in "Four Years On," p. 9.

30. Roger Southall, "The Beneficiaries of Transkeian 'Independence,'" *Journal of Modern African Studies* 15, no. 1 (1977): 11.

31. Quoted in G. Maré, "Class Conflict and Ideology among the Petty Bourgeoisie in the 'Homelands': Inkatha—A Study" in Development Studies Group, *Conference on the History of Opposition in South Africa* (Johannesburg, 1978); Maré also documents tensions between Buthelezi on the one hand and some members of the Kwazulu commercial petty bourgeoisie on the other over his "liberalizing" support for the entry of "white" commercial capital (e.g., the Checkers supermarket chain) into the homeland economy.

32. See Southall, "African Capitalism," for this comment and subsequent quotations.

33. Anna Starcke, *Survival* (Cape Town, 1978).

34. On these various organizations see "A Black Politics Review," in Barry Streek, ed., *South African Pressclips* (Houtbay), March 1981.

35. Catholic Institute for International Relations (CIIR), *South Africa in the 1980s* (London, 1980).

36. Slovo, "South Africa—No Middle Road," p. 126.

Chapter 4

1. *The African Communist* 83 (1980). More recently, in May of this year, the Minister of Police Louis Le Grange "blamed the combined forces of the African National Congress and the South African Communist Party for the wave of terrorism [sic] sweeping the country" as the regime's carefully orchestrated Republic Day celebrations were turned into a fiasco by the force of popular protest. See *Eastern Province Herald* (Port Elizabeth), May 26, 1981.

2. *Strategy and Tactics of the African National Congress;* the position is further elaborated in Slovo, "South Africa—No Middle Road."

3. See their "South Africa: The Workers' Movement, SACTU and the ANC—A Struggle for Marxist Policies" (London, n.d.); also *Inqaba Ya Basebenzi: Journal of the Marxist Workers' Tendency of the African National Congress,* its first issue published in London in January 1981.

4. For the former see Callinicos and Rogers, *South Africa After Soweto,* and for the latter see Ernest Harsch, *South Africa: White Rule, Black Revolt* (New York, 1980).

5. Ruth First, "After Soweto: A Response," *Review of African Political Economy* 11 (January-April 1978): 98.

6. CIIR, *South Africa in the 1980s.*

7. For a useful history of SACTU see Ken Luckhardt and Brenda Wall, *Organize . . . or Starve! The History of the South African Congress of Trade Unions* (London, 1980).

8. See "Reagan's Views on South Africa Praised by Botha," *The New York Times,* March 5, 1981, and "U.S. Seeks to End 'Polecat Status' of South Africa," *The Globe and Mail* (Toronto), May 30, 1981.

9. Chester A. Crocker, "South Africa: Strategy for Change," *Foreign Affairs* 54, no. 2 (Winter 1980-81).

The Crisis Deepens
by JOHN S. SAUL

Writing five years ago, in 1981, Stephen Gelb and I spoke of a "crisis in South Africa."[1] If the phrase was accurate then, it is all the more so now. In fact, the level of resistance to the apartheid state in South Africa has continued to rise dramatically, especially since mid-1984; moreover, the diffuseness and semi-spontaneity of the activities that we identified (following Rosa Luxemburg) as beginning to constitute a virtual "mass strike" in South Africa have since been complemented by an ever greater—and often quite inspiring—degree of political focus and organizational capacity on the part of those who seek to overthrow that country's cancerous system. Since this impressively growing resistance movement has been the main factor keeping crisis on the agenda in South Africa it is, self-evidently, a reality that must be examined in considerable detail in·this essay. But Gelb and I also sought, in 1981, to assess the apartheid regime's own response to crisis, specifying the way in which it was attempting to take "formative action" (its so-called reforms) as a means of diffusing rising resistance and of shifting the defense of its sharply contested system onto what it was hoped would prove to be somewhat more promising terrain.

These efforts have continued and, indeed, the question of their substance and adequacy has become the focus of sharp debate within the ruling circles. In particular, capital, worldwide and local, has become skeptical to an unprecedented degree as to the likely ability of the National Party regime to steer the system through dangerous waters. Despite this, the most salient feature of the South African state's response has not, after all, been further reform; rather, there has been an attempted intensification of repression vis-à-vis virtually all those pressing for fundamental and meaningful change. Since there are very real limits to the state's ability to wield such repression and since, in any case, this approach shows every sign of being a self-defeating one in the long-run, its continued prominence as an apparently desperate "last resort" demonstrates just how much of the initiative, in historical terms, the apartheid state has lost.

Resistance, Repression, and "Reform"

In *The Crisis in South Africa* Gelb and I examined the first round of "formative action," action most notable for its attempt to deal with the perceived threat of the "urban African." Prominent in this regard was the 1979 Wiehahn Commission, centerpiece of an effort to coopt the newly emergent independent (and primarily black) trade unions. It was increasingly apparent that even if these latter could be further harassed in various ways, they could not be crushed outright; hence the beginnings of a move to legalize them—the better to ensnare and domesticate them within the framework of a closely supervised industrial relations system. But Wiehahn dovetailed, in turn, with the 1979 Riekert Commission, this latter proposing measures designed to differentiate ever more sharply between urban and rural Africans and between the more permanently settled and the migratory workers. By (marginally) distinguishing in favor of the "urban insider" in terms of rights and privileges granted it was hoped that a wedge might be driven between the two groups, the better to coopt and to divide and rule. Such, too, was the intention behind granting some slight expansion of the political space available to African urban politicians through the introduction of new "community councils" in the townships and to Indian and "Coloured" notables through inclusion of members of these "racial groups" in the freshly minted President's Council.

The immediate results of such attempted formative action were none too promising for the regime, of course. For example, although the unions debated among themselves the possible perils of accepting registration, it was soon apparent that such was the momentum they had already gained and such the active working-class base they had begun to consolidate that the mere fact of registration could not be expected to deflect such unions' continuing assertiveness. True, it is still only about 15 percent of the black workforce that is unionized, but membership continues to grow, one notable area of expansion being in the mining sector, where the National Union of Mineworkers (NUM) has surged forward dramatically in the past few years. Despite recession, there is considerable militancy; the number of strikes, legal and illegal, of union and nonunionized provenance, is high,[2] and there is an even greater tendency for the unions to take a more directly political role within the resistance movement, broadly defined. The strength of the pull toward trade union unity, culminating in the formation, in late 1985, of the Confederation of South African Trade Unions (COSATU), is also of great significance, present and potential.

Nor could community councils and the like be expected to absorb the spirit of resistance that was already afoot in the urban townships. In fact, as the government sought further to elaborate its "reform" agenda in the years after 1981, the palpably manipulative character of the "concessions" made served primarily as a focus for the intensification of resistance rather than the reverse. Certainly this was the case with the extension of the President's Council multi-racial initiative into the establishment of a new constitutional format centered on a tricameral parliament (this parliament encompassing separate assemblies for whites, "Coloureds," and Indians within a structure carefully crafted to guarantee overall white control).* This new dispensation was a blatant affront to African opinion since it further institutionalized their exclusion from the central policy (blithely

---

* In the South African context multi-racial has come to connote reformist efforts at desegregation which have produced organizations open to all races yet firmly controlled by whites. Non-racial, in contrast, is used to designate policies and organizations whose objective is racial equality.—*Editors.*

advising that Africans rest satisfied with seeking to realize their most basic political demands primarily through participation in their so-called homelands).

But the almost blanket limitation on the amount of real power to be devolved to them through this new parliamentary system—as well as the starkly divisive intent of the whole exercise—was also perfectly apparent to the vast majority of Indians and "Coloureds." Perhaps only an official of the Reagan administration could have been disingenuous enough to applaud such an initiative, U.S. Undersecretary of State Lawrence Eagleburger hailing (in June 1983) the "indisputable fact" that the "South African government has taken the first step toward extending political rights beyond the white minority."[3] In South Africa itself, however, the backlash against the sham involved was explosive. Thus the massive campaign in 1983-1984 to resist the imposition of the constitution and subsequently to boycott the elections for the Indian and "Coloured" chambers gave important initial focus to the emergence of the United Democratic Front (UDF), an impressive instrument of national political mobilization. And the dramatic success of the boycotts substantially undercut diplomatic gains made by the apartheid regime earlier in the year, when P. W. Botha had parlayed the signing of the Nkomati Accord with Mozambique into a tour of Western European capitals.

Less immediately dramatic but cumulatively even more telling has been the deepening resistance to the further evolution of government policy toward the African urban townships, a policy exemplified most clearly in the range of legislation designed to implement the Riekert proposals and known, collectively, as the "Koornhof bills." Included among these was some further up-grading of the already discredited community councils into "Black Local Authorities" (viz., the Black Local Authorities Act of 1982), presented as a bow in the direction of providing certain additional "political rights" for urban Africans. However, the function of these authorities was to be much the same as that of their predecessors (and, indeed, to be something of an urban variant on the bantustan pattern). Through them, the white-dominated government sought to establish a stratum of privileged intermediaries between themselves and the urban Africans. These, in implementing the government's policies, might help legitimate such policies—or, at worst, provide a lightning rod for popular protests against them. Ironically, from the government's point of view this tactic worked all too well. Even more than had been the case with the community councils, these authorities came to provide so much of a focus for popular grievances that they have virtually collapsed under the strain, thus taking the townships themselves even further outside the range of effective government control.

The reality of resistance had long been present in the townships, of course. Students and unemployed youth have continued to be a dynamic element ever since the "Soweto uprising" in 1976 and this has been all the more the case as the government has continued to fumble with the issue of black education in recent years and as the rate of black unemployment has risen.[4] New was the higher level of self-organization of such elements, as witness the emergence of youth "congresses" in many townships and the impressive and effective role played by the Congress of South African Students (COSAS), at least until the point of its being banned by the government in September 1985. Equally striking has been the further emergence and evolution of various "civic associations" since 1981, these being township political groupings formed precisely to resist both the "neo-colonial" political structures exemplified by the local authorities *and* the various policies perpetrated by the white government and its local puppets vis-à-vis township dwellers. These "civics" have helped quarterback the boycotts of the structures themselves, producing the postponement of elections, low polls when elections have occurred, resignations by councillors, and even direct physical reprisals against the most compromised of local participants. But they have also become the mobilizational focus for the plethora of rent strikes, bus boycotts, and the like that have come increasingly to characterize political life in so many of the black urban areas.

Moreover, it was just such organizations that became some of the most important primary building blocks for the alliance-like structure of the UDF (even as, simultaneously, the UDF held the promise of stimulating more such grassroots entities into existence). And when civic organizations have been able to link up with youth and student organizations on the one hand and trade unions on the other in more coordinated campaigns, the impact has been especially powerful. Indeed, this kind of development was precisely what began to occur in the Transvaal in late 1984, the "Vaal uprising"[5] (as it came to be known) beginning in a one-day stay-away that spread across the Vaal "triangle" (Pretoria-Witwatersrand-Vereeniging) and was directed against proposed service charge increases in the townships. Other grievances were added (police presence in the townships, the victimization of boycotting students) as additional stay-aways followed in, first, Soweto and then KwaThema, the pattern culminating in a massive two-day stay-away (November 5 and 6) throughout the triangle, which saw some 600,000 workers and 400,000 students participating. There seems little doubt that the November stay-away in particular gave severe cause for alarm to the business community, prompting more serious doubts than previously about the wisdom of the existing course. The government, too, was gripped with alarm, its violent reaction to the Vaal uprising—involving vastly expanded and ever more ruthless police activities but also drawing the army into the township struggles—marking a qualitative intensification of conflict. Indeed, it suggested a pattern of "mass revolt met by massive resistance" that was to characterize the following year (1985) even more dramatically. As one writer has put it, "If 1984 was the year which saw the emergence of mass resistance organizations, leading to the collapse of the tricameral and local authority elections, then 1985 was the year the state hit back at the mass organizations, pulling out all stops in a bid to smash them."[6]

One might reasonably ask what remains of "reform"—formative action—in such a context. But before exploring further the tense debate that continues in ruling circles over the precise blend of reform and repression which is appropriate to the present crisis, something more must be said regarding the economic basis of this crisis. Not that it is any simple matter to disentangle its political and economic dimensions, most obviously because the intensifying political resistance—and the government's inability either to preempt or repress it—has been so important in exacerbating the country's economic problems. Thus, as mentioned, the growing unease of capital, worldwide and local, stems primarily from the fact that the extent of popular mobilization has rendered South Africa's future uncertain in a quite fundamental manner. When in 1985, in an unprecedented move, many foreign banks refused to roll over South African loans, and some private capital (domestic as well as foreign) began to pull out of the country, these were probably more "market-led sanctions"—negative responses on the part of investors to that uncertainty—than responses to the pressure of disinvestment lobbies in Western countries. At the same time, it is evident that South Africa's crisis does have a certain economic logic of its own, one that has fed political unrest even as the latter, in turn, has reinforced economic difficulties.

The downturn of South Africa's open, trade- and import-dependent economy took its cue, in considerable measure, from the global international crisis, and South Africa's continuing and extreme vulnerability to worldwide trends has become increasingly evident in the 1980s. Thus, as the United States revived its economy by beggaring much of the rest of the world (allowing interest rates and the dollar to ride up), the gold price, the rand, and South Africa's balance of payments all took a severe beating. As Gelb and I argued, such problematic features link up, in turn, with constraints upon growth specific to South Africa's own racially structured brand of capitalism: the very pattern of racial stratification that has, historically, made cheap labor so readily available has begun to show some costs—especially as South Africa's economy has become more sophisticated and complex (semi-industrial)—in terms of shortages of skilled labor and inherent limitations upon local consumer markets. It is these and other factors that explain why "stagflation"—a crippling combination of high rates of both inflation *and* unemployment—has become an even more marked feature of the South African economy than it was when we wrote in 1981.

Moreover, government policies have themselves contributed to a worsening of the situation. It is not surprising, perhaps, that so right-wing a government as that in South Africa should be seduced by the nostrums of monetarism, seeking to restore growth by undercutting the claims of labor, curbing inflation and "excessive government spending," and bettering the profitability of the hardier of capitalist entrepreneurs. As Geoffrey Spaulding has recently written from Johannesburg, "This involved raising interest rates which reduced market demand, resulting in massive layoffs of black workers; allowing the exchange rate to float freely—it promptly sank like a stone; boosting inflation via higher import costs; and attempting to slash the government's own budget deficit by rolling back subsidies— on basic food and fuel items, as well as to black local government, and introducing a general sales tax."[7] These cuts have in part been necessitated by the fact that certain other key areas of government expenditure have proven to be difficult to curb, notably defense, salaries to white civil servants, and hand-outs to white farmers (key bases of support for the Nationalist government), black education (where expenditures are relatively high owing to the combination of the economy's need for more skilled labor on the one hand and black student demand on the other), and subsidies to the bantustans and their bloated puppet administrations (this being one of the more grotesque distortions of the budget necessitated by apartheid's grand design).

As Spaulding continues, "Blacks were therefore faced with a severe economic squeeze—rising unemployment combined with downward pressure on wages and a rising cost of living. This came at the same time as the new political structures were being implemented, and reinforced their lack of legitimacy. For example, newly established Black Local Authorities, elected by tiny percentage polls, were forced to increase rentals in their areas, to try to obtain essential financing." It will be readily apparent how much momentum such developments gave to the community organizations, and why action against rising rents, transport fares, and the like have been so important in seeding urban unrest. And all this without permitting any kind of economic turnaround. Indeed, as the crisis deepened, a *volte-face* occurred on many policy fronts. By late 1985, for example, the very government that "had declared itself in favor of freeing the financial and exchange markets from official interference [was] suddenly interfering on a hitherto unheard of scale (through suspending the stock exchange, reintroducing the financial rand, reneging on foreign debt repayments, and supporting the currency)."[8] But these and other recent steps (e.g., short-term reflationary measures) have really been counsels of desperation, not likely in and of themselves either to restore business confidence or to get the economy out of the doldrums.

The Limits of Formative Action

As 1985 drew to a close, however, the economic recipe was merely more of the same. The South African government announced plans to extend its original four-month freeze—due to expire on December 31—on repaying its foreign loans and to introduce strict exchange controls to bolster the severely stricken rand (down from U.S. $.85 to $.36 in less than two years). Predictably, business circles remained less than impressed. As Audrey Dickman, senior economist at South Africa's giant Anglo American Corporation, said of the measures, "They don't get to the heart of South Africa's fundamental problem, which is a lack of confidence.... [F]or this [latter] political and economic stability are crucial." Similarly, Arthur Hammond-Tooke, chief economist of South African's Federated Chamber of Industries: "The measures imposed can be seen as a holding operation which may be successful in the short-term, but it is important for the government to put forward a credible package of political reforms and economic reconstruction."[9] In short, "reform" lives, even winning some surprising—and surprisingly frank—converts. Witness Louis Luyt, Afrikaner millionaire, long-time apologist for apartheid, and notorious bag-man for the National Party during the Muldergate scandal period (fronting the government's purchase of *The Citizen,* for example), who now vouchsafes that "we must do away with a system that has been wrong for forty years. If the political situation changes, I can see a tremendous future for this country."[10] Now Luyt can even favor us with a pretty good Marxisant analysis of his country's racial capitalism:

Whether business likes it or not, it has benefitted from apartheid. It is only now that apartheid has turned against them that they are seeking its removal. For years big business did not want the situation changed. . . . [F]or far too long the private sector has paid lip service to real change. The big companies could have done much more to influence change.

Such a call for "change" was echoed throughout 1985 by many more respectable capitalists than Luyt—Gavin Relly, chairman of Anglo American, for example:

As the causes for the run on the currency were not economic but political, any economic measures that the authorities may introduce will have no more than a short- to medium-term effect unless they are accompanied by a new political dispensation.

What is needed for the short-, medium-, and long-term health of the country is an acceleration of reform, in particular in regard to citizenship, influx control, a positive urbanization policy, and the development of a unitary education policy. Above all, it is necessary for the government to enter into genuine negotiations with representatives of all groups in SA for a new political system of genuine power sharing.[11]

Change? Reform or repression? From its first days, of course, Botha and company's "total strategy" to defend their system was defined as including both reform and repression, a point reiterated by Botha himself in a recent gloss on widespread police and military action in the townships: "Official security action [sic] protects the process of peaceful reform and ensures the necessary stability without which reform will be undermined by violence and revolution."[12] Certainly preemptive "security action" became, with Botha's ascendancy in 1978, an ever more marked feature of South Africa's policy beyond its borders in southern Africa. Building on the precedent of the 1975 invasion of Angola and subsequent destabilization efforts there (via UNITA), Botha proceeded to generalize this approach throughout the region, unleashing, most dramatically and brutally, its MNR puppet against the Mozambican regime while employing a mix of similarly shadowy bands of counter-revolutionaries and occasional direct attacks elsewhere as well (Lesotho, Botswana, Zimbabwe). One goal of such actions was to weaken logistical support for the African National Congress (ANC), although South Africa has also been interested in undermining the credibility of the nationalist and/or socialist experiments being attempted in such countries and in forcing their damaged economies back in under South African regional hegemony.[13]

The apartheid government has paid a surprisingly low cost for such ruthless aggression, both internationally and domestically—even being praised in some quarters as "peacemaker" when Mozambique's government finally capitulated to South African military pressure at Nkomati. Moreover, the destabilization tactic may have scored some success in disadvantaging the ANC, however temporarily. Perhaps if use of the stick had proved to be as effective inside South Africa itself, less criticism would have been heard, in business and other circles, of Botha's overall policy package. Fortunately, this has not been the case, though not for want of trying on the part of the state. Of course, repressive state action has always been close to the surface in apartheid South Africa, but its scope expanded markedly in 1984 and 1985 as resistance grew. At the beginning of 1984 it was directed primarily against student protestors, in August against those working to boycott the tricameral elections in the Indian and "Coloured" communities. Yet, as already noted, it was the dramatic scale of police and military response to developments in the Transvaal beginning in September—dozens killed, hundreds detained—that really set the tone for what was to follow. When the state of emergency was declared in many parts of the country in July 1985, it was primarily a formalization of the prevailing situation, even if it did give the forces of repression a somewhat freer hand. Not surprisingly, the death toll continued to mount: the South African Institute of Race Relations recently documented that in the sixteen months from September 1, 1984, to the end of 1985 nearly one-thousand people (992) died in township unrest.[14]

No need to elaborate: this latter is a reality known to every television viewer outside South Africa—or at least this was the case up to the time that the South African government banned coverage of township "incidents" (thereby seeking to duplicate overseas the news blackout it had already imposed on inhabitants of its own country). A little less starkly visible, if even more potentially debilitating politically, has been the toll of bannings and detentions, the minimum total number of emergency and security detainees between January 1 and December 12, 1985, at one time reaching a figure of 10,836, with over one-thousand still being held, including a large number of children; moreover, during this period, at least eighty-five people have died "in detention or police custody for an alleged political offense or during a period of political imprisonment."[15] The targets have been carefully selected, the UDF being especially prominent among them. As Trevor Manuel of the UDF's national executive wrote in August 1985, "Two years and one month after its inception, the UDF finds itself bearing the full brunt of the government's onslaught. Two-thirds of our national and regional executive members are out of action through death, detention or trial. At least 2,000 rank and file members of the UDF are in detention. A major UDF affiliate, COSAS, has been banned.... This repression ... is the consequence of the effective challenges we have mounted to the government's 'reforms.' "[16] Moreover, this grisly national pattern could be extended with examples drawn from virtually every South African black community, though the small town of Cradock in the Eastern Cape provided a particularly graphic instance. There Mathew Goniwe—"the dead man who haunts all our futures," in the words of Anton Harber—helped lead the Cradock Residents' Association (CRADORA) to mount an impressive, broad-gauged program of political mobilization (among other things, convincing local councillors to resign their posts and then effectively facilitating their reintegration back into the community). The result? One night in June 1985, the car driving Goniwe and three of his close associates was "intercepted" on the road by unknown assailants; over the next four days, according to Harber, "the mutilated and charred bodies of the four men were discovered in isolated posts on the outskirts of the city."[17]

Not surprisingly, the UDF, in an official statement regarding Goniwe's murder, felt "forced to conclude that the 'defenders of apartheid' were bent on a 'murderous path' to eliminate all popular leaders."[18] At the same time, such developments did begin to make some spokesmen for vested interests in South Africa uneasy. Was it possible that the "leaders" who were thus being peeled away were in fact important potential intermediaries in the kind of dialogue with the mass of the population that might eventually become necessary? Was the day arriving when a more rather than less organized resistance movement would be welcome as providing some minimal guarantee of a reasonably orderly transition to a new dispensation? These were questions given all the more urgency by the fact that the government's fierce crackdown seemed merely to heighten the black population's spirit of resistance, rather than the reverse. As Spaulding has written,

... even official brutality of the sort which has characterized the Emergency has not proven to be the short, sharp death-blow to resistance which the government, and big business, clearly hoped it would be. Their model was the previous Emergency, in 1960, when popular resistance collapsed like a pricked balloon. This time around, black militancy, especially amongst youth and students, has not been so easy to smash. The ten years since Soweto, formative for most of these activists, have seen an escalation of political struggle, including actions by ANC guerrillas and sustained periods of open defiance against apartheid. Having seen so many people killed or maimed by police action during this time, including such heroes as Steve Biko and Solomon Mahlangu, the hanged ANC militant, a certain fatalism has developed amongst young blacks. ... No wonder the security forces' activities—not just detentions and torture, but also substantial harassment of township dwellers in their homes, their schools, on the streets, and even in the clinics—has hardened attitudes and increased militancy, rather than puncturing it.[19]

Those in capitalist circles were also aware that the image of civil war that South Africa now projected was the very worst kind of publicity abroad, not only making the global corporate community profoundly uneasy but also giving fresh strength to more politically motivated anti-apartheid forces. What a dangerous turn when even Ronald Reagan could be forced by public opinion to make a bow—however tame and tactically motivated it might be—in the direction of governmentally imposed sanctions.

In consequence, as several quotations cited above have indicated, it is the business community that has been most desperate to discover a more adequate reform agenda. Thus when P. W. Botha appeared to fumble the ball with his ill-starred "Rubicon" speech to the National Party Congress in Natal in August—a speech much ballyhooed as likely to announce significant change but, in the event, characterized by an all too familiar defensive truculence—the headline for the story in the influential *Financial Mail* was a blunt "Leave Now":

... the man has gone as far as he can—he has nothing more to offer—and he should therefore pay the appropriate penalty. ... [He] is hopelessly out of his depth and should, forthwith, go into a well-earned retirement.
Nothing new. Nothing specific. No timetable. Influx control to be "reviewed," Mandela stays in Pollsmoor. The backtracking on the denationalization policy implicit in the homelands policy was done in guarded and obscure terms. Everything, in short, suggests that if Botha ever had a "hidden agenda" for change, it was that the blacks would be linked to the homelands; urban blacks given their say in community and regional service councils; and everyone else represented through the tricameral Parliament.
There have been tinkerings—or, to be more correct, promises of tinkerings—to the system. But it is in shambles. That is where P. W. has led us.[20]

To be sure (as this quotation suggests) the government continues to flash the reform card and one move—the scrapping of the Mixed Marriages Act—even had Ronald Reagan, as late as August 1985, momentarily "hailing South Africa for an American-style solution to racial segregation."[21] Moreover, in the wake of the disastrous reception, both at home and abroad, of his intransigence at the Rubicon, Botha spent the next few months whistling up the prospect of other changes, proposing, for example, to include some Africans in the President's Council, talking of return to a common South African citizenship (to be a dual citizenship for those in the already "independent" bantustans, as it turned out, and to carry with it *no* claim to participation in the central government) and of the possible lifting of "influx control" and certain features of the pass laws (though not the Group Areas Act, which dictates geographical separation by race and continues to rationalize massive forced removals and the arbitrary incorporation of certain black urban townships into the bantustans). This was probably just enough to strengthen a backlash among whites to the right of the National Party, a backlash visible, for example, in several October by-elections for the whites-only parliament. But it was nowhere near enough, at the other pole of the political spectrum, to assuage international opinion—much less the opinion of South Africa's black population. Indeed, what tended to come across most clearly was a sense of considerable disarray on the government side as it oscillated wildly, caught uncertainly between, on the one hand, a reliance on the jack-booted repression its gut racism and crude survival instinct seemed to dictate and, on the other, some real move toward the "reform" its economic and political vulnerability seemed to demand.

What, then, of the business community's own reform agenda? Certainly the most prominent and powerful of capitalist interests are relatively less boxed in by the ideological parameters of "white supremacy" than is true of denizens of the state structure and, as Gelb and I observed, can thus more readily conceptualize a shift away from racial capitalism. For all the benefits that have accrued historically to capital (the availability of cheap black labor, in particular) from South Africa's unique marriage of economic exploitation and racial oppression, this marriage can begin to have its costs, economic costs (as we have mentioned), but, perhaps more importantly, political costs. After all, South African-style racial oppression tends to etch class contradictions in color, race and class contradictions then reinforcing each other in a manner that can become quite revolutionary. Take, for example, the current politicization of the trade unions. A recent pro-reform policy statement by a consortium cf South Africa's leading business groups worried that this was inevitable—and quite dangerous—unless there were profound political changes:

If effective channels of political expression for blacks up to the highest level are not developed, they will increasingly be forced to employ industrial relations mechanisms to voice grievances. Such a development is unsound and would put the business community in an invidious position.

Indeed, this is merely one among a number of reasons why these business representatives feel that, in the current escalation of conflict, it is "the traditional 'business way of life'—the private enterprise system—[which] is fundamentally at stake." Defending capitalism (and pre-empting revolution), not defending white privilege per se, becomes the bottom line here, as does an awareness that the most successful capitalist systems are (relatively) color blind and legitimate themselves through (relatively) open democratic institutions. "It is essentially both self-interest and social responsibility which are driving the business community towards promotion of reform," the statement concludes.[22]

In consequence, the business community has begun to hedge its bets, the current sense of urgency producing, as its most adventurous outcome to date, an expedition to Lusaka, Zambia, by a group that included three of South Africa's most important capitalists—Relly, Mike Rosholt of Barlow Rand, and Tony Bloom of Premier Milling—in order to hold exploratory meetings with the banned and exiled African National Congress. We must be circumspect, however. As Gelb and I noted in 1981, even for the most sophisticated actors in the capitalist camp "the passage from racial capitalism to liberal capitalism seems a particularly hazardous one. . . . [The] dominant classes, mounted on the tiger of racial capitalism, now find that they can neither ride it altogether comfortably, nor easily dismount."[23] Thus, even if they could hope to deliver a quite advanced model of reform through the dense underbrush of the whites-only polity (a considerable challenge in itself), such actors sense that they might not easily keep the democratization process within its "proper" channels. Given the deeply engrained social and economic inequalities that would continue to exist in South Africa, they have the nagging fear that the granting of any real political power to blacks must lead to a revolutionary challenge to those inequalities as well. Small wonder that even a Gavin Relly draws back at the water's edge: "I don't think our generation is going to see majority rule" (although "it may be an option for some future generation"), he averred at year's end.[24] Nor is it difficult to decipher Louis Luyt's further gloss on his own death-bed conversion to reform, quoted earlier: while the "black vote must come," he found himself agreeing with recent comments by his sometime liberal antagonist Helen Suzman to the effect that "we are not going to give this country away. There is no point in exchanging a bad white government for a bad black government."

Reform if necessary, but not necessarily reform. But just how do the "liberal minded" propose to become half-pregnant in South Africa? The formulation by the aforementioned Gavin Relly, published almost simultaneously with his meeting with leaders of the ANC, is among the most sophisticated, and warrants quoting at length:

[In] thinking about how to create a new coherent society that offers reasonable equity to all . . . there seem to be two fundamental approaches. . . . The first is to continue to modify the present system . . . [an] approach [which] appears to take into account . . . the necessity of a form of power-sharing, which at least would recognize various real power centers in the country, some of which would be tribal, such as the powerful Zulus, some of which may be the independent homelands (which can by no means be disregarded), some of which may be urban and multiracial, and some of which may even be white.

In our highly complex society I would by no means reject this line of thinking as impractical, and provided it were able to establish a balance of power in a free society shared by everyone, I would not regard it as morally offensive. Nor would it exclude everyone's having the vote, though not necessarily in a single, directly elected assembly. There are of course many possible models within this reformist approach, but whichever one is chosen will have to take account of vast cultural diversity, basic communication problems flowing from the fact that a large part of the population uses a vernacular language rather than English or Afrikaans, and traditions in Africa that are not always democratic.

The other approach stems from the view that any modification of the present structure would be simply serving the same pie in a different dish. It bluntly declares that nothing short of immediate universal suffrage with no protection for minorities or safeguards for institutions is acceptable. This attitude is supported by the African National Congress. I myself have no hesitation in believing that implementation of such a policy would have a devastating effect on the country and the subcontinent.[25]

A slippery text indeed—typical of what happens to the reform impulse when it moves beyond the eternal (albeit newly redis-covered) verities of freeing up the marketplace (removing the "irrationalities" of influx control, for example) toward the ques-tion on "one person, one vote, in a unified South Africa." There is the arrogance of power, of course, the same arrogance that led "reform-minded" Anglo American offhandedly to sack 14,000 workers from its Vaal Reefs mine in early 1985 when they had the temerity to take strike action. Nor is the kind of constitution-mongering bruited about by Relly something new. It surfaced in Natal at the beginning of this decade with the report of the Buthelezi Commission, which sought to theorize a novel (and highly qualified) redivision of power between Chief Buthelezi's KwaZulu administration and Natal's white polity. And Frederik van Zyl Slabbert and his Progressive Federal Party, the voices of liberal capitalism in South Africa's white parliament, have long been hawking just such "confederal" and "consociational" constitutional models, models that reflect the PFP's stated preoccupation with what they choose to label South Africa's "plural society" and with the dangers of "majority dom-ination."[26]

Put more honestly, such proposed constitutional gimmickry seems chiefly preoccupied with so dividing and counterbalancing black political inputs—all in the name of democracy—as to blunt any eventual challenge to white social and economic power. But perhaps under such a dispensation the qualifier "white" would become somewhat less important, giving further point to Roger Southall's conclusion to his careful study of the Buthelezi Commission that the "common objective of consocia-tional strategy at this point is to recruit subordinate racial elites to a front that is deliberately counter-revolutionary"—thus marking one further and quite sophisticated attempt, in the name of reform, "to forge a class alliance across racial lines."[27] We shall no doubt hear more of such schemes, if, as, and when a third round of "formative action" gets underway. Indeed, re-cent evidence suggests that the government, too, is laying the groundwork, through programs of industrial decentralization and regional administrative reorganization, for various possible "federalist" solutions of its own.[28] It need scarcely be added that none of these possible developments has much to offer the mass of the African population. What will be evident, however, is just how much harder the state and business community will have to be pushed before the matter of genuine democratization and transfer of power to the black majority is likely to be placed firmly on the negotiating table.

Consolidating the Liberation Struggle

We have seen, in previous sections, just how much of a push there is already, from students, civic associations, trade unions, and the like. In the five years since Gelb and I wrote, the apartheid state's ability to retain the initiative, to set the pace, to "form" the terrain of political struggle, has weakened considerably. When, at the beginning of 1985, the African National Congress distributed widely in South Africa a call to "make apartheid unworkable," to "make the country ungovernable," that task, as we have seen, was already well underway. Indeed, it is, first and foremost, the extent to which blacks in South Africa have made apartheid "unworkable" that has won fresh allies to the anti-apartheid cause. It is this, too, that has helped make the ANC so much more unavoidable an actor— witness, again, its well-publicized meetings in exile with Relly's team but also with van Zyl Slabbert, with Afrikaner editors and students, with prominent South African church leaders—in the current South African drama. These are recent meetings, of course. Yet one particularly well-informed observer has already underscored the drama of the ANC's increased ascendancy in June—before the Emergency, before the Rubicon speech:

The most vivid contrast between the ANC of today and the exile movement of the late sixties and early seventies is the broad political context within which it operates in South Africa. This week sees the thirtieth anniversary of the Freedom Charter, an anniversary which will be celebrated with enthusiasm by those UDF affiliates which can rightly be considered as representing the mainstream of township political life. The youthful political sub-culture which is increasingly to the forefront in the ritual and ceremony of black political protest, at funerals, church services, cultural events, and mass meetings, has, as its mentors, incorporated into its slogans,

songs, and dances the iconography provided by the heroes of Robben Island [Mandela in particular—JSS] and the soldiers of Umkhonto. In the last nine months, *oorbeligte* Afrikaner Nationalists,
the Student Representative Council presidents of Stellenbosch and
RAU, the deputy editor of the *Beeld,* and 43% of the whites
polled in an HRSC survey, have all expressed themselves in favor
of negotiations with the ANC. All these facts testify to the increased
legitimacy of the ANC—or at least to the measure with which it is
regarded as a central and inescapable fact of South African political life.

In short, as Tom Lodge has concluded, "It could be reasonably
contended that [the ANC] *has largely won the battle of ideas.*"[29]
    It is one thing, however, to win a "battle of ideas," quite
another to win the struggle for power. As Lodge adds, "A bomb
a week does not add up to a full-scale guerrilla war, and the
prospect of the ANC being able to present a really formidable
set of obstacles to the functioning of the state and the economy
is still remote." Not that the struggle for power in South Africa
is likely to look like some clearly recognizable rerun of guerrilla
warfare elsewhere in Africa. Nonetheless, the mobilization of
actions across a broad front which constitutes the "mass strike"
(and which cumulatively saps the confidence and capacities of
the defenders of the status quo) needs to obtain greater firepower if it is to shake more profoundly the powers-that-be. Small
wonder that when the ANC held its Second National Consultative Conference (the first took place in Morogoro, Tanzania, in
1969) in Zambia in June 1985, this was a key issue for discussion. Clearly, Nkomati had undermined some of the ANC's
freedom of maneuver in the region. But, given the high level of
popular combativeness inside South Africa, it was clearer than
ever that the center of gravity of the ANC's activities would in
any event have to be inside the country.
    Not that the ANC had not made significant advances in
this respect even before Nkomati. Lodge, for example, saw clear
indications in mid-1985 that "to maintain Umkhonto [Umk-
honto we Sizwe, the ANC's military wing] activities at their
present level does not require uninterrupted external lines of
communication, recruitment, and support. Trials have produced
evidence of recruitment and simple training within the country,

externally trained men function inside South Africa for lengthier periods, and the speed with which guerrillas react to internal political events demonstrates the extent to which they operate on their own initiative."[30] Nevertheless, the Consultative Conference took as a frank point of departure that the ANC was still too weak in this respect. The point was certainly underscored that in 1985, the year that the ANC had officially designated as the "Year of the Cadre," a first priority would be the strengthening of the ANC's political network in order to bring it into even closer contact with all the various focuses of resistance in the country. But, beyond that, the military and political dimensions of underground work in South Africa also would have to become more effectively meshed than in the past. Certainly, the ANC's "armed propaganda" has had an extremely positive impact in recent years—witness the enthusiastic popular response to the May 1983 Pretoria car bomb explosion reported by Joseph Lelyveld ("Blacks Jubilant ANC Finally Hitting Real Targets") in the *New York Times*,[31] for example, and to the attacks on the Anglo American offices in Johannesburg in almost immediate response to the company's having sacked thousand of workers in 1985. But the strengthened political network that is envisioned would now serve, in turn, to help develop the capacity to lend fire power and paramilitary clout to popular actions in the townships and workplaces in any confrontation with the South African army and police.

Events since June 1985 suggest that the ANC is still a long way from being able to provide enough of this kind of clout to the resistance movement. Government bullets still tend to be met by sticks and stones; defenseless Africans die while white policemen escape reprisal and the rest of the white population remains cocooned in its comfortable suburban lifestyle. However, there are signs that this is changing. Africans are beginning to shoot back in the townships. There seems less reluctance on the ANC's part—a point that was apparently discussed at length at the Consultative Conference—to eschew the kinds of attack in which white civilians might perish. Of course, this grim necessity, unwelcome to the ANC since it is the apartheid state and not the liberation movement that harbors the terrorists and psychopaths

in South Africa, is merely one way in which the resistance movement must "take the struggle to the white areas," in the words
of a recent ANC leaflet distributed inside South Africa.[32] But it
reflects an awareness that the large majority of the white population that continues to support the apartheid state, either actively or tacitly, must be made to comprehend more clearly the
precise scope and seriousness of the black challenge that confronts it. Much depends on the ability of the ANC to deliver
on its promise in this regard.

But what of consolidating the politics of the mass strike and
giving it an ever stronger thrust in sheer mobilizational terms?
Here, too, there are challenges. Thus the questions of the precise weight to be assigned to race consciousness and racial solidarity in developing South Africa's resistance movement has
always been a problematic one. The Pan Africanist Congress's
split from the ANC in the late 1950s had a distinctly cultural
nationalist edge to it, and while the PAC has more or less self-
destructed in exile, the Black Consciousness Movement (BCM*,
which did so much to revive the spirit of resistance in South
Africa in the late 1960s and early 1970s, evoked some of the
same sentiments. Though many BCM people have since found
their way into the Congress Alliance, the cultural nationalist
legacy lives on, providing, in the organizational forms of the
Azanian People's Organization (AZAPO) and the National
Forum, a current dissident from the UDF–ANC–Freedom
Charter mainstream.* This has led on occasion to inter-organ-
izational tensions, although useful efforts have also been made
to resolve them when they have threatened to get out of hand.
It is worth noting, as well, that cultural nationalism has also
had some impact on the trade union movement, the Azanian

---

* There is also attached to this cultural nationalist wing of the resistance movement, broadly defined, a distinctly leftist element, of apparently Trotskyist provenance, one that safeguards its left project on
such paradoxical terrain by emphasizing the role of the *"black* working
class." Perhaps the logic of this link lies in the fact that AZAPO and company provide the only other "game in town" on the side of liberation, an
available platform, therefore, from which to challenge the potential for
petty-bourgeois and/or Stalinist deviations that activists in this group see
to exist in the Charterist movement.

Congress of Trade Unions (AZACTU) and the more important Council of South African Trade Unions (CUSA) both having refrained from joining the impressive new trade union central, the Congress of South African Trade Unions (COSATU), launched in November 1985. At the same time, it should be emphasized that CUSA's intransigence on this question cost it the affiliation of what was far and away its most important unit, the National Union of Mineworkers (NUM), which did join COSATU.

In fact, cultural nationalism has been far less divisive than one might anticipate, given how graphic is the counter-reality of white racism. Certainly the UDF has eschewed it completely in stitching together its formidable alliance of some six hundred to seven hundred base organizations. Moreover, the UDF's firm line on this issue may have influenced the ANC, at its June conference, to remove its last remaining restriction on the role of non-Africans within the movement, membership on the National Executive Committee. Rather more complicated has been the question of the relationship between the UDF and the trade union movement. Thus a number of unions, particularly those linked to the Federation of South African Trade Unions (FOSATU), have held back from joining the UDF. One misgiving they had was historically rooted, springing from a sense that in the 1950s trade unions—given the close ties of the South African Congress of Trade Unions (SACTU) with the Congress Alliance—had rushed too readily into national level political campaigns without adequately consolidating the kind of shop-floor presence—power at the point of production—so necessary over the long haul. They were anxious to avoid making the same mistake.

Moreover, one of the most striking features of the independent trade unions that have emerged since the 1970s is their strong emphasis upon internal democracy and accountability to the membership. It was just such unions that tended to be most suspicious of the actual functioning of the UDF, being wary not merely of its size and the catholicity of the organizations affiliated to it, but also of the possibility that its top-heavy structure and commitment to high-profile political activity would, in Spaulding's words, "almost inevitably make [it] less democratically linked to [its] base than the unions themselves."[33] Nor is this all. As Spaulding continues:

Some unionists have apparently worried that the UDF—and possibly the ANC—were just a bit too petty bourgeois in their make-up and too exclusively preoccupied with the mere transfer of formal political power to push big business on the questions of socialism and working-class power in post-liberation South Africa. For such unionists, further consolidating a working-class base on the shop-floor is crucially important, not only in order to make possible a continuing confrontation with capital but also to help pull to the left any ANC-led alliance which might eventually rise to power.[34]

It seems evident, for example, that it was just such a concern that Alec Erwin, national education officer of FOSATU, sought to raise in a suggestive recent speech entitled "The Question of Unity in the Struggle." Distinguishing between the "politics of liberation"—ever "in danger of co-option"—and the more radical politics of "transformation," he stressed the necessity for workers to begin what he termed "building tomorrow today."[35]

This "workerist" tendency of FOSATU does not stand alone in the camp of the independent trade union movement. There are certainly unions and unionists of a more "economistic" bent, for example, whose reluctance to enter the political arena has been grounded in a much narrower definition of the legitimate scope of union activities. Moreover, misgivings about particular kinds of political involvement have, upon occasion, even led to tensions between workplace and residence, between trade unions on the one hand and civic and youth organizations on the other. This was notoriously the case with the Eastern Cape stay-aways in March 1985—directed against massive retrenchments, the AMCAR-Ford merger and, most centrally, increased petrol prices—and especially in Port Elizabeth (but less so in Uitenhage).[36] Nonetheless, it remains generally true that all South African trade unions have been drawn ever more firmly into the political arena. Witness our earlier discussion of the November stay-away in the Transvaal, but also the fact that, in some townships, groups of shop stewards have formed the backbone of community organizations; that demonstrations organized to mark May Day or to commemorate a fallen leader like Andries Raditsela have struck such sparks; that many unions have played prominent roles in mounting the consumer boycotts that became so effective in 1985 in bringing pressure to bear on some segments of the white business community and, through them, on the political system. Moreover, some unions, those of what might be called a "politicist" tendency (the South African Allied Workers' Union—SAAWU—for example), have actually linked themselves quite closely with the UDF (and, by extension perhaps, with the SACTU/ANC tradition of trade union activity as well).

Indeed, one of the most interesting aspects of the newly formed COSATU is that—in addition to the sheer number of pre-existing unions (33) and workers (over 500,000) it represents—it brings together a wide variety of perspectives on the question of trade union activity: workerist, economist, politicist. Yet, to quote Spaulding once again, "This kind of diversity is [not] likely to prove a negative thing. Such tensions within the new union will throw up crucial questions about the very nature of the movement for liberation in South Africa, as well as about the nature of post-liberation society."[37] Of course, even in terms of strengthening the union movement for industrial action there is much to be done. Union activity, particularly in a period of retrenchment, is still highly vulnerable, as the National Union of Mineworkers, in particular, has found out; there are also vast numbers of nonunionized workers to organize and links with the unemployed to be forged. More immediately, a primary task of the new union has been to restructure itself internally—the "general unions" which have joined are now reorganizing, in conjunction with the others, along industrial union lines, for example—the better to do battle with capital on a day-to-day basis. In addition, however, the first indications as to what COSATU's political role will be are encouraging.

Thus Chris Dlamini, COSATU's first vice-president, led off the union's inaugural rally at King's Park Stadium in Natal in early December by announcing that "time has run out for employers and their collaborators." Indeed, the "unity gained through the formation of COSATU has foiled the rulers' divide-and-rule strategy." Then it was the turn of Elijah Barayi, now president of COSATU, to speak and he immediately called for the resignation of P. W. Botha and all homeland leaders. Barayi also delivered a quite specific ultimatum to Botha: abolish influx control laws within six months or COSATU would take (unspecified) action. There were other pronouncements: support for disinvestment now and for the nationalization of the mines and other large industries in the future; for equal pay for equal work, especially for black women; and for the immediate lifting of the state of emergency and the withdrawal of troops from the townships.[38] It remained to be seen how these and other demands would be followed up on, but it was hard to avoid the impression that another important step had been taken toward consolidating a distinctive "working-class politics" in South Africa. This impression was given even more force a few days later when Jay Naidoo, COSATU's general secretary, met with the ANC in Zimbabwe. In that meeting, he later reported,

I told the ANC and SACTU delegation we did not want superficial changes, or black bosses to replace white bosses, while the repressive machinery of state and capital remained intact. I expressed very clearly to them our commitment to see a society which was not only free of apartheid, but also free of the exploitative, degrading and brutalizing system under which black workers suffered. This meant a restructuring of society so that the wealth of the country would be shared among the people.

In short, "COSATU was looking at alternatives which would ensure that any society that emerged would accurately reflect the interests of the working class."[39]

It may be that this and other kinds of strong opinion will give rise to tensions within the resistance movement, broadly defined. But as with the tensions that we have seen exist specifically within COSATU itself, it is not inevitable that these will turn sharply antagonistic or become debilitating. Indeed, one of the most exciting things about contemporary South Africa—for all the likely horrors of the transition period still to come—is precisely the vibrant quality of its liberatory politics, the number of "big questions," which, being alive and well, give promise for the South Africa that will ultimately emerge. Not that all "antagonisms" within the black population can be so positively defined. The regime has found its allies, even in the black townships, although it is no accident that these latter have been markedly the targets of popular outrage there. Nor are the actions taken against them quite the outbreaks of anarchic "black-on-black" mob violence that the media (with South African official blessing) would often have us believe. As noted, an organizational infrastructure that exemplifies a very high level of political creativity generally underpins and guides township political actions (this in spite of the government's most brutal efforts to decapitate successful organizations whenever it can safely do so, as witness the Goniwe case). As the well-informed Catholic Institute of International Relations correctly insists, the so-called disorder in South Africa is, in reality, a "mass movement." The CIIR is even more out-spoken about the targets, both institutional and individual, of this "movement":

South African blacks are proving that they cannot be governed as a people colonized from the white enclave, either by black collaborators, or by the naked violence of security forces and riot police. They reject the garrison state. . . . Most significantly, they have identified the new black local authorities, the community councillors, as the key to the state's attempt to control the town-ships and co-opt blacks. Community councillors have been dealt with mercilessly, killed and their houses burnt. Almost 200 have resigned; only 3 out of 34 councils set up in 1983 still function. Black resistance has thus struck hard at the lynch-pin of state strategy towards urban blacks.[40]

Other "internal" enemies of liberation are even more familiar, if a little less immediately vulnerable: the bantustan elites, in particular. Thus, in 1983, the crackdown on SAAWU activists and on East London bus boycotters was even more vicious inside Lennox Sebe's Ciskei than it was outside. And such is the authoritarian and unapologetically servile nature of Mangope's regime in Bophutatswana that when, as 1986 dawned, over 20,000 miners were sacked by Gencor for striking its Impala Platinum Mines inside that bantustan, they had even less hope for redress than their 14,000 counterparts fired by

Anglo American, a number of months earlier, in the so-called white area. Examples could be multiplied endlessly. However, it can safely be said that the actor in the "homeland" drama who is most deleterious to the cause of liberation has been Gatsha Buthelezi, chief minister of KwaZulu. The only black South African leader of any real visibility to have come out in strong opposition to economic sanctions against South Africa, this immoderate stance has made him the darling of certain influential Western circles and a boon to the South African business community and the apartheid government.

Yet his real value to the latter is manifested inside the country. Although he is just ambitious and independent enough to be an occasional embarrassment to it, the government has nonetheless found that, given a long leash, Buthelezi serves their basic game plan of divide and rule very well indeed. He is an outspoken foe of both the ANC and the UDF, and recent months have found his *impis* (squads of bully boys) and youth corps—working with tacit police support—acting as the physical hammer of the UDF and of community activists in Natal (while also exacerbating tensions between Africans and Indians there). This need come as no surprise. In fact, Buthelezi has built his power base among the Zulu at least as much by force and intimidation as by charisma and tribalist rhetoric. This is especially true in the most rural areas of KwaZulu, where the combination of isolation and of chiefly power structures has hung heavy over local communities. But the menace of Inkatha's strategy of intimidation has always spread more widely than that: among the ugliest of numerous relevant incidents was the 1983 assault on the Ngoye campus of the University of Zululand, where Inkatha thugs killed, beat, and raped dozens of students for the "disrespect" they had shown toward Buthelezi. Like so many other frightening facts about Buthelezi, this event was little publicized abroad.[41]

Never quite the "spokesman for the 6 million Zulu" that his publicists have sometimes claimed him to be, Buthelezi's recent excesses in attempting to savage the growing mass resistance movement have reduced his popularity even further. According to the Community Resource and Information Centre:

An opinion survey conducted by the Institute of Black Research showed that most Africans blamed Inkatha for the recent unrest in Durban. It was found that Inkatha and the police were seen as starting the trouble and being the most active in it thereafter. The survey reflected a considerable loss of support for Chief Buthelezi—a finding that was supported in other recent surveys.[42]

Still, Buthelezi remains credible enough—and pliable enough—for van Zyl Slabbert to have taken him on board the PFP's "Convention Alliance," a recently proposed moderate "middle way" forward to constitutional reform. True, the fact that Buthelezi was alone among black leaders in linking himself to such an initiative is equally significant, while Slabbert's decision to join the trek to Lusaka to meet with the ANC may serve to remind us that it is definitely not Buthelezi who is "winning the battle of ideas." At the same time, there can be little doubt that he remains on offer for any "consociationalism"—he had, of course, attempted to take out a patent on that scenario with his own Buthelezi Commission—or "confederalism" that may be forthcoming. Other blacks may be available, if, as, and when the "endgame" bargaining process becomes a more pressing reality. For reasons that we have discussed, however, it will not be easy for any such blacks to deliver a sufficiently large popular constituency to render workable any of the (limited) range of formative options South African ruling circles seem willing to risk, now or in the foreseeable future.

The Revolutionary Dialectic

Speaking in a self-critical vein at its Consultative Conference, the ANC assumed some responsibility for Buthelezi's present prominence, admitting to having encouraged him to build Inkatha—albeit a very different Inkatha than that which ultimately emerged—in the first instance. But Buthelezi was seen to be "our fault" in another, more basic, sense as well. For "we have not done and are not doing sufficient political work among the millions of our people who have been condemned to the bantustans. The artificial boundaries purporting to fence them off from the rest of our country do not make them any less a vital and integral part of the popular masses fighting for national liberation and social emancipation in our country."[43] This suggests that the rural areas may become an even more important additional front for action than they have been in recent years. Nor should the category "rural areas" be taken to exclude the often overlooked white farming zones (where in fact—at least along the borders—there has actually been a recent stepping up of sabotage activity). Nonetheless, as we have seen, it is the struggle in the urban areas that is central, and it is likely to remain so for the foreseeable future.

What, then, of the future? Even if developments since 1981 seem to have confirmed much of the analysis of South Africa's crisis that Gelb and I advanced at that time, and even if that crisis has deepened along lines we might have predicted, it is not much easier now than it was then to set out with any real precision (or, indeed, confidence) a scenario for racial capitalism's ultimate demise. There will be some ebb and flow that springs from the degree of intensity of state repression (that degree of intensity being itself affected by the unprědictable balance of forces—and arguments—within ruling circles, even if unlikely to diminish markedly in the near future). In this regard, the dismissal at year's end of treason charges against a significant number of imprisoned UDF leaders has been hailed as a major political victory. Not that bannings, detentions, and killings will cease to take their toll. Nonetheless, the UDF's brand of aboveground, mass-based opposition seems likely to take fresh strength from these acquittals, the newly released leaders almost immediately throwing themselves back into political work.

Their renewed efforts, in combination with continuing pressure on the state on all the internal fronts we have examined (from the post-Consultative Conference ANC, from the postunity trade union movement, from the township mobilization which will not disappear), must continue to take a toll of the state's capacity to repress the struggle. As for the precise "content" of this resistance movement, even the advances it has made since 1981 do not make its future entirely predictable. Gelb and I wrote then of the simultaneity, within the South African struggle, of the proletarian and the "popular-democratic" moments (the latter evidenced in broad organizational—and class—alliances and constructed around the ideologies of nationalism, racial consciousness, and democratic self-assertion that seem so effective in focusing much of the experience of lived oppression in South Africa). We suggested that the pressure of events in South Africa made it likely that these two moments would be complementary rather than contradictory, each drawing out the progressive potential of the other. As we have seen, the past five years have brought a further strengthening of both the "popular-democratic" and the "working-class politics" terms of South Africa's revolutionary equation and this has been, unequivocally, all to the good. Moreover, these two components have, indeed, tended to reinforce one another, the strength of popular-democratic assertions helping further to politicize the trade unions (to take one example), the growing assertiveness of the working class helping further to deepen the saliency of class considerations and socialist preoccupations within the broader movement.

Precisely how these strands will interweave, organizationally and ideologically, and in terms both of the further development of the liberation struggle itself and of the efforts to shape a new, post-liberation South Africa remains openended, of course. It may be true that the ANC, at least as regards organizational linkages, stands in most immediate and overt harmony with the UDF, this latter being, in turn, the most important aboveground manifestation of the "popular-democratic" current in South Africa. Moreover, the ANC remains most comfortable with a relatively populist projection of its programmatic intentions; it is reluctant, certainly, to proclaim any very straightforward socialist vision of the future, a "two-stage" theory of the struggle (national liberation first, then, possibly, socialism) still being the most that many of its spokespersons will offer publically on this subject.[44] Yet this need not imply that the ANC is fundamentally out of step with the most important bearers of "working-class politics" (those within the trade union movement, for example); nor that Jay Naidoo spoke to deaf ears during his Harare meeting with the liberation movement.

It is even less likely that the ANC, already so deeply rooted inside the country, could be very far out of step with the crystallizing mood of the black townships. There "popular-democratic" assertions are not easily distinguished from even more radical sentiments. As Patrick Laurence has written in assessing "capitalism's uncertain future," "South Africa's major extra-parliamentary opposition movements bristle with anti-capitalist sentiments. There is no doubt that there is a growing hostility towards capitalism among black youth. The reason is simple: capitalism is seen as the driving force behind apartheid."[45]

It is not surprising, then, that the 1985 Consultative Conference underscored more strongly than ever a familiar ANC theme: the centrality of the working class to its revolutionary endeavors. As for its recent spate of meetings with businessmen, politicians, editors and churchpersons, not only has the ANC refused to compromise on the question of the full democratization of South Africa, but it has also stuck, quite explicitly, to the basic intimations of a socialization of production that are to be found in the Freedom Charter: "The national wealth of our country, the heritage of all South Africans, shall be restored to the people; the mineral wealth beneath the soil, the banks and monopoly industry shall be transferred to the ownership of the people as a whole."

Both resistance and radicalization have grown apace, then, and the process cuts across the entire field of organized opposition. Certainly there are strong grounds for reasserting—even reinforcing—the conclusion Gelb and I reached in 1981: "Just as the ANC is at the center of things, so the center of things is increasingly within the ANC: the continuing dialectic between this movement and the considerable revolutionary energies at play within the society has become the single most important process at work in South Africa's political economy."[46] True, there is little more room than there was in 1981 for "jejune optimism"; it remains true that the "crisis is still a long way from being resolved in favor of the popular classes or in socialist terms." Nonetheless, the evidence and arguments presented above do suggest that as the South African crisis has deepened in recent years, it has moved much closer to a positive resolution on both counts.

Notes

1. See John S. Saul and Stephen Gelb, *The Crisis in South Africa* (New York: Monthly Review Press, 1981).

2. See Sheryl Raine, "Strikes: A New Intensity" in *The Star* (International Airmail Weekly) (Johannesburg), 23 December 1985, where it is documented that "strike activity reached an all-time high during 1985, with the mining industry hardest hit" (p. 12).

3. Quoted in Sanford J. Ungar and Pete Vale, "South Africa: Why Constructive Engagement Failed," *Foreign Affairs* 64, no. 2 (Winter 1985-86).

4. For example, in 1983 the government rejected the recommendation of its own de Lange committee that there be a single ministry of education. For a useful account of student protest—embodied in boycotts relating to such issues as the demand for democratically elected Student Representative Councils, an end to excessive corporal punishment, and sexual harassment of schoolgirls and the like, and, ultimately, to much broader issues, including the actions of the military and the police in the townships—see South African Institute of Race Relations, *Race Relations Survey 1984* (Johannesburg, 1985).

5. See, in particular, Labour Monitoring Group, "The November Stay-Away," *South African Labour Bulletin* (Braamfontein) 10, no. 6 (May 1985).

6. Anton Harber, "Politics in the Year of the Wagging Finger," *Weekly Mail* (Johannesburg), 20-26 December 1985, p. 4.

7. Geoffrey Spaulding, "Apartheid's Death Throes," unpublished paper; see also the interview with Spaulding under the title "One Person, One Vote, in a Unified South Africa," in *Southern Africa Report* (Toronto) 3, no. 2 (December 1985).

8. Duncan Innes, "The Policy that Sunk in the Rubicon," *Weekly Mail,* 15-21 November 1986, p. 13; see also Stephen Gelb and Duncan Innes, "Economic Crisis in South Africa: Monetarism's Double Bind," *Work in Progress* (Johannesburg) 36 (April 1985): 31-39.

9. Dickman and Hammond-Cooke are both quoted in a Reuters story, "Pretoria's Controls Seen as Short-Term," printed in *The Globe and Mail* (Toronto), 10 December 1985.

10. This and the following quotation appear in Peter Farley, "SA Must Come Back to Its Senses, Says a Laid-Back Luyt," *The Star* (Johannesburg), 19 September 1985.

11. Quoted in a survey of prominent businessmen entitled "Business and Reform," *Financial Mail* (Johannesburg), 6 September 1985.

12. Quoted in Spaulding, "Apartheid's Death Throes."

13. On this subject, generally and with specific reference to Mozambique, see my "Mozambican Socialism and South African Aggression: A Case Study in Destabilization," paper presented at the (American) African Studies Association, New Orleans, November 1985.

14. See the report "Unrest Death Toll near 1000," *The Star* (Weekly Edition), 23 December 1985.

15. For these figures see "Apartheid Barometer," *Weekly Mail,* 20-25 December 1985.

16. Article reprinted from the *Cape Times,* 28 September 1985, in *ANC News Briefings* (London), 10 October 1985.

17. See the related stories by Anton Harber and Molly Blackburn in the *Weekly Mail,* 12-16 July 1985.

18. Cited in Harber, "Politics in the Year of the Wagging Finger."

19. Spaulding, "Apartheid's Death Throes."

20. *Financial Mail,* 6 September 1985.

21. Ungar and Vale, "South Africa." In a telephone radio interview, Ronald Reagan said, to the subsequent embarrassment of his aides, that South Africa had "eliminated the segregation that we once had in our own country—the type of thing where hotels and restaurants and places of entertainment and so forth were segregated—that has all been eliminated. They recognize now interracial marriages and all."

22. See the statement presented in September 1985 to the United Nations hearings on transnational corporations in South Africa and reprinted, under the headline "Business Sets Out Its Reform Role," in *Business Day* (Johannesburg), 20 September 1985. Signatories to the statement were Die Afrikaanse Handelsinstitutet, the Association of Chambers of Commerce, the National African Federation of Chambers of Commerce, the Federated Chambers of Industry, and the Urban Foundation.

23. See above, p. 95.

24. From an interview with Relly published under the headline "We Need a Free Market—and a Free Society," *The Star* (Weekly Edition), 16 December 1985, p. 13.

25. Gavin W. H. Relly, "South Africa: A Time for Patriotism," from the *Washington Post,* as reprinted in the *Manchester Guardian Weekly,* 6 October 1985.

26. On van Zyl Slabbert, see the article, "The Centre Cannot Hold: White Liberalism and Beyond in South Africa," *Southern Africa Report* 1, no. 3 (December 1985).

27. Roger J. Southall, "Consociationalism in South Africa: The Buthelezi Commission and Beyond," *Journal of Modern African Studies* 21, no. 1 (1983): 108.

28. See the extremely suggestive paper by William Cobbett, Daryl Glaser, Doug Hindson, and Mark Swilling entitled "South Africa's Regional Political Economy: A Critical Analysis of Reform Strategy in the 1980s," presented to a seminar at the University of the Witwatersrand, in Johannesburg in 1985.

29. Tom Lodge, "The ANC After Nkomati," address to the South African Institute of Race Relations, Johannesburg, June 26, 1985, subsequently circulated as a SAIRR "Topical Opinion" paper (p. 8); emphasis added.

30. Ibid., p. 6.

31. Article by Joseph Lelyveld, as reprinted in *The Globe and Mail* (Toronto), 26 May 1983.

32. Reproduced in *Sechaba* (Lusaka), December 1985, p. 2.

33. Some have worried that these features of the UDF have sometimes made it too parasitic on local youth and community action organizations as well. Certainly mantaining a judicious balance between local

political action and energies and nationally focused efforts will be a continuing challenge for the resistance movement.

34. Interview with Spaulding, "One Person, One Vote."

35. Alec Erwin, "The Question of Unity in the Struggle," *South African Labour Bulletin* 11, no. 1 (September 1985): 62, 68. In his article "Superunion: Born into Defiance" (*Weekly Mail*, 6-12 December 1985), Patrick Laurence reminds his readers of a 1981 speech by Joe Foster, FOSATU general secretary, which made some related points. There Foster contended that "political movements are often controlled by the 'petty bourgeoisie' who fear genuine worker-controlled trade unions. They strive to dissolve worker-controlled movements into a mass political movement dominated not by the workers but by the 'petty bourgeoisie.' According to them, the workers are only useful as a kind of battering ram they themselves seek to lead." See also Rob Davies and Dan O'Meara, "The Workers' Struggle in South Africa—A Comment" in *Review of African Political Economy* 30 (1984).

36. Labour Monitoring Group, "Report: The March Stay-Aways in Port Elizabeth and Uitenhage," *South African Labour Bulletin* 11, no. 1 (September 1985).

37. Interview with Spaulding, "One Person, One Vote."

38. Dlamini's and Barayi's statements are quoted in Mike Siluma, "Botha Must Resign—COSATU President," *The Star* (Weekly), 9 December 1985.

39. See the article entitled "COSATU Spells Out Its Aims to ANC," *The Star* (Weekly), 23 December 1985.

40. Catholic Institute for International Relations, *South Africa in the 1980s: Update No. 3* (London: June 1985), p. 30.

41. Inkatha's tactics of terror and intimidation are well documented in Community Resource and Information Centre, *Inkatha: Black Liberation or National Reaction* (Braamfontein, n.d. [1985]). See also Patrick Laurence, "Buthelezi Hasn't Got Majority Urban Zulu Support, Shows Poll," *Weekly Mail*, 11-17 October 1985, and the picture story "Here's the Proof: Top Inkatha Men *Are* Leading the Notorious Impis in Their Terror Campaigns in Durban," *City Press*, 22 September 1985.

42. Community Resource and Information Centre, ibid (section on "Inkatha and the UDF," p. 20).

43. African National Congress, *Documents of the Second National Consultative Conference of the African National Congress* (Lusaka, 1985), p. 21.

44. For a particularly dramatic recent statement on this subject by a senior ANC cadre, see Thabo Mbeki, "The Fatton Thesis: A Rejoinder," *Canadian Journal of African Studies* 18, no. 3 (1984). In his response to an (extremely fatuous) article by Robert Fatton in the same issue, Mbeki asserts that the "ANC is not a socialist party. It has never pretended to be one, has never said it was, and is not trying to be."

45. Patrick Laurence, "White Capitalism and Black Rage," *Weekly Mail*, 13-19 September 1985.

46. See above, p. 200.